Night and Day:

The Interaction Between an Academic Institution and Its Evening College

by

Myrtle S. Jacobson

The Scarecrow Press, Inc.
Metuchen, N. J.   1970

To

Albert Salomon

dear friend and teacher

Acknowledgements

Night and Day began to take form as an analytical
study within the context of formal organizational theory at a
conference on "Dynamics of Change in the Modern University, "
held at Syracuse University in 1966. There I met Peter Blau
of the University of Chicago, well known for his studies in
bureaucracy and formal organization, and Burton Clark of the
University of California, equally well known for his research
in the field of formal organizations with particular emphasis
on higher education. Both Dr. Blau and Dr. Clark gracious-
ly encouraged me to make an organizational study of the dynamics of interaction between the parent college and one of
its component units.

The analysis here is not limited to formal organizational structure and function. At relevant points, the dynamics of informal groupings and relationships are introduced.

The research involved examination of a vast number
of official documents, correspondence, policy statements and
other original data. For generously making a mass of this
documentary material available to me, I wish to express my
deepest gratitude to Dr. Edwin H. Spengler, Dean of the
School of General Studies. In addition, he spent countless
hours with me in discussing theoretical and practical
questions and in critically evaluating inferences and interpretations. Without his gracious and unstinting cooperation,
completion of this study would have been immeasurably more
difficult.

To Dr. Deborah I. Offenbacher, colleague and friend, I am indebted far more than I can adequately express. Her sensitivity as a human being, and her critical judgments as a scholar contributed very substantially in converting a heavy burden into a scholarly adventure.

I gratefully acknowledge the assistance of Dr. Arthur Vidich and Dr. Sol Miller who made many suggestions from the point of view of sociological theory.

My sincere thanks are also expressed to Dr. Stanley Diamond, Director of the "Culture of Schools Program" research project under which I was privileged to receive a grant from the U. S. Department of Health, Education and Welfare. (Grant No. OEC 1-7-008725-2005. Project No. Br 6-8725)

To my husband, Dr. Sol Jacobson, whose wisdom and advice, patience and encouragement sustained me throughout, I am ever grateful.

Myrtle S. Jacobson

Foreword

Night and Day is the story of the development of educational opportunity for adults in the School of General Studies
at Brooklyn College in a period when it was established dog-
ma that educational budgets were to be exclusively devoted to
the young. It is a tale of dedicated administrators on the
one hand and highly motivated adult students on the other who
together developed a vital and sprawling educational program
of adult opportunity on a skimpy budget financed by tuition
fees when the accepted educational and fiscal conventions provided a constantly growing tax budget for a tuition-free baccalaureate program for relatively highly qualified current
academic graduates of New York City high schools.

For some thirty years, Brooklyn College developed
for the qualified young an academic program of growing excellence. It was a liberal arts program characterized by
relative freedom of choice. It experimented with "functional
majors" expressing the student's individual vocation in
contrast with the usual departmental rigidity. It was a curriculum that pioneered for New York State with so-called
exemption examinations designed to accredit and to develop
academic achievements that were measurable and that had
no visible antecedents recorded in the student's transcript of
his preceding academic record. It was a college that experimented with a two-year terminal program which was
vocationally oriented before the State of New York accepted
the idea as the basis for its community college programs.

vii

It is the story of administrators and teachers who transferred their achievements in the regular baccalaureate program financed by a handsome tax budget to a growing variety of programs appealing to adult students which were subsidized by the existence of idle buildings in the afternoon and evening hours and by a "shoe-string" budget financed by the tuition payments of the adult students themselves.

Dr. Jacobson is not only a careful student of this development but was intimately involved in the process of its growth. She records all the details of the story of the struggle with entrenched institutional rigidity, with professorial lack of imagination camouflaged as the "defense of standards," along with the story of impressive achievement with highly motivated adult students as their records were evaluated by orthodox standards such as the number of graduates who went on to diplomas with departmental honors and to subsequent graduate and professional careers.

In the light of our present relaxed standards of admission of young people to tuition-free programs and in the perspective of the permissive practices that have become characteristic of present curricular administration, some of these achievements may appear to be merely "historical." The story of the Special Baccalaureate Program for Adults which is told in Chapter III of this book has a message for the future that is already in the process of recognition in current developments. We live in a period in which educational opportunity has been so generously extended to youths with constantly decreasing levels of preparation and motivation that it becomes more and more probable that large numbers of adults, who for one reason or another could not take advantage of collegiate opportunities in the past, are now in terms of academic potential and in personal motivation a more promising risk for educational investment.

"Motivation" is one of the most difficult topics in education at all levels. We have little difficulty in recognizing it when we encounter it, but we know little about its development or its initiation. It is clear, however, that our present-day undergraduates are frequently not potential scholars. They are merely candidates for a diploma. We have imposed statutory or conventional periods of scholastic servitude on a growing multitude of the young, and they resent the frustration incurred from periods of prolonged dependence upon adults. The final outcome produces a painful contrast with the lush harvests of adult achievement which are within reach if we could only change our deeply worn grooves of academic habit and rationalization with regard to the age of the students for whom we design our programs. Brooklyn College's Small College Program with its "Accent on Adults" is now developing a response on the basis of the earlier Special Baccalaureate Program for Adults to many of the questions that we currently seek to answer in our program for a younger age group.

I find it easy to imagine that the college president of the next decade or so may find many of his present problems with prolonged adolescence that are anchored in lack of motivation, modified in scope and intensity, if we should begin to aim at a variety of programs responding to the keen motivation of adults who are in many ways impressively endowed with intellectual potential that has not been developed because of deficiencies in fiscal or in vocational opportunity. The student body of the future may well have an average age of over 30 with an intensity of adult commitment or dedication that will materially affect the sense of perspective of the younger fellow students. The benefits will therefore

ix

be shared by both the young and the more mature students, and the productivity of the educational investment--in economic as well as in moral terms--will be enhanced for society as a whole.

On a national scale we are not ready for this move since the creative and innovative work on the methods of instruction and the structure of curricular design have not been completed, or even initiated. Dr. Jacobson's story of these programs in Night and Day, including the painful record of the frustrations inherent in entrenched professional self-righteousness, is here to hold a lamp to a path into the future that is full of creative and liberating promise. Those who confuse the euphoria of complacency with the defense of professional standards, need only to glance at the record of the adult programs in the Brooklyn School of General Studies. This is a story of qualitative achievement under severe fiscal handicaps, and it offers a refreshing contrast with conventional rhetoric anchored in a smug reliance upon handsome fiscal support geared to the young which hold out a promise for nothing but quantified mediocrity. In the splendid words of Isaiah incorporated in the Brooklyn College seal: "See and be radiant!"

Harry D. Gideonse
New School for Social Research
New York, N. Y.

Table of Contents

	Page
Acknowledgements	v
Foreword	vii
List of Tables	xiv
Introduction	15

Chapter

I. Organizational Structure	21
The Multiversity	22
The City University of New York	23
Brooklyn College	25
School of General Studies Administrative Structure	31
School of General Studies Student Body	34
Budget and Finance	37
Problem Areas	38
Brooklyn College Organizational Chart	43
School of General Studies Organizational Chart	44
II. Organizational Goals	46
Goals of the City University	47
Goals of Brooklyn College	47
Historical Emergence of SGS Goals	50
Reorganization and Expanding Goals	52
The Take-Off Period of Growth	54
Contraction and Goal Succession	62
Moving and Reaching Out	64
Efforts to Retain SGS Jurisdiction	72

The Verdict on Jurisdiction 74

Looking to the Future 78

The Dialectics of Change 80

III. Innovation through Cooptation 85

The Tensions With the Status Quo 86

Democratic and Bureaucratic Obstacles 88

The Principle of Organizational Cooptation 90

The Special Baccalaureate Degree Program
for Adults 91

The Associate Degree in Nursing Science 118

Summary: Variations on a Theme 141

IV. Authority and Responsibility: Internal
Structure and Dynamics 149

Formal Academic Organization 150

Authority Interrelationships 152

Annual Line Personnel 154

Deputy Chairmen and SGS Administration 177

Roles of CLAS Faculty in SGS 185

The SGS Majority Group: Lecturers 192

Summary: Reverberations of Limited
Authority 203

V. Stress and Strain: The Effects of
Environmental Pressures 209

The Focus on SGS 212

Pressure from the City University 214

Transmitted Pressure from the College 226

Pressure from the Board 236

Summary: The Varieties of Organizational
Interaction 245

VI. Image and Identity 253

Evening College Images 254

Projecting a Positive Image 257

Image and Marginal Status   262

Image and Academic Standards   265

Comparability of Admission Standards   270

Image and Perception   275

Is There an SGS Image?   291

Conclusion   295

VII.   Retrospects and Prospects   300

The Problem of Goals   301

The Problems of Innovation and Cooptation   302

The Problems of Authority and Responsibility 308

The Problems of Image and Identity   316

A Typology of Evening Colleges   319

A Blueprint for Better Balance   325

To Mold the Future   331

Appendix   335

Bibliography   339

Index   345

List of Tables

Page

Table

Comparative Enrollment CLAS and SGS   35

SGS Student Enrollments 1950-1965   65

Annual Line Personnel   155

SGS Line Appointments   158

Faculty Promotions - Comparison of SGS
    with CLAS   173

Length of Service - Off-Campus Lecturers SGS
    Division of Liberal Arts - Fall 1965   199

Length of Service - Off-Campus Lecturers SGS
    Division of Vocational Studies - Fall 1965   199

SGS Enrollment - Fall 1966   272

1. Percentage Comparison of Total Staff and
    Respondent   276

2. Characteristics of Students - Responses (in
    percentages)   278

3. Problems in SGS - Responses (in percentages)   286

4. Problems in SGS - Responses (in percentages)   287

5. SGS Student: Positive and Negative Responses
    (in percentages)   288

6. Advise to Choose Day College (Reason for Choice)   289

7. Advise to Choose SGS by Reason for Choice   291

xiv

Introduction

The central theme of this book is the organizational interaction between a parent academic institution and one of its component units, the evening college. Specifically, it is a case study of the relationships of Brooklyn College and its School of General Studies, the sub-unit that administers degree programs in the evening.

Part-time Students in Evening Colleges

Approximately one-third of total college enrollments in the United States consists of part-time students in evening colleges. This form of mass education is a unique American phenomenon. No other country in the world has developed a comparable system of higher education. To a large segment of the urban population, part-time study in the evening toward a college degree represents the only educational means by which to achieve upward mobility. For many it is the only method of preparing against the threat of human obsolescence brought about by the technological advances of automation and cybernetics.

In their essential characteristics--goals, student body and instructional staff--evening colleges are quite distinguishable from their day-time counterparts. Evening students are, in general, a more heterogeneous group than are day students in terms of age range, life's experiences, interests and educational objectives. Most significant is the difference in commitment to education: the evening student's commitment, because of inescapable responsibilities to job or

15

family, is necessarily secondary or even tertiary in contrast
to the primary commitment of the day student to education.
With respect to institutional goals, the Chairman of the
Board of Higher Education of the City University of New
York once stated that "evening students need a different approach, different courses and teaching methods from those
of the regular undergraduate."[1] It is these needs that give
rise to distinctive identity and goals for the evening college.
Moreover, in contrast to the day college, the teaching staff
of the evening college typically consists of a high ratio of
part-time teachers recruited from the day college, other
educational institutions, the professions and the business
community. Only a small proportion of its staff is permanent, full-time faculty. It is this diversity in goals, staff
and student body that gives the evening college a flavor and
culture recognizably different from that of the day college.

Dynamics of Interaction

The School of General Studies of Brooklyn College[2]
is an evening college that offers diverse programs of study
to a wide variety of part-time students. While it has a
distinct identity, separate administrative leadership, and
teaching staff in part distinguishable from the college faculty,
it nevertheless functions totally within the orbit of Brooklyn
College of which it is a suborganization. SGS has a student
body of more than 10, 000 and an instructional staff of over
600. It is a typical evening college in an urban setting.

The central focus of this study is the patterns of
organizational interaction which emerge from the relationship
of sub-unit to parent organization. The dynamics of the
interaction are analyzed from two points of view: (a) the
relationships between component unit and parent in the context
of the sociology of formal or complex organizations; (b) the

implications of the relationships as they apply to practical
questions of policy concerning the allocation of authority from
parent to sub-organization.

The organizational interaction between the parent institution and one of its components involves many facets of
sociological analysis. For example, the composition of the
teaching staffs with their varying perquisites and opportunities is relevant to formal organizational theory. Critical
with respect to professional status of a staff member is the
locus of power for recruitment, selection, retention and promotion. This power resides in the instructional departments
of the parent college. Also, the roles of the evening staff
members are prescribed not only by the instructional departments but also by the School of General Studies. Thus a dual relationship exists which may harbor the seeds of tension
in the interactive process. Other points of pressure in the
interaction between the parent organization and its component
pertain to administrative standards and controls concerning
student admission and retention policies, academic standards,
course and curricula content and, finally, requirements for
the degree.

Though a "public . . . actually a part of the organization,"[3] the student body of evening colleges is not as yet
a significantly active force in determining institutional goals
and the means of achieving them. To be sure, these are
formulated in light of the characteristics of the student body,
and the students are involved in the political processes. Up
to this point, however, students as "clients" still occupy a
subordinate position to administration and faculty in determination of policies and procedures.[4] Although the student
body is rapidly becoming an active element in the interactive
process, this study will exclude that segment in order to fo-

cus on the existing organizational structural elements.

Sociological analysis of formal organizations since
Weber's seminal study of bureaucracy has developed to a
point where an impressive body of systematic knowledge exists. A vast literature, in large part based on empirical
studies, also exists with regard to the informal groups within formal organizations. Within the context of the theory of
formal organizations, this study may be seen as a contribution to the analysis of organizational "sets." In the existing
literature, two types of sets have been conceptualized:

a) the role-set model, which studies the focal organization in its relationship to other organizations
with which it interacts in various capacities.[5]

b) the status set model which studies the effects of
differentiation of prestige among organizations
which have similar goals and purposes.[6]

The study presented here may be seen as an analysis
of a third type of organizational set which, following Drucker,
we may call the federated type, i. e. , a set consisting of
semi-autonomous organizations with common or complemen-
tary purposes and certain legally defined administrative relationships.[7] While Drucker analyzes such organizational sets
in industry, there is, to our knowledge, no study which deals
with such federated organizational sets as they appear in the
non-profit sector of society.

The basic intention of this study is to contribute to the
understanding of the complex and dynamic forces operating in
formal organizations by focusing on the pushes and pulls
which occur as a sub-organization endeavors to maintain its
character and integrity vis-a-vis the parent organization.
Emphasis will be placed on the dynamics of cooperation, competition, conflict, and accommodation within the framework of

two interlocking social systems. In addition to the investi-
gation of the structural and formal aspects, the study ex-
plores the informal arrangements and behavioral patterns
which operate within the context of the social and organizational pressures. These informal arrangements and patterns,
when seen within the matrix of the formal organization, add
insights to the meaning of the social dynamics involved.

Ideal Types of Organizational Patterns

From the point of view of organizational patterns, the
relationship of evening colleges to parent institutions may be
classified into three ideal types. One type--a relative mi-
nority--is not separated as a sub-unit in terms of administrative authority and responsibility. The evening college is
fully integrated with the day college and the same administrative authority covers the total operation. A second type,
also in the minority, is the fully autonomous operation administratively independent of the day college. Operated as a
separate college--most usually designated as University Col-
lege--administrative authority is vested in the dean of the
evening college who is responsible directly to the president
or vice-president. The most typical organizational structure
--the subject of this study--is that of parent/sub-unit where
the evening college has limited authority and is subject to a
variety of controls by the day deans and the college-wide instructional departments.

The "ties that bind" are both functional and dysfunctional in the sub-organization's quest for self-identity and individualized goals. The extremes on the scale are autonomy
versus dependency. Between these extremes is a vast number of possible combinations. As in every facet of individual or societal life, value judgments must ultimately determine the point on the continuum which will promise "the best

of all possible worlds." In essence, the question is one of
maximum effectiveness in relationships where tensions are
inevitable and where the adjustment process is a complex
one.

While this case study focuses on the organizational
interaction between parent and sub-unit at Brooklyn College,
from a broader point of view, light will be shed on the relative merits and disadvantages of this type of organizational
structure for all evening colleges.

Notes

1. A Broader Mandate for Higher Education, Report of the
   Chairman of the Board of Higher Education (1946-
   1948), p. 32.

2. Hereinafter referred to as SGS.

3. Peter Blau & W. Richard Scott. Formal Organization
   (Chandler Publishing Co. , 1962), p. 79.

4. The International Association of Student Evening Councils
   --an evening student organization--has a voice in decision-making but, as yet, has not achieved a position of influence. On the impact of the client on organizational goals and procedures in a different setting
   see: Peter M. Blau and W. Richard Scott, op. cit. ,
   p. 78-86.

5. William M. Evan. "Toward a Theory of Inter-Organizational Relations," Management Science, Vol. II, No.
   10, August 1965.

6. Theodore Caplow. Principles of Organization (Harcourt
   Brace, 1964).

7. Peter Drucker. The New Society (Harper and Row,
   1962).

Chapter I

Organizational Structure

"Architecture is a sort of ora-
tory of power by means of
forms."

Friedrich Wilhelm Nietzsche

If avowed goals are to be accomplished by a formal
organization, a rational and systematic method of organizing
authority and obedience must be introduced. Regardless of
the rigidity or flexibility of the particular organizational system, centers of authority must be clearly identified and the
character of delegated authority defined with reasonable clarity and precision. Such identification and definition imply
recognized rules and regulations concerning structural and
functional areas that carry with them sanctions more or less
compulsory. Since these definitions cannot wholly be trusted
to fallible memory, it is not surprising that they are most
frequently reduced to writing as official documents, properly
authenticated, whether called charter, by-laws, directives or
memoranda, etc. Since these involve a complex set of structural and human relationships, the framework is typically depicted by an organizational chart. In an architectural sense,
the table of organization graphically clarifies the lines of authority and obedience, of function and responsibility. In addition, the table of organization reveals the system or network of communications both up-the-line and down-the-line.

Weber long ago pointed out that in formal organizations, specific functions may be viewed as tasks authoritatively assigned where there is an expectation as well as a duty of obedience resting on a sense of the legitimacy of the authority to assign.[1] But formal rules, especially in a professional organization, do not usually spring full-blown from organizational charts. In the face of changing conditions and circumstances, the formal rules must grow and change with experiences, convictions and aspirations as well as the reasoned and affective ambitions of those who will be both personally and professionally affected by them. Thus degrees of latitude must necessarily be provided--either explicitly or implicitly--for experiment, for trial and error, for validation and for adjustment.[2] The degrees of freedom are like spatial openings in the structure, making it possible to frame and reframe codes, to interpret and to reinterpret what was written, and to endeavor to perceive now what was intended then. Thus modification in system, in relationships, in interactive processes and in goals is an ever-present potential.

The Multiversity

As was so brilliantly pointed out by former President of the University of California, Clark Kerr, universities are being called upon to produce knowledge as never before in man's history and, as a consequence, they are undergoing revolutionary changes.[3] Their very nature and quality are in a state of flux. His acutely descriptive term "multiversity" was coined to clarify that American university tradition is not a "community of masters and students with a single vision of its nature and purpose" but many communities--even related gesellschaften--of students, faculty, public authority

and administration.   Most crucial is the fact that all are
competing for power in the process of incessant change.

An increasingly important part of multiversity government no doubt rests with the administration.   This stems, at
least in part, from the immense growth of federal grant
funds--in large measure the reason for the conflict among
"scientists affluent and humanists militant. " The alleged deterioration of undergraduate teaching has been attributed by
many careful observers of the academic scene to the competition for grants which are, to some extent, directly related
to a "publish or perish" imperative.

The symbolic head of academic administration is, of
course, the president.   In the view of Kerr, however, Hutch-
ins of Chicago was one of the last great giants (Harold Dodds,
former president of Princeton disagrees with Kerr on that
score).   As Kerr views the present role of the multiversity
president, his function is chiefly that of "mediator-innovator"
whose task is first to keep the peace among the competing (even
warring) units and second to promote progress.   Kerr argues
that the university president "wins few clear-cut victories; he
must aim more at avoiding the worst than seizing the best.   He
must find satisfaction in being equally distasteful to each of
his constituencies. "[4]

The City University of New York

Though the City University of New York is not a colossus comparable to the University of California, on which
Kerr chiefly based the multiversity concept, it nevertheless
partakes of the essential character of the large American
university--a whole series of communities and activities held
together by a common name, a common governing board and
a universal adherence to a tradition of lernfreiheit and lehr-

freiheit. Whether from the vantage point of the colossus
exemplified by the University of California, or the lesser
giant, like the City University of New York, an understanding of the multiversity first requires a broad rendering of
its structure. While the central theme is Brooklyn College's
SGS--a component of lesser authority, responsibility, influence and power in the structure of the giant City University
complex--a structural representation of the totality is essential for a clearer understanding of SGS.

Some statistics of the magnitude of the City University will be enlightening in order more fully to comprehend
the parameters involved. It is comprised of a total of seven
senior colleges, each with a distinctive name, faculty, administration, student body and physical site.[5] All are under
the jurisdiction of the Board of Higher Education which, under statute, constitutes the board of trustees.[6]

Also included in this complex are six two-year community colleges, administered by the Board of Higher Education under the program of the State University.[7] These community colleges offer two-year curricula in liberal arts leading to the associate in arts degree and curricula in various
technologies leading to the associate in applied science degree. Qualified graduates with the necessary prerequisites
may transfer to four-year institutions. Total enrollment in
the City University in the Fall 1966 semester was about
142, 600, of which 110, 561 were in the senior colleges,
29, 332 in the community colleges, and 2, 710 in university
doctoral programs and City University College Centers.

The colleges are financed primarily by the City of
New York, the State of New York, and by fees and gifts.
The 1966-67 operating budget amounted to $135, 000, 000. The
initial plans for capital construction for the next three years

total some $260,000,000 to be financed under the City University Construction Fund, a recent legislative creature.[8]

Tuition for baccalaureate degree programs is free for qualified residents of the City and for qualified residents of the State who are preparing to teach or are enrolled in the fifth year teacher education program. New York State students not preparing to teach may enroll for baccalaureate study. For them, tuition is $400 a year. Tuition is now free for matriculated community college students who are qualified residents of the city. For other New York State students, tuition is $300 a year. Tuition fees are paid by all other students in undergraduate, graduate, and adult education courses. Laboratory and service fees are also paid by all students.

Brooklyn College

Brooklyn College was established in May, 1930, as the third liberal arts college supported and maintained on a tuition-free basis by the City of New York. Prior to that time both City College and Hunter College had maintained two-year units in Brooklyn. For their junior and senior years, students in these Brooklyn branches transferred to the appropriate main centers in Manhattan.

The first space occupied by both the two branches and the new infant college was in rented quarters in a number of office and loft buildings in what is commonly known as the Borough Hall sector of Brooklyn. In 1930, the branches were combined into a new, independent college and named Brooklyn College. At that time, there were 2,800 men and women attending Day Session classes, another 5,000 in Evening Session classes. Two-thirds of the teachers (who were largely those who had taught in the Brooklyn branches of the parent college) were in the "apprentice" ranks of fellow, tutor and instructor.

Admission of students was strictly on the objective basis of the high school average and course units taken in high school.   Unlike other public colleges in some parts of the country, Brooklyn College did not have to admit merely on the basis of a high school diploma without other quantitative and qualitative criteria.   From the beginning, then, academic achievement and promise were factors of concern. This concern was deeply felt throughout the students' college career; they were constantly encouraged to seek scholarships, fellowships, assistantships and to pursue graduate studies. The number of graduating seniors in this area of honors and awards has grown from a modest start to an impressively substantial record.

Although Brooklyn College was born and had its infancy in the period of the depression, when hundreds of students received modest financial assistance through federal programs--like the National Youth Administration--and engaged in part-time employment off-campus, the pursuit of academic excellence marked its spirit from the outset.   In 1931, an A. A. U. P. chapter was established at Brooklyn College.   In 1933, the American Council on Education and the Middle States Association of Colleges and Secondary Schools granted accreditation.   The next year, 1934, the Council of Medical Education and Hospitals of the A. M. A. also bestowed recognition.   The Institute of International Education and the Association of American Colleges followed suit shortly thereafter.   The Association of American Universities conferred its approval in 1936 as did the American Association of University Women in 1951.   Rho Chapter of Phi Beta Kappa was installed in 1950 and the Society of Sigma Xi, the scientific honor society, established a campus chapter in 1954.

The obvious shortcomings of the commercial and industrial Borough Hall area where the College operated through its first half dozen years--in several buildings separated by ten to fifteen minutes walking distance from each other--early impressed public officials, college authorities and members of the Board of Higher Education. Combined efforts resulted in the acquisition of a forty-acre tract in quiet, residential Flatbush. Ground was broken on October 2, 1935 for the first of the five buildings. The first students were moved to the new campus in a delayed fall 1937 opening. At last, a genuine college campus in Brooklyn was attained.

Administrative Organization

As previously stated, Brooklyn College is a unit of the City University of New York under the jurisdiction of the Board of Higher Education, the governing body. A Brooklyn College Committee of the Board, comprised of five men and women, is equivalent to the trustees designated for Brooklyn College. Bimonthly it reports to the full Board on academic and financial matters for appropriate action.

The President of Brooklyn College, elected by the Board, is the chief administrative and educational officer. His major administrative officers, appointed by the Board on his recommendation, are: Dean of Administration, Dean of the Faculties, Dean of Students, Dean of Studies, Dean of the School of General Studies,[9] Dean of the Division of Graduate Studies, Director of Teacher Education, Associate and Assistant Deans, Business Manager and Assistant Business Managers. In this connection, the concluding observations

of President Harry D. Gideonse in his inaugural address,
delivered on October 19, 1939, are still revealing:

> I might properly conclude with a remark which I
> also addressed to the student body of this college
> at our first meeting this fall: Brooklyn College
> has some 13,000 students working for the regular
> bachelor's degree. Some other institutions in the
> city have a larger total enrollment--none of them
> has a larger arts and sciences enrollment. It is
> difficult to visualize 13,000 students. If we could
> add up the total student body of Barnard College,
> Columbia College, Williams College, Vassar Col-
> lege, Amherst College, Colgate University, Smith
> College, Mount Holyoke College, and all of Prince-
> ton University, we would still be several hundred
> short of Brooklyn College's thirteen thousand. The
> administrative officials of these other nine institu-
> tions would number nine college presidents and
> some thirty deans. We have one president and the
> equivalent of four deans, to match that army of ad-
> ministrative talent, and I think almost anyone would
> agree that the students in a big city college are
> far more urgently in need of administrative guidance
> than the students in most of the colleges enumer-
> ated. My final plea: If we go slow--and if we
> seem somewhat impersonal--keep the arithmetic in
> mind. [10]

Faculty Organization

The faculty is organized in instructional departments
and serves in the customary ranks of professor, associate
and assistant professor, and instructor. Also enjoying faculty status are members of the Registrar and Library staffs,
organized as distinct instructional units. Some members of
the Educational Clinic and the Early Childhood Center, as
well as of the Speech and Hearing Center, also have faculty
status. [11]

With the aim of "democratizing" the organization and
administration of the colleges under its jurisdiction the Board
of Higher Education adopted Bylaws in 1938 in which it provided for an elected Faculty Council as the legislative body

in each college.   Its members include the elected chairman
and one elected delegate from each instructional department,
from six to eight elected delegates-at-large elected by the
departments in the three main branches of learning--humani-
ties, social sciences and natural sciences.   The President
of the College is chairman and presiding officer of the Faculty Council.   Other members are the Deans, Registrar and
Business Manager.   The members of the Council are elected
triennially.[12]

Department chairmen are similarly elected for a
three-year term with one-third of the instructional departments holding elections each year.   At the time the department chairman is elected, elections are also held for a delegate to the Faculty Council and a departmental appointments
committee of five members, which includes the chairman.
Not more than one of the four elected members may be in
the Instructor rank.   The appointments committee is responsible for recommending new appointees, reappointment
of individuals serving during a probationary period of three
years, termination of appointment of those serving on probation, and finally, tenure for those to be granted permanent
status after the three-year probationary period.[13]   Departments also have various other committees, some elected,
some appointed by the department chairman.

Faculty Council functions largely through elected standing committees which render reports at times deemed appropriate.   All committees file annual reports in April.   A
Committee on Committees of Faculty Council annually circu-
lates a questionnaire to all faculty members inquiring as to
the committees on which they will be available to serve.
Based on the replies, the Committee on Committees makes
its nominations for committee appointments.

Committees of Faculty Council are responsible for curricular offerings, orientation and counseling of students, student organizations and activities, among other matters. Policies established by these committees and approved by Faculty Council are the guidelines for such officers as the Dean of Students and his department of Student Services, the Dean of the Faculties and his Associates, faculty advisers to student clubs and other groups.

There is also a host of committees appointed by the President as presidential advisory committees on such matters as space and facilities, safety, athletics, ceremonials and business enterprises. The Business Manager reports directly to the President. His responsibilities include payroll, collection of fees, purchasing, book store and food services, plant operation and maintenance, and preparation of the annual budget. Reporting to him are the Assistant Business Managers and the Superintendent of Buildings and Grounds.

The Bylaws establish a Committee on Faculty Personnel and Budget, the members of which are departmental chairmen and the Dean of the Faculties. Other deans are members ex-officio. The President is the chairman and presiding officer of this Committee.[14] All departmental recommendations for appointment to the instructional staff, with or without tenure, salary levels, promotions, and special increments are subject to its review and recommendation to the President. While the President has the initial responsibility of preparing the annual tentative budget, he is required to submit it to the Committee on Faculty Personnel and Budget for its recommendations. The tentative annual budget is then submitted to the Chancellor of the University by the President together with his comments and recommendations.[15] In addition, the Committee has the power to receive and con-

sider petitions and appeals from members of the instructional staff with respect to matters of status and compensation.
Its power extends solely to that of making recommendations
to the President; it does not have decision-making power of
a binding quality.[16]

The General Faculty meets twice during the college
year. Its elected Committee on Review examines the minutes and reports of Faculty Council to determine whether any
matters should be submitted for review by the faculty-at-
large. These meetings are called by the President. Customarily he uses each occasion to discuss matters of common interest and concern to the general faculty.

Two organizational charts appear at the end of the
chapter. The first one gives a bird's-eye view of the structure and lines of authority and responsibility of Brooklyn College in broad, sweeping perspective. On the page following
is a detailed organizational chart of SGS, the component unit
with which this study is centrally concerned. The detailed
SGS chart is essential to bring into clear and sharp focus
the direct lines of authority and responsibility as well as the
coordinating and advisory relationships with the College of
Liberal Arts and Sciences (hereinafter referred to as CLAS).
Chapter IV on "Authority and Responsibility" is devoted to
an organizational analysis of the various lines graphically depicted on the detailed chart.

SGS Administrative Structure

Deans

The Dean of the School of General Studies is its chief
executive officer and is directly responsible to the President.
He meets with the College Committee on Faculty Personnel
and Budget, is a voting member of Faculty Council, and rep-

resents the College on the Council of Deans and Directors
of all the municipal colleges.

The Associate Dean has administrative responsibility
for all divisions in the School of General Studies in the areas
of admissions, dismissals, discipline, refunds, loans, and
special course and standing appeals. He is also charged
with maintaining liaison and coordinating effort with other
College officers of administration in their respective areas
of responsibility. He is deputy for the Dean of the Faculties and for the College-wide Committee on Course and
Standing with regard to all policy matters concerned with
Faculty rules and regulations. Similarly, he is deputy for
the Dean of Students on decisions involving disciplinary action, or in matters relating to admissions policies, relations
with the high schools, and entrance and guidance tests.

Assistant Deans are responsible for the administration of their respective divisions of Liberal Arts, Vocational
Studies, and Nursing Science. They receive delegated authority from the Dean and the Associate Dean to develop educational programs, organize and supervise staff, survey teaching loads and the quality of instruction, maintain admissions
and retention standards and, in general, conduct the several
divisions within the framework of college-wide policies and
procedures.

Deputy Chairmen and Coordinators

The deputy chairmen[17] serve as the official spokes-
men, in School of General Studies matters, for their respective departments and for their chairmen. Among other duties, they assist in planning curriculum offerings for evening
college needs, staffing of courses with qualified teaching personnel, controlling the size of sections, instructing and ori-

enting new teachers in standard operating procedures, visiting classes and rating teachers, holding staff meetings, advising majors on the selection of courses, and evaluating for
academic credit those courses taken at other institutions.
A Council of Deputy Chairmen, chaired by the Dean, serves
as a consultative body concerning questions of mutual concern, and for the formulation of recommended action.

The Division of Vocational Studies is similarly structured, except that the "coordinators" (who parallel the role
of the deputy chairmen) have broad jurisdiction over their respective subject matter areas. They do not represent any
department in the College of Liberal Arts and Sciences. A
Council of Coordinators, chaired by the Assistant Dean, Division of Vocational Studies, meets periodically for the exchange of ideas and information.

Advisory Council and Policy Committee

In the absence of a full time faculty,[18] the Advisory
Council serves as the official representative body of the
School of General Studies. Chaired by the President, this
Council receives reports of standing committees, advises on
proposals for changes in admission requirements and curricular offerings, as they relate to the School of General
Studies, and considers all matters pertaining to the aims and
objectives of educational programs and the maintenance of
academic standards. It also acts upon lists of candidates
recommended for degrees and diplomas. Decisions of the
Advisory Council are submitted to the Faculty Council or to
appropriate faculty committees, where necessary, for ratification. Recommendations that do not necessitate Faculty
Council action are referred, through the President, directly
to the Board of Higher Education.

The SGS Policy Committee is composed of the executive officers of the School of General Studies. It meets weekly and serves as a clearing house for the discussion of immediate problems, particularly those involving overlapping areas of responsibility. Efforts are directed toward the maintenance of a high degree of coordination among the SGS divisions, and between SGS and all other departments, agencies, and divisions of the College in order to achieve a proper administrative and functioning coherence. Toward this end, minutes of the Policy Committee are regularly circulated among the deans and other administrative officers of the College.

SGS Student Body

Comparative statistics on student enrollment in CLAS and SGS for the decade from Fall 1955 to Fall 1965 show substantial growth in both divisions. Significant, however, is the fact that the total enrollment in SGS exceeded that in CLAS by approximately 25%. In other words, the student enrollment of the component unit was larger, in each of the periods compared, than that of the parent, though not in total credit work done.[19]

As shown in the statistical table below, in the fall of 1965, 11,202 students were enrolled in SGS. Almost 2,000 men and women, eligible for the baccalaureate degree but unable or unwilling to attend during the day--because of other responsibilities to job or family--were enrolled as part-time students in the liberal arts curriculum. Another 1,115 matriculants were CLAS day-session students who, for a variety of reasons, elected to enroll in one or more SGS courses offered in the evening. Still another 2,500 students were enrolled in the two-year A.A. degree liberal arts cur-

Comparative Enrollment CLAS and SGS

	Fall 1955	Fall 1965
CLAS		
Baccalaureate Matriculants	7, 785	10, 162
Others (Permits SGS)	292	128
	8, 077	10, 290
SGS		
Baccalaureate Matriculants	2, 171	1, 939
Matriculants for Assoc. Degrees	2, 610	3, 702
Matriculants for Diplomas	1, 652	28
Non-Matriculants	2, 313	4, 418
Others (Permits CLAS)	215	1, 115
	8, 961	11, 202

riculum and were working toward a change to matriculated
status so that they might be permitted to continue as baccalaureate students.   In the Division of Vocational Studies,
approximately 1, 100 students were enrolled in curricula leading to the A. A. S. degree in a variety of career-oriented
curricula, including accounting, business, industrial relations, real estate, insurance, secretarial studies and police
science.   Post-baccalaureate students, technically classified
as non-matriculated students, numbered about 650; these
students were enrolled in undergraduate courses which would
help them become eligible for new positions, special li-
censes or admission to graduate and professional schools.
The balance of the enrollment, amounting to nearly 4, 000,
consisted of non-matriculated students attending for a variety of reasons: Some were interested in earning matriculation, others were enrolled in specific courses for retraining or for general educational background, some were regu-

lar college students at other institutions, and still others,
while they may have had the qualifications for full matriculation, filed applications too late for matriculation. The
status of the last group as non-matriculants is, therefore,
temporary and is changed when the necessary application and
records are duly filed.[20]

On the average, SGS students are older than their
CLAS counterparts. The span of ages ranges from seven-
teen to seventy. The heterogeneity is also manifested in the
varying degrees to which these students are responsible
"breadwinners." Some of the younger students work only to
provide for their individual needs. Others are heads of
households whose full-time employment is indispensable to
the well-being of children and spouse, parents and other
members of the family. The heterogeneity appears again in
the student's life experience and capacity to meet the challenge and standards of a liberal arts curriculum. These
students range from those whose environment appears to have
been devoid of intellectual experiences to those who have had
broad experiences. Among the latter, independent study and
life experience have placed many on an intellectual and cultural level above students with extended formal training only.
As a consequence of this kind of variation, classroom groupings will include students who are matriculated and students
who are not; some who hold one or more academic degrees
and others who lack necessary high school units. Still others may be struggling to attain eligibility for matriculated
status previously denied because of poor scholastic performance at high school or other colleges attended, or because
of poor grades received in courses taken at Brooklyn College
either in SGS or CLAS.

Matriculated baccalaureate degree candidates in SGS

meet the quantitative and qualitative entrance requirements
of CLAS.   They choose evening study for personal, job or
family reasons.   But a large group of young people who did
not meet the qualifications for admission to the B. A. program were eligible for matriculation for the two-year Associate in Arts degree.   For them, the quantitative and
qualitative requirements for admission were lower.[21]   This
category is diminishing in numbers as the community colleges increasingly take over the role of the Associate Degree
programs.

Non-matriculated students are permitted to enroll in
SGS after passing an entrance examination administered by
it.   This category is especially important for mature individuals who have been out of school for appreciable periods
of time.   Past records in formal education, it is felt, provide a less reliable index for predicting probable success in
college than would factors such as experience, maturity and
motivation.   The "poorest risks" are weeded out by a strict
retention policy which drops those who cannot maintain a
"C" average.

Budget and Finance

The budget for the School of General Studies is officially provided by the Budget Director of the City of New
York.   Each year a budget request is prepared by the Dean
and submitted to the President of the College.   The President then reviews the request, makes whatever revisions he
deems advisable, and submits the total College budget to the
Board, which incorporates it in the budget request of the
City University.   The total budget recommendation is then
transmitted to the Budget Director.

From the point of view of SGS administration, budg-

etary allocations to it are always inadequate. The budgets
have, from the early days of the predecessor evening sessions, been a mere pittance in comparison with day college
budgets. In 1956-66, for example, the average cost per
student credit hour in SGS was approximately $15. Ex-
pressed in terms of a full-time equivalent program on an
annual basis (15 credits per term; 30 credits per annum)
this amounts to a cost of approximately $450 per student.
Comparable costs for full-time day students have been vari-
ously estimated at $1400-$1800 per year.[22] This financial
discrepancy places the part-time instructors, who constitute
the bulk of SGS faculty, in an inferior salary level compared
to the full-time staff. In general, compensation per course
of a part-time instructor in SGS is approximately 60% of the
pay of a full-time staff member computed on the basis of
teaching load to annual salary.

Problem Areas

As a suborganization, SGS continues to wrestle with
certain obstacles and weaknesses. Most of these are deep-
rooted and closely associated with problems that have vexed
evening colleges for a generation or longer.

> They stem from the fact that evening sessions or
> branches were traditionally supplemental functions,
> i. e. , adjuncts to the day sessions, and not major,
> first-line commitments of the institutions that cre-
> ated them. Consequently they had to operate with
> whatever financial resources, personnel, and physi-
> cal facilities were available after provision had
> been made for the central purposes of the institu-
> tion. [23]

The Major Problems

The following major problems face SGS:

1. Employment of teaching and supervisory staffs on a part-time basis at salary rates considerably lower than those paid to full-time personnel.

2. Ambiguities and conflicts in lines of authority and responsibility.

3. Lack of physical facilities for the development of educational programs especially designed for adults.

4. Inadequate budget.

5. Heterogeneous nature of the student body.

These problems have played an influential role in creating the impression that SGS lacks status on the campus; that its personnel are "second-class citizens" and that the standards of excellence and high repute of the institution as a whole are being compromised. Without a full-time faculty of its own, and often confronted with a college-wide faculty which is indifferent or even hostile to its stated aims and purposes, SGS has frequently found itself severely restricted in conducting its operations along lines that would best serve the interests and needs of its students.[24]

The relative harmony at Brooklyn College, despite the problem areas, is to a large extent due to the support of SGS by the President of the College and to the widespread involvement of so many CLAS faculty members in one or more phases of evening college work.[25] This active participation has served to give them an understanding and appreciation of SGS goals, aspirations and programs. The Dean of the Faculties has expressed the opinion that: "Generally speaking, the faculty has shown a sympathetic interest in affairs and has been unusually cooperative in supporting policies that would strengthen the school and improve its status."[26]

Nevertheless, the fact remains that the problems persist in greater or lesser degree. SGS is still under-staffed in terms of annual lines, underprivileged in terms of hourly rates of pay, in terms of part-time employees not eligible for benefits of sick leave, paid vacations, tenure, pension and welfare privileges, and disadvantaged in terms of staff-room facilities. Very significant is the fact that the financing is still "shoestring" in character; the funds assigned for SGS functions are a small fraction of the total college budget. Equally significant are the limitations on its envisioned goals, its jurisdiction and role. These problems will be treated more fully in the chapters that follow.

Notes

1. Talcott Parsons, (ed.). The Theory of Social and Economic Organization (Free Press, 1947), p. 152.

2. Howard S. Becker. The Teacher in the Authority System of the Public School, in Etzioni, Amitai, Complex Organizations (Holt, Rinehart & Winston, 1965), p. 243-257.

3. Clark Kerr. The Uses of the University (Cambridge, Mass. 1964), passim.

4. Ibid., p. 40.

5. City, Hunter, Brooklyn, Baruch, Queens, Lehman, Richmond and York Colleges offer curricula leading to the baccalaureate degree, open to bona fide residents of the city and state. Masters' programs are offered in a wide variety of fields. The John Jay College of Police Science offers degrees with majors in police science. Doctoral programs are offered in many fields by the City University of New York.

6. The Board has a membership of twenty-one men and women appointed by the Mayor for nine-year terms, and one member ex officio, the President of the Board of Education. Board members are drawn from many areas of the city's life and serve without salary.

Board headquarters are at 535 East 80th Street, New York, New York 10021.

7. Borough of Manhattan, Bronx, Kingsborough, New York City, Queensborough and Staten Island.

8. New York State Laws of 1966, chapter 782, Article 125B.

9. Until 1966, this title was Director. The current title is Dean and it will be utilized hereafter.

10. Quoted in A Report to the Middle States Association of Colleges and Secondary Schools, June 1, 1966, Brooklyn College of the City University of New York, p. 5-6.

11. Bylaws, Art. VIII.

12. Ibid., Sec. 8. 6.

13. Ibid., Art. IX. (In 1969, the probationary period was extended to five years.)

14. Bylaws Sec. 8. 7 (a).

15. Ibid., Sec. 8. 7 (b).

16. Ibid., Sec. 8. 7 (c).

17. The Bylaws provide for election of department chairman (see p. 29 this chapter) but no specific provision is made for an administrative head of the department in SGS. The deputy chairman is recommended by the chairman to the Dean and approved by the President. For a detailed description of this administrative role, see Chapter IV, "Authority and Responsibility," p. 175-183.

18. The SGS teaching staff consists predominantly of part-time teachers, though there is a small core of college faculty members or SGS "lines."

19. CLAS students customarily take an average of fifteen credits per semester; the average for SGS students is seven credits, or approximately one-half the full-time credit load.

20. See p. 160-161 of Report cited in footnote 10.

21. This group is no longer admitted to SGS.   They may
    now (since 1966) apply for admission to community
    colleges.   See Chapter II,"Organizational Goals."

22. "Annual Report of the Dean," School of General Studies,
    1965-66, p. 25.

23. See p. 173 of Report cited in footnote 10.

24. Ibid. , p. 173-174.

25. See Chapter III, "Innovation Through Cooptation."

26. See p. 174 of Report cited in footnote 10.

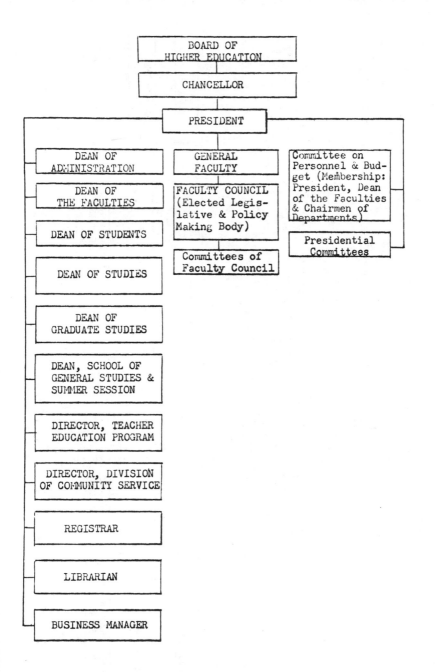

BOARD OF
HIGHER EDUCATION

CHANCELLOR

PRESIDENT

DEAN OF
ADMINISTRATION

DEAN OF
THE FACULTIES

DEAN OF STUDENTS

DEAN OF STUDIES

DEAN OF
GRADUATE STUDIES

DEAN, SCHOOL OF
GENERAL STUDIES &
SUMMER SESSION

DIRECTOR, TEACHER
EDUCATION PROGRAM

DIRECTOR, DIVISION
OF COMMUNITY SERVICE

REGISTRAR

LIBRARIAN

BUSINESS MANAGER

GENERAL
FACULTY

FACULTY COUNCIL
(Elected Legis-
lative & Policy
Making Body)

Committees of
Faculty Council

Committee on
Personnel & Bud-
get (Membership:
President, Dean
of the Faculties
& Chairmen of
Departments)

Presidential
Committees

43

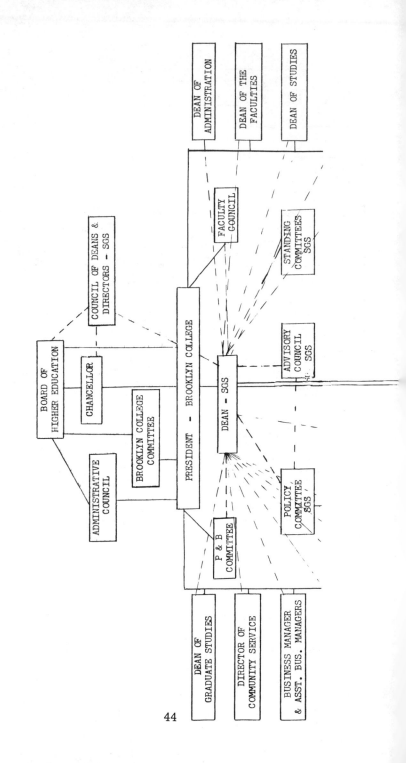

BOARD OF HIGHER EDUCATION

CHANCELLOR

ADMINISTRATIVE COUNCIL

BROOKLYN COLLEGE COMMITTEE

COUNCIL OF DEANS & DIRECTORS - SGS

PRESIDENT - BROOKLYN COLLEGE

DEAN - SGS

DEAN OF ADMINISTRATION

DEAN OF THE FACULTIES

DEAN OF STUDIES

FACULTY COUNCIL

STANDING COMMITTEES SGS

ADVISORY COUNCIL SGS

POLICY COMMITTEE SGS

P & B COMMITTEE

DEAN OF GRADUATE STUDIES

DIRECTOR OF COMMUNITY SERVICE

BUSINESS MANAGER & ASST. BUS. MANAGERS

44

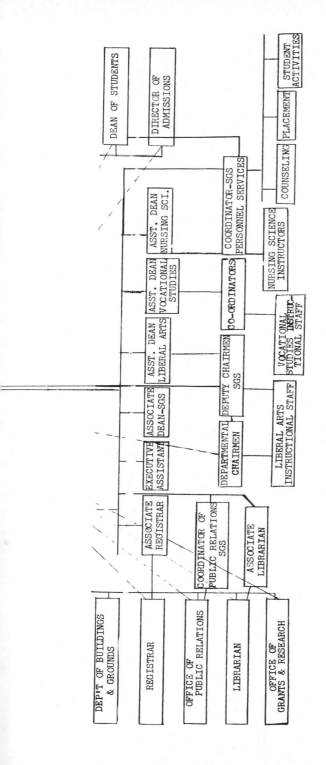

Chapter II

Organizational Goals

> "If a man does not know to
> which port he is steering, no
> wind is favorable."
>   Seneca

Every charter, constitution or proclamation begins
with a statement of purpose. The preambles of the Charter
of the United Nations and the Constitution of the United
States, for example, first declare the reasons for the formation of the collectivity and in lofty language proclaim its
goals. The goals thus formulate a raison d'etre and legitimize the claim for a sphere of activity.[1]

In addition to conferring legitimacy on activities,
goals reveal the manifest aspirations of the organization as
an entity. Whether these are consistent with the aspirations
of the actors within the organization is a separate problem.
The fact is that the entity itself sets goals which it hopes to
achieve. These goals provide targets for the actors toward
which they are expected to strive in the interests of the organization.

The extent to which stated goals are achieved is often
considered a measure of the effectiveness of the organization. Thus goals also serve as a standard against which actual performance is evaluated.

Goals of the City University

The goals of the City University are broadly stated
in its Master Plan:

> The City University of New York aims at meeting
> the need for publicly-supported education beyond
> the high school, principally for the men and wo-
> men who live in New York City, to insure that
> each one of them who has a reasonable expectation
> of success in education beyond the high school may
> have the opportunity to profit by such education.
> It must, therefore, provide the fullest possible
> range of opportunities in higher education, reach-
> ing from the most advanced research at one ex-
> treme to the sub-professional technical training of
> much-needed specialists on the other . . . The
> only limits which the University recognizes are
> those set by the limitation of the individual stu-
> dents' and scholars' desire to learn and to con-
> tribute to the learning of others . . . The goal is
> educational excellence at all levels.[2]

Fulfillment of these goals rests primarily with the
constituent colleges that make up the City University as an
educational system.   Like American Telephone and Telegraph
Co. , the City University may be viewed as an integrated system of a number of operating companies.   While the holding
company--the City University--establishes guidelines for action, it decentralizes management in the individual operating
companies, the component colleges.   The individual colleges
in the City University, like subsidiary companies in any holding company complex, then proceed to individualize their
goals within the framework of the total system's guidelines.

Goals of Brooklyn College

Diversity within unity is a typical consequence of complex organizations, for the component units in the system acquire their own history, traditions, programs and aspirations.

While governed by the broad aims and objectives of the total system as an entity, each component unit forms and expresses its own particular goals. This is the essence of
decentralized management in the matrix of coordinated control.

Brooklyn College is a liberal arts college and it de-
clares its goals in the highlights and shadows of the liberal
arts tradition. Catalogues of practically all colleges offering the bachelor of arts degree contain similar language describing the institution's objectives. The differences are
mainly in literary style. Brooklyn College expresses its
liberal arts goals in the following words:

1. Providing the opportunity for the acquisition and
   assimilation of a liberalizing and useful body of
   knowledge;

2. Developing the ability to think critically, reason
   and generalize logically and express one's
   thoughts and experiences with clarity and precision;

3. Developing the acquisition of a strong sense of
   individual responsibility;

4. Fostering an understanding and appreciation of
   human personality;

5. Promoting an understanding and appreciation of
   the need for effective practices of good social
   relations;

6. Meeting the needs of the student, as an individual and as a member of society for the stimulation and continuing development of activities related to his intellectual life, his career, his
   home life, his community life.[3]

These general principles indicate the broad goals of
Brooklyn College at the undergraduate levels with respect to
CLAS as well as SGS. In conducting the daily affairs of the

organization, however, such general principles must be translated into operational terms.   It is at this point that differences in student population, instruction and staff lead to a
divergence of specific pragmatic goals between the parent
organization and its sub-unit.   Though both readily subscribe
to the broadly stated purposes of the institution, the specific
activities they undertake and the goals which legitimize these
activities may no longer be congruent.

The primary commitment of the parent college is to
matriculated students enrolled for the bachelor's degree.
However, it was recognized for a long time that a large segment of the SGS student population is interested not only in
a degree but also in individual courses.   In addition, there
are many high school graduates who do not meet the eligibility entrance requirements for full matriculation who nevertheless seek an opportunity to gain this status while at college.   This quest for a second chance to prove scholastic
promise is a cogent appeal to a tax-supported educational
system.   The open-door policy to higher education, within
the reasonable limits of student capacity and motivation,
plainly subserves the democratic ideal of equality of opportunity.   Hence a non-matriculated category of students was
established so that "Every mature resident of the City of
New York, of either sex, who can profit by the work, may
be admitted to particular courses in the Evening Session as
a non-matriculated student, upon the payment of the required
fees, and may receive certificates of work in particular
courses."[4]

Despite identity of courses, curricula and degrees,
SGS is not, in any decisive sense, a facsimile of the day college.   Recognition of the differences in student composition
has been a constant theme of the evening college.   For ex-

ample, in an official communique to the staff the distinguish-
ing feature of the student body was stressed by referring to
the evening, part-time student as "more mature than those
in the College of Liberal Arts and Sciences . . . (they) attend evening classes because they are employed during the
day . . . (going) to school at considerable personal sacri-
fice and . . . their reaction to college work is therefore
more serious, practical and decisive than that of other college students."[5]

Historical Emergence of SGS Goals

In 1941, the Evening Session, predecessor of SGS,
developed new goals in order to provide the equivalent of a
"junior" college education in liberal arts.   An organized,
balanced curriculum embracing the humanities, arts, natural
and social sciences, and consisting of half the number of
credits required for the baccalaureate degree, was constructed
for those evening students whose high school grades evidenced lower than "senior" college potential or for those evening students whose interests did not extend to the long-term
grind (from seven to eight years) necessary to achieve the
B. A. degree in an evening program.   This program led to
the Associate in Arts diploma and later to the Associate in
Arts degree.   The entrance requirements for the diploma or
associate degree programs were significantly lower than those
required for admission to the regular B. A. degree.

To a large extent, many students who formerly would
have been classified as non-matriculants for the B. A. degree now became qualified as matriculants in the diploma or
associate degree program.   While these students, like non-
matriculants, also paid tuition fees, the rates were lower
than those for B. A. non-matriculated students.   As a conse-

quence, three rather than just two categories of students
came into being.

The rationale for this development was explained by
Ordway Tead, the Chairman of the Board of Higher Education, in his 1944 annual report as follows:

> For thirty-five years the city colleges have offered
> evening session courses paralleling the day cur-
> riculum for which the student could eventually get
> the regular baccalaureate degree. This was de-
> signed to give students who needed to work, during
> the day, the opportunity to earn a college degree
> at night. The demands upon the evening student
> in terms of time and energy are extraordinary, for
> it normally takes concentrated evening study for
> seven or eight years to earn a degree. The natur-
> al consequence has been a far too high mortality
> between those who start and those who finish . . .
>
> Recognizing this fact and after a careful study of
> the whole problem both by a committee of the
> Board and by the College itself, Brooklyn College
> embarked upon a terminal evening course in the
> Fall of 1941. This is the Associate in Arts Cur-
> riculum and is designed to meet more expeditious-
> ly the requirements of evening students. It in-
> cludes a program equivalent to two college years
> in general education and normally can be completed
> in three and a half years of evening session
> work . . .
>
> It is to be hoped that a similar attack upon the
> problem of shorter evening instruction curricula
> will be worked out in the other colleges at the
> close of the war.[6]

After World War II, SGS experienced a huge influx of
returning veterans financially assisted by the G. I. Bill of
Rights. These veterans represented an older, more mature
age-group. As a result, the differentiation in character between the day and evening student populations became even
more pronounced. This development again highlighted the
critical question of whether content and method appropriate

for one division were necessarily valid for the other. Further probing of this question, especially by the Directors of the Evening Sessions, led to the visions of still wider horizons for the evening divisions. As stated in the 1946-1948 report of the Chairman of the Board of Higher Education:

> All these (evening) students need a different approach, different courses and teaching methods from those of the regular undergraduates; and their needs must be met if the colleges are to fulfill their obligation to serve the educational requirements of the people of our City. It has been proposed that for this service an educational unit, newly named, be set up in each of the four colleges, which would embrace and develop the present adult education and other kindred offerings. . .[7]

Reorganization and Expanding Goals

These germinal ideas finally came to fruition on April 17, 1950, when an "educational unit, newly named" the School of General Studies, was designated by the Board of Higher Education as the successor to the old Evening Session. The name School of General Studies apparently was chosen to connote the broad spectrum of educational activities to be encompassed. The newly named division was characterized as a "major Division of Brooklyn College" and was "charged with the administrative responsibility for Liberal Arts work offered during the evening and given full jurisdiction over all diploma curricula and the enrollment of non-matriculated students."[8]

Jurisdiction over associate degree and diploma curricula and over non-matriculated students was thus vested exclusively in the School of General Studies. SGS consequently experienced a sense of advancement toward a greater level of autonomy, even though "in the degree granting area, the Schools of General Studies would continue to provide in-

struction and services consistent with existing regulations of
the faculties concerned through cooperation with regular Day
Session departments. "[9]   Referring to the creation of the
School of General Studies, its Dean significantly stated in his
1950–1951 annual report:

> This development represented far more than a
> change in name. For the first time since the
> founding of Brooklyn College, students attending
> its afternoon and evening "branches" or "sessions"
> were offered the stature and dignity of a separate
> school, possessing a certain amount of autonomy
> and devoted primarily to the interests of this ma-
> jor segment of the student body. [10]

As constituted in 1950, SGS embraced both credit and
non-credit programs. It offered both four-year baccalaureate degrees and two-year associate degrees and diplomas.
In addition, it conducted a myriad of community services
such as a speech clinic, a symphony orchestra, a children's
theater and similar cultural enterprises. As far as the
four-year baccalaureate degree was concerned, curriculum
and staffing were quite intimately tied to the administrative
controls of the day college's instructional departments. Room
for expansion, therefore, centered principally in those programs which were unique to SGS: non-matriculant students,
two-year liberal arts and vocational curricula and community
services. [11]   It was in these areas that sustained growth was
envisaged. To provide the implemental means for growth,
SGS reorganized its component units into functional divisions.

Six divisions to absorb old and newly planned functions were established, with the approval of the President.
Each division was placed under the administrative control of
a "supervisor" recommended by the then Director (now Dean)
of SGS. These divisions were:

1. The Division of Liberal Arts: Administrative con-

trol of two-year and four-year liberal arts degree curricula
in which matriculated as well as non-matriculated students
were enrolled.

2. The Division of Vocational Studies: Administrative
control of two-year career oriented curricula in business and
sub-professional areas which led to diplomas and to the Associate in Applied Science Degree.

3. The Adult Education Division: Administrative control of a liberal arts, vocational, cultural and recreational
character for everyone interested.

4. The Division of Community Services: Conduct of
a vast variety of cultural enterprises consisting of concerts,
theater, dance, speech therapy and like services for the
community.

5. The Division of Counseling and Guidance: A service department consisting of clinical and other psychologists,
and a battery of counseling and guidance personnel to advise
students on curricular, personal and educational objectives.

6. The Division of Audio-Visual Services: A service
department to provide audio-visual and related instrumental
aids for lectures and classroom instruction.

Girded by this new divisional organization, SGS embarked on an energetic program to expand the variety of offerings and the size of student enrollment.

The Take-Off Period of Growth

Like any underdeveloped country or organization which
feels the initial stirrings for growth and development, SGS,
after its first year, critically reviewed its resources and
current "market position" and appraised its potential for expansion.   For sustained growth it first sought to diversify
its offerings in those areas where consumer (student) demand

and need were most evident. Second, it attempted to attract additional students to its existing programs as well as
to its newly developing programs. Implemental measures in
both directions were simultaneously adopted, for the two
goals were mutually dependent. Achievement of these new
goals demanded the highest degree of imagination and re-
sourcefulness since, at that time, colleges generally were
not in a "seller's market" but rather in a "buyer's market."
Competition among colleges for students was extremely vigorous in those days. Though structural and operational patterns of the college were exceedingly tradition-bound, SGS
perceived its condition as a seminal one. Eagerly, it accentuated bold experimentation with novel products and new
clientele. Such market expansion and diversification are
characteristic of a young, striving organization.

Experimentation with new offerings on a large scale in
a relatively brief period of time was, however, practically
impossible in the liberal arts four-year degree. In that
sphere, SGS exercised very limited controls and was not
free to innovate without the prior approval of CLAS. And
CLAS approval involved a long and arduous clearance procedure from a multitude of administrative officials, instructional departments, faculty committees and Faculty Council.
Consequently, the expansion movement was concentrated
mainly in the areas where SGS was not dependent on paren-
tal authorization and where it had exclusive jurisdiction.
These, of course, were primarily in the two-year vocational
curricula, in the Adult Education Division and in the Community Service Division.

1. Adult Education Division
The most dramatic expansion occurred in the Adult

Education Division.   A host of new non-credit courses of
highly popular appeal--i. e. "How to Become Effective in Con-
versation," "How to Remember," etc. --were added to the
offerings.   Accelerated courses in real estate and insurance
brokerage, qualifying the student for the State licensing examinations, were widely advertised.   Practical courses in
security analysis, bookkeeping, salesmanship, small business
techniques, production planning, foremanship and supervisory
techniques, among others, were designed for veterans seeking
to readjust to a competitive but strangely peaceful society.
A wider variety of recreational and hobby courses--drawing,
painting, dancing, sculpture, graphic arts, etc. --were added
to the list of selections.   Serious reading and study courses
in literature, drama, creative writing, philosophy, psychology, sociology, foreign languages, etc. , augmented the ever-
increasing size of the announcement brochures.   From an
enrollment of 4, 794 in the academic year 1950-1951, registration grew to 6, 408 in 1952-1953. [12]   SGS looked with satisfaction at this 33% rise in fee-paying enrollment attained in
a short period of two years.

2. Division of Vocational Studies

        This Division, which offered 48-credit diploma cur-
ricula and 64-credit Associate in Applied Science Degree curricula, also embarked on an expansion program and experienced a substantial rise in enrollment in the initial period of
SGS growth.   In a period of three years, it, too, advanced
33%.   The rise was from 1, 216 students in 1950-1951 to
1, 610 students in 1953-1954.

        This substantial rate of growth was achieved, in large
measure, by broadening curricula offerings to embrace wider
choices.   New associate degree and diploma programs in ad-

vertising, merchandising, business management, industrial
relations, insurance, real estate and secretarial studies were
established.   Experimental diploma programs in food service
administration and in police science were instituted to test
student interest in these fields.   Cooperative arrangements
with large restaurant chains and institutional cafeterias were
consummated for the food service administration program;
similar arrangements were developed for the police science
program in cooperation with the Port of New York Authority
and other law enforcement agencies.   The objective was to
expand these areas from diploma into associate degree offerings if sufficient student interest materialized.[13]

Another venture in college-community cooperation was
initiated at the same time in the field of Nursing Science.
Classes in the natural sciences and general education for student nurses were organized in September, 1953 under contracts with the schools of nursing of the Norwegian Lutheran
Deaconess Hospital and the Prospect Heights Hospital.   The
experience gained from these ventures laid the groundwork
for the establishment in the Fall 1954 semester of fully organized two-year curricula in Nursing Science leading to the
Associate in Applied Science degree.   Funds for this project
were provided in 1953 by the Board of Higher Education in
order to assist in the alleviation of the severe shortage of
nurses in New York City.   These funds made it possible to
conduct a tuition-free program to train students to become
registered nurses.

3. Division of Liberal Arts

Even though SGS faced time-consuming administrative
obstacles in innovating in the liberal arts area, novel ideas
were nevertheless advanced.   The need for a full-scale cur-

riculum in accounting, leading to the bachelor of science degree to prepare students for the New York State C. P. A. license examinations, was discerned. At the time, this curriculum was being offered only at the Baruch School of Business Administration, the downtown branch of City College in
Manhattan. This monopoly position was not easy to overcome.[14] Enlisting the enthusiastic support of the CLAS Economics Department which offered a series of courses in accounting, the project was made a joint venture between the
department and SGS. Parenthetically, it should be pointed
out that the Dean of SGS was also a full professor in the
Economics Department and a life-long colleague of the senior
faculty member teaching accounting in that department. These
formal and informal relationships were of vital importance in
the formation of the joint venture to introduce a B. S. in Accounting degree in a liberal arts college. Finally, in 1954,
the project was approved by the Board of Higher Education
after the State Education Department granted preliminary registration of the curriculum. It might be added that this program has proven a highly successful one to the present day.

For adults interested neither in a 48-credit liberal
arts diploma nor in a 64-credit associate in arts degree, SGS
promulgated in 1952 a "guided and balanced program of liberal education for adults at the collegiate level."[15] No eligibility requirements for admission based on high school scholastic record or scholastic aptitude tests were imposed. Any
mature person who appeared able to profit from the course
of study, after a counseling interview, was eligible for admission. The intent was to reach reasonably intelligent a-
dults--housewives, workers, small businessmen, civil service workers, immigrants, etc.--who aspired to a moderate
level of intellectual stimulation and study.

The curriculum, known as the Diploma in General
Education, consisted of a prescribed core of night courses,
two in each of the four main branches of learning: humanities, natural sciences, social sciences and written and oral
communication.   In addition, the student was expected to
elect a total of eight additional courses from the humanities,
communication, social sciences and natural sciences.   The
inspiration for the program and its structure were germinated
by a quotation from a Ford Foundation publication, Education
in a Democratic Society:

> Education must meet the needs of the human spir-
> it.   It must assist persons to develop a satisfactory
> personal philosophy and sense of values; to culti-
> vate tastes for literature, music and the arts; and
> to grow in ability to analyze problems and arrive
> at thoughtful conclusions.

In essence, this Diploma in General Education curriculum was neither a non-credit nor a credit program in
the accepted senses of those terms.   Indeed, courses taken
in this curriculum were not creditable toward the B. A. degree should a student later transfer to the baccalaureate program.   It was in the nature of a straddle between credit and
non-credit programs.   It was also designed for the purpose
of exploring the magnitude of community interests and to
gain insights into new directions.   In the Fall 1953 semester, 86 students were enrolled in this "balanced" program:
enrollment dropped to 72 in the Spring of 1954.   Despite
heroic efforts to enlarge enrollment through contacts with
parent-teachers associations, community centers, women's
social and business clubs, labor unions and community organizations, the program had to be withdrawn in 1954 because
of inadequacy of registration.   Students indicated that a "diploma" was accorded little recognition in the community;

serious students preferred to register in two-year "degree"
programs.

Release of manpower from this area furnished the human resources to concentrate on another novel idea, an experimental baccalaureate degree project for mature adults
with rich life experiences. Conferences on this experimental project were held with the Center for the Study of Liberal Education for Adults, a Chicago-based institution financed
by the Fund for Adult Education, an organization supported
by the Ford Foundation. The object was to obtain a grant
of funds to initiate a pilot operation with a carefully selected
group of mature adults who had documentary and other evidence of scholastic and intellectual promise. In 1954, this
pioneering experiment was instituted. The techniques employed to achieve it are so critical to the theories of organizational cooptation that an analysis of this program, which
has gained national recognition and prominence, is reserved
for the next chapter.

4. Division of Audio-Visual Services

Recent success by various institutions in using tele-
vision as the medium of reaching wide listening audiences at
home, such as New York University's Sunrise Semester, currently refreshes memories of the early start of SGS in insti-
tuting home-study courses via radio. At the time, this concept was truly a pioneer effort, but it apparently was historically too early for mass educational techniques. The
basic idea was enrollment of students in home-study courses,
obviating typical class attendance. Courses in music, literature, speech and socio-economic problems were conducted on
radio with the aid of syllabi prepared for each course. Students were then given course credits applicable to the A. A. S.

degree after successfully passing an examination. Lack of
adequate student response after four years of effort to place
this imaginative venture on a meaningful foundation, regrettably dictated its discontinuance.

5. Division of Community Services

As one of its responsibilities, SGS visualized its role
to be that of contributing to the improvement of the cultural
level of the community. From its very beginning, SGS organized a symphony orchestra, a children's theater and a
speech clinic. But it constantly endeavored to engage in
more extensive community activities. In the performing arts,
it proceeded within two years to organize a community chor-
us, a symphony and choral society and a theater group.
Amateur performers from the community were invited to participate in these artistic endeavors. Recitals and perform-
ances were regularly given.

To advance another significant community service,
SGS expanded the original speech clinic by broadening its
scope into a Speech and Hearing Center. Manned by pro-
fessionally-trained personnel, the functions were to diagnose,
treat and improve persons with speech and hearing impediments. Broader community influence was attained by SGS
in establishing a Speakers' Bureau. Published lists of faculty members available as public speakers and lecturers were
circulated to groups desiring a lecturer for an evening. A
broad spectrum of subjects in the learned disciplines, from
anthropology to zoology, was included. The rates were exceedingly moderate and many local associations, clubs, con-
gregations, community houses and other groups were able to
secure a speaker for the evening from the Speakers' Bureau.

Contraction and Goal Succession

These extensive innovations on a broad front by SGS
represented appreciable strides in extending the scope of its
activities.   The deliberate intention was to expand old goals
and also to expand the range of activities.   The high degree
of success in most areas made the future look bright.   But
then pressures arose from sources external to SGS.   The
pressures stemmed chiefly from the parent organization,
which clipped SGS's wings in important respects.   Curtailment of its domain presented a serious threat of contraction.
To overcome the effects of these restrictions, additional and
new goals had to be created.

In the literature, goals succession is seen as a result of either of two situations:

   a) when the organization has reached its goals and
      its services are no longer required;

   b) when it becomes clear that the goals cannot be at-
      tained. [16]

SGS experience demonstrates a third source of goal
displacement: that is, an organization demonstrates that
certain goals are desirable and attainable but this very demonstration causes a more powerful body to usurp these goals,
leaving the sub-organization to find new ones.

In terms of legal and bureaucratic structure, the three
SGS divisions of Adult Education, Audio-Visual Services and
Community Services had the most tenuous link to the administrative and instructional officialdom of CLAS.   In these divisions, SGS exercised the highest degree of administrative
autonomy.   While its decisions were subject to presidential
review, SGS did not share divided authority in those spheres
with the various deans or permanent faculty of the parent

college. Indeed, the Adult Education Division, which offered only non-credit courses to serve a variety of interests
--intellectual, business, vocational, recreational, etc.--car-
ried out its functions outside the CLAS "system" of credit
and degree programs. These areas were free of the CLAS
administrative and instructional hierarchy. Similarly with
the Division of Community Services. Hence these Divisions
constituted virgin territory in which SGS was free to explore
and to stake out operational activities. Indeed, during the
first three years, SGS made substantial progress in ventur-
ing into this territory in many novel and exciting directions.
But then came the ides of March, 1953.

On the ground that "the community services must
have the single and primary attention of a director if the
latter was to exercise a creative touch,"[17] the President
proposed that the Adult Education and Community Service
divisions be separated from SGS and be merged into a new
Division of Community Services under the jurisdiction of a
separate director. Separation of the credit and non-credit
areas was desirable, he declared, because of "the steadily
increasing enrollments" in the instructional divisions, both
credit and non-credit.

The proposal was approved by the Board of Higher
Education by means of delegating authority to the President
to determine relative boundaries of jurisdiction. Apparently
the presidents of the other three senior colleges in the municipal system--City, Hunter and Queens--though experienc-
ing substantially similar steady increases in enrollment, did
not deem it advisable to reorganize their Schools of General
Studies along the same lines. Brooklyn College was the only unit in which this organizational spin-off and merger came
into being. The "supervisor" of the former Division of Com-

munity Services was named the Director of the reorganized
Division of Community Services.

Severance from SGS of two other divisions occurred
somewhat later.   To centralize operating budget and authority over technical personnel concerned with audio-visual material and equipment, the Division of Audio-Visual Services
was merged in 1955 with its day-college sibling and placed
under the jurisdiction of the Office of the Dean of the Faculties. [18]   Two years later, after a long debate involving a
jurisdictional contest between the Dean of Students and the
Dean of the School of General Studies, the Division of Counseling and Guidance was dissolved by presidential directive
and the functions of this division transferred to the Department of Personnel Service of which the Dean of Students was
the chief officer.

After these territorial partitions, SGS's jurisdiction
was reduced exclusively to authority over credit and degree
programs in the two instructional Divisions of Liberal Arts
and Vocational Studies.

Moving and Reaching Out

Analogizing the university to a living plant or animal
that adapts to a changing environment, one observer of the
academic scene views the university as "always adjusting its
parts internally, and always moving, reaching out as long as
it is alive."[19]   The metaphor may be aptly applied to SGS.
To maintain vitality, it energetically embarked on a process
of "moving and reaching out" for greater expansion in student enrollment in the remaining two instructional divisions.
That these goal successions bore a bountiful harvest is indicated by the enrollment statistics in five-year intervals over
a period of fifteen years from 1950 to 1965.

SGS Student Enrollments*
1950 - 1965

Year	No. of Students
1950	7, 766
1955	8, 961
1960	9, 105
1965	11, 202

*Based on Fall Semester

The steep rise in total student enrollment from 1950 to 1965 was attributable to several factors. First, undergraduate enrollment on the national scene rose from 2. 2 to 4. 2 million. Coupled with the population explosion was the significantly higher ratio of college-age students desiring to attend college. In fact, the staggering rate of growth in student population is expected to continue for the next decade. Projected for 1970 is a potential undergraduate enrollment of 6. 9 million, and for 1975 one of 8. 6 million. To accommodate the potential enrollment will require an estimated outlay of $3 billion for new academic facilities, the sum needed to triple the quantity of academic facilities built during the last decade. [20]

By 1965, Brooklyn College was already operating at excess capacity. New construction was desperately needed to alleviate the extraordinarily crowded conditions. As evidenced by the enrollment figures, SGS obviously participated in the efforts to accommodate larger and larger entering classes.

A second factor that accounted for the steep rise of enrollment in SGS was the inability of CLAS, in terms of its limited physical space, staff and budgetary resources, to admit all applicants. For many years, the total number of

applicants for admission to the day college far exceeded the
number that could be accommodated.   For example, in the
Fall 1962 semester, 4, 767 students applied for admission
but only 2, 780 could be admitted.   Admission standards were
thereupon raised to a high school average of 85% from the
previous 83%.   In the Fall 1963 semester, applications for
admission rose to 5, 133 and the high school average for entrance was then raised to 87%.   Admissions were limited in
order to maintain enrollment levels within reasonable relationship to plant and personnel resources. [21] Concomitantly,
there was an upsurge of tuition fees in private institutions.
Many students, therefore, chose to enroll as A. A. matriculants or as non-matriculants in SGS to take advantage of substantially lower tuition fee.   Thus the economic circumstances
of students also had a strong impact on the rising SGS enrollment figures.

Finally, the expansion and diversification of course
and curricular offerings by SGS, as a component of a prestigious college, attracted many students who did not wish to
compromise, for economic or status reasons, on a less
prestigious but more expensive private college either in the
city or out-of-town.   For still others, SGS was the only solution if one had to work during the day in order to support
self and family.   For many others it was the temporary
back door, dependent upon scholastic achievement, ultimately to gain entry after a year or more to CLAS on an advanced standing basis.   In addition, it provided many with
"junior" college education--the A. A. and A. A. S. degrees--
which met their individual levels of educational aspiration.

Plans for Affiliated Community Colleges

One of the developments which had a decisive influ-

ence on the goal structure of SGS was the expansion of community colleges. Over the years efforts were exerted to
achieve consolidation of the two-year curricula into community college organizations "on the campuses of the several
city colleges."[22] A major aim was to qualify for State aid
and other benefits available under the New York State Education Law. Under the law, operating costs are borne one-
third by the State, one-third by the municipality and one-
third by student tuition fees. With respect to capital budget,
the State bears one-half and the municipality bears the other
one-half of the capital cost.[23] The financial advantages to
be gained from a community college set-up for the two-year
liberal arts and vocational programs under the aegis of the
School of General Studies was, therefore, a powerfully in-
triguing organizational move.

Prior to 1965, New York City had only two independent units for two-year terminal programs: the New York
City Community College of Liberal Arts and Applied Sciences, located in downtown Brooklyn in a rather blighted
area of the borough at that time; and the Fashion Institute of
Technology, located in mid-Manhattan, which specialized in
the textile and apparel industries. These community colleges
did not enjoy the enhanced status that inevitably comes from
being closely associated with a senior college of high reputation. In this respect, the New York City Community College was not generally regarded as a serious competitor of
the School of General Studies of Brooklyn College.

As early as 1950, the SGS Directors of the City University proposed that community colleges, as affiliated but
separate units, be established on the four senior college
campuses. In 1954, the Board of Higher Education approved
the proposal upon the recommendation of the Administrative

Council (composed of the senior college presidents). Authorization was granted for the opening of negotiations with State and City authorities to accomplish this goal.

The plan contemplated the creation of community colleges which would be responsible for the two-year liberal arts and vocational matriculated as well as non-matriculated students. The four-year baccalaureate curricula would remain in the Schools of General Studies.

The organizational structure of the proposed community college on the Brooklyn College campus was depicted as follows by Brooklyn College's SGS Dean in his 1954 annual report:

1. The President of Brooklyn College would become the President of the community college. Immediately responsible to him would be an Executive Officer of the community college.

2. For purposes of coordination the above-mentioned Executive Officer would meet with similar officers of other community colleges in New York City in a Council of Executive Officers.

3. The internal structure of the community college would include the appointment of appropriate administrative officers in charge of such areas as liberal arts, vocational studies, counseling and guidance, student life, athletics, etc., as well as such officers as registrar, bursar, etc.

In the interests of economy certain functions performed by executive officers of Brooklyn College might well be extended to the community college rather than set up duplicate administrative posts. This would include such categories as Business Manager, Custodial Engineer, Librarian, etc.

Provision would also be made for an autonomous faculty with all of the rights and responsibilities normally accorded to a faculty body. [24]

Why did the Directors of all the Schools of General Studies propose a separate, though an affiliated, community college on the senior campuses? At first blush, such proposal would appear to be inconsistent with their dominant goals of inducing expansion and growth of the Schools of General Studies. Surely they would not be willing to surrender an appreciable part of their jurisdiction in return for State fiscal aid to a separate organization. Several underlying reasons explain the motivation.

No doubt the first reason was genuinely on grounds of educational policy. Contrasting the isolation of the New York City Community College and the "social setting" of a community college on the Brooklyn College campus, the Dean stated in his 1954 annual report:

> It is expected that the proposed community college will attract large numbers of students who would otherwise not have gone to college at all. These young men and women, educated in some field of vocational study or in a well-rounded curriculum in the liberal arts, are very much needed by the community. Although these students will enroll in two-year terminal curricula, there is good reason to believe that after the experience of a year or more on the campus, some of them will develop an interest in higher education and apply for further studies leading to the four-year degree. In some respects, therefore, the two-year programs offer educational stimulation for students who originally had not contemplated an extended program in higher education. [25]

The second cogent reason rested on the factors of increasing enrollment in both the undergraduate and graduate divisions of the parent college which deprived SGS of the necessary lebensraum for expansion. As a matter of fact, the number of classrooms made available to the Division of Vocational Studies for daytime use was being more and more

limited with each passing semester; as a result further expansion in this area became exceedingly difficult.   New plant
and facilities for the entire college were sorely needed.   It
was hoped that under the community college formula the
State would furnish the necessary capital funds for the construction of buildings.   Should this occur, SGS would be able
to reduce sharply its utter dependence for space and facilities on the parent senior college.   Said the Brooklyn College
Dean:

> The Brooklyn College campus has sufficient land
> space available for (such) new construction . . .
> and an expansion of plant facilities could . . .
> bring about an increase of 100 or 200 percent in
> the initial enrollment. [26]

Though the proposal spoke in terms of an "autonomous
faculty" for the community college only, a fair inference is
that the Directors also meant "an autonomous faculty with all
of the rights and responsibilities normally accorded to a
faculty body" for SGS, too.   This goal probably rested on
the rational expectation that the Directors of the Schools of
General Studies, as the persons with the greatest knowledge
of and experience in the two-year programs, would also be
designated as the Executive Officers of the Community College while retaining directorship of the School of General
Studies.   It may be reasonably inferred that the belief was
held that if autonomy were achieved for the community college unit under the same administrative authority, the road
toward autonomy for the other unit would be strategically
improved.

Establishment of Independent Community Colleges
        While the Council of Directors proposed, the Board
of Higher Education disposed (on the recommendation of the

State Education Department).   Instead of organizing community colleges on the campuses of the senior colleges, the
Board of Higher Education directed the establishment of separate and independent community colleges for each borough
with their own buildings and grounds, administrative and
teaching staffs, courses and curricula and student bodies.
Thus Staten Island Community College was formed in 1955,
Bronx Community College in 1957, Queensborough Community College in 1958, Manhattan Community College in 1963,
and Kingsborough Community College in 1963.   In addition,
supervision and control of the New York City Community College, heretofore governed by a separate Board of Trustees,
was transferred in 1964 to the Board of Higher Education by
action of the City administration.   Thus the City University
acquired a string of subsidiary units represented by the community colleges.

It was generally assumed that the community colleges
would not preempt the programs developed by the Schools of
General Studies but that these sister institutions would live
side by side.   But the financial and space pressures against
the Schools of General Studies persisted.   Indeed, they
steadily grew stronger.   A measure of fiscal relief was accomplished in 1960 through an amendment to Section 6215 of
the State Education Law which added State financial aid to the
extent of one-third of operating costs for the first two years
of liberal arts education, regardless of whether it led to an
A. A. or B. A. degree.   Scarcity of space, however, became
increasingly acute as enrollment pressures rose.   Questions,
therefore, continued to be raised as to whether it would not
be desirable to transfer all two-year programs of the senior
colleges to the community colleges.   To justify the retention
of such programs by the Schools of General Studies--despite

demands for the space they occupied--the Dean at Brooklyn
College wrote in his 1960 annual report:

> However, the School of General Studies has one
> significant characteristic that distinguishes it from
> the two-year junior colleges. This is its intimate
> relation to a parent four-year institution, both
> physically and administratively. Without any doubt
> this very structured feature, which has provided
> so many advantages to the School of General Stud-
> ies, has been the major stumbling block for sever-
> al years in preventing the application of the State
> community college law to our associate degree pro-
> grams. Now, despite our dissimilar structure, the
> log-jam appears to be breaking, as evidenced by
> the provision of State-aid along the lines of the
> community college formula. The School of Gener-
> al Studies should now strive to utilize state finan-
> cial assistance in a manner that will preserve its
> identity as completely as possible. The mutual
> help that is derived from having the College of Lib-
> eral Arts and Sciences and the School of General
> Studies share in library and laboratory resources,
> athletic facilities, and in the services of staff and
> professional personnel are advantages not enjoyed
> by the independent two-year colleges. Moreover,
> because of their liaison in curriculum planning and
> in course and standing, there is almost no prob-
> lem between CLAS and SGS concerning transfer-
> ability of credit and eligibility for higher degrees.[27]

Efforts to Retain SGS Jurisdiction

In connection with a comprehensive study of the City
University system in all its ramifications by the Board's
Committee to Look to the Future,[28] the Directors of the
Schools of General Studies were requested in 1961 to prepare
a document describing their operations, resources and goals.
In a section entitled "Degree Programs in the Schools of
General Studies and in the Community Colleges; Similarities
and Differences," the Directors urged the following points:[29]

1. Associate degree programs, 'planned to provide the student with substantial studies in general education along with a limited concentration in a field of specialization,' are available at both the Schools of General Studies and the Community Colleges.

2. Programs in the associate degree curricula in the Schools of General Studies provide 'a greater variety of sources from which students may choose their liberal arts studies than is true in the Community Colleges.'

3. The programs in the Schools of General Studies are more intimately oriented toward the four-year liberal arts college aims.

4. The Associate in Applied Science programs in the Schools of General Studies are 'broader in their liberal arts emphasis and less vocational in the area of concentration than those in the Community Colleges.'

5. The associate degree programs of the Schools of General Studies serve recent high school graduates who are employed but 'principally' they serve older students, many of whom return to college after having interrupted their formal education; the community college 'serves almost exclusively students continuing their education immediately following their high school graduation.'

6. 'The community colleges are wholly dedicated to the first two years of college level work; consequently their curricula consist of basic courses designed for freshmen and sophomore students. The Schools of General Studies, on the other hand, provide a full four-year program leading to the baccalaureate degree and a sizable proportion of their enrollments are in upper level work.' Degree candidates (both two- and four-year), therefore, have a wide choice of advanced elective courses, all of which are available during evening hours.

7. The Schools of General Studies have, historically, offered education beyond the high school to students not qualified for matriculation at entrance. These students have been given the opportunity to 'demonstrate their ability to do acceptable college work'

and, if they so demonstrate, they may qualify for
admission to the four-year baccalaureate program.
In this connection the Schools of General Studies
have pioneered in assisting those "who do not conform to the rigid pattern of undergraduate admission requirements.' [30]

The Directors concluded this section by emphasizing
that the "central concerns" of the Schools of General Studies
are "the education of those students who seek the baccalaureate degree and who can attend college only in the evening."
The central purpose of the Community Colleges, on the other hand, was "to meet specifically defined vocational needs
of students."[31] While the Directors acknowledged that the
community colleges would become increasingly important in
associate degree programs, they again stressed the point
that there will "continue to be advantages for the associate
degree students (at the Schools of General Studies) in facilities, staff, library resources and laboratory facilities, as
well as in the accumulated experience and viewpoints in the
four-year colleges."[32] Indeed, "because large numbers of
adults in the metropolitan area are able and willing to attend
classes during the day, separate facilities should be provided
for the Schools of General Studies for day as well as evening
programs."[33] Furthermore, the Directors urged that the
School of General Studies be accorded the status of a "college" or school with its own core faculty. This last decla-
ration was a most important thrust for autonomy.

The Verdict on Jurisdiction

In June 1962, the Long Range Plan for the City University of New York was transmitted to the Board of Higher
Education by the Committee to Look to the Future. With respect to the future role of the Schools of General studies,

it stated:

> It is (further) recommended that, at such time as
> physical facilities are available, two-year degree
> curricula now in the Schools of General Studies
> of the Senior Colleges be transferred to the Com-
> munity Colleges.[34]

It further recommended that "for the most part, the
Schools of General Studies confine their associate degree curricula to the kind generally described as transfer."[35]   In
other words, terminal programs for the associate degree
should be surrendered to the community colleges.   With respect to the Directors' proposal that associate degree curricula be extended into full daytime operations, with special
facilities to accommodate these students, the Long Range
Plan disapprovingly commented that this "would appear to
create new community colleges on the campuses of the senior
colleges.   While the Schools of General Studies should be encouraged to provide daytime activities for their regular clientele (i. e., shiftworkers, housewives, the aging and other
part-time students) there seems to be no logical reason for
changing their character by adding a full-time community college division for young day students."[36]

Though the Board of Higher Education did not adopt in
its Master Plan all of the recommendations of the Long Range
Plan, it did accept most of the recommendations with regard
to the Schools of General Studies vis-à-vis the community
colleges.   The Master Plan was, however, more radical in
recommendations for transfer to the associate degree programs.   Under the heading Guide-lines for Second Quadrennium, 1968-72, Section B, Community Colleges, it stated
that "crucial to the development . . . of the Community Colleges . . . is . . . the transfer to these colleges, as soon
as their capacity warrants it, of the A. A. and A. A. S. pro-

grams now being conducted in the Schools of General Studies
of the Senior Colleges . . . "[37]

The following significant footnote accompanied the
statement:

> When the aggregate daytime enrollment capacity of
> our six community colleges reaches 15,000, it is
> estimated that they will be able to accommodate,
> in addition to their present categories of students,
> those who now use the A. A. and A. A. S. programs
> in the Schools of General Studies of the Senior Col-
> lege as a gateway to matriculation in our bacca-
> laureate programs. [38]

With relation to the Schools of General Studies, the
Master Plan observed that:[39]

> It is anticipated that the extent of upper division
> work will continue to grow in the Schools of Gen-
> eral Studies as increasing numbers of community
> college graduates seek to further their education
> in the junior and senior years. This development
> will probably be accompanied by a reduced enroll-
> ment in freshman and sophomore courses in the
> Schools of General Studies, with a corresponding
> growth in the number of part-time students regis-
> tered in the evening divisions of the Community
> Colleges. [40]

The establishment and planned growth of community
colleges with their mandate to . . . "provide two-year programs of post high school nature combining general education
with technical education relating to the occupational needs of
the community" . . . and to provide "special courses and
extension work . . . for part-time students"[41] had an obvious and immediate effect at Brooklyn College on the School
of General Studies. For out of a total enrollment of approximately 11,000 students more than two-thirds were either matriculated in the two-year programs or classified as non-
matriculated students. Only about one-third of the student

body consisted of fully matriculated candidates for the four-
year baccalaureate degree or of post baccalaureate students
(classified as non-matriculated students for technical reasons)
interested in individual courses.

Following the establishment of Kingsborough Community College in 1964, the President of Brooklyn College in-
structed the SGS Dean to open negotiations immediately with
the President of Kingsborough Community College to fix a
timetable for the discontinuance of the two-year associate
degree programs by SGS. By setting up a schedule of terminal dates for the admission of entering two-year degree students to Brooklyn College's SGS, recent high school graduates would necessarily be channeled to the community colleges. The timetable had to be a gradual one for two reasons: first, to afford sufficient time to the community college to build staff, curricula and facilities to accommodate
all the high school graduates desiring to enroll in these programs; second, to enable SGS to provide the opportunity to
currently enrolled students to complete their courses of
study. Thus the two-year programs at Brooklyn College
would be eliminated by the technique of closing its doors to
new entrants, while in the interim, a gradual process of attrition through graduation and resignation would work itself
out.

The phasing out timetable that was agreed upon was
to begin immediately with the transfer of the nursing science
program and then to transfer additional curricula in six
month intervals. The nursing science program would be fully
phased out by 1967 and the remaining curricula by 1969.

Looking to the Future

SGS was thus at the crossroads as a result of forces set in motion by the external community and by the hierarchy of authority external to SGS's internal organization. It is axiomatic that an organization will strive with all resources at its command to perpetuate itself. The question is how to respond to external pressures which tend to diminish or eliminate the foundations on which its survival as a separate organization depends. For to survive it must have organizational integrity and a distinctive function. It is well recognized that "each social organization or bureaucracy secures its existence not by being in the service of another but by fulfilling a somewhat different social function."[42]

Faced with the elimination of a major segment of its curricula and student body, SGS had to weigh a number of alternative choices. It could:

1. Continue to function as a smaller organization after making structural changes in its administration, curricula, faculty and student body;

2. Accentuate and expand those functions which it has retained;

3. Seek new goals and objectives within the boundaries of its assigned jurisdiction;

4. Develop new approaches to old problems, such as recruiting formerly disinterested groups, such as housewives, senior citizens, retired workers and businessmen eager for a second career.

To explore these alternative choices and, to the extent possible, to implement the choices made, SGS established a new Division of Program Development in 1966. Its mandate was taken from a statement prepared by the Council

of Directors in 1964 and submitted to the Board of Higher
Education when the Master Plan was being drafted.   Pointing
out that the accent in recent years had been mainly on youth
and that the more mature adult had scant and inadequate attention at best, it stated that:

> Such citizens, given the opportunity to enroll in
> college level courses, are as valuable and impor-
> tant to society as are the young high-school gradu-
> ates beginning their college courses. [43]

It further emphasized that:

> The responsibility of the evening college extends
> to an older, more mature and quantitatively larger
> segment of the population.   Students in this cate-
> gory are not preparing to become responsible citi-
> zens; the burden is already upon them . . . The
> need to assist the adult, who is making economic
> and social readjustments has a commanding pri-
> ority. . . . It is in these terms that the Schools
> of General Studies perform their most crucial roles
> for the individual and the society.   They signifi-
> cantly give opportunity to the economically threat-
> ened, to the culturally deprived, to the scholasti-
> cally challenged.   They offer a chance for the
> realization of new aspirations in a changing so-
> ciety. [44]

Though adequacy of space is still the most critical
factor, SGS is, nevertheless, intensively examining new goals
in light of the contemporaneous automating and space-explor-
ing society.   Admittedly, the current explosion of knowledge
makes previously acquired knowledge and skills rapidly obsolete.   Moreover, the high school diploma that was adequate
for productive work in modern society only a quarter of a
century ago is no longer adequate in an accelerating number
of instances.   College training is, to a sharply increasing
extent, becoming the minimum education for meaningful job
placement.   Also, there is the blot of our affluent society with

its deplorable pockets of poverty inhabited by socially and
economically disadvantaged persons who desperately need
broader horizons.   For them, hope for a better future lies
in the opportunity for a college education.   It is these realities that SGS is scrutinizing in order to determine the directions in which it should move.   As an educational institution,
it seeks to find its raison d'etre in "offering a chance for
the realization of new aspirations in a changing society" to
those who thirst for such chance.

The Dialectics of Change

The dialectics of expansion, contraction, and reaching
out for new areas of function are historically reflected in
SGS goal successions.   At SGS's inception, its goals were
broadly defined to include credit and non-credit programs--
both baccalaureate and associate degrees as well as diplomas
--coupled with a variety of community services.   Then, in
spite of the acknowledged success of these programs, SGS
jurisdiction was sharply curtailed.   First, SGS, by directive
of the President, relinquished the non-credit and community
service programs.   Then, with the expansion of community
colleges in the City, SGS was directed, by the Board, to
phase out and transfer to these colleges all of the two-year
degree programs.   Thus SGS came full circle back to the
original goals of its predecessor Evening Session; i. e. , credit programs toward the B. A. degree.

But the search for identity and distinctive goals, dif-
ferentiated from those of CLAS, persists.   As a sub-organization subject to a division of authority with the parent college, SGS may not embark on enterprises which might be regarded as transgressions upon the authority of the parent.   In
light of its limited jurisdiction, SGS cannot risk placing it-

self in the vulnerable position of being charged with the usurpation of powers not directly conferred upon it. Though its jurisdiction is now restricted to credit programs, it seeks again to expand its sphere of influence by formulating new goals within that framework. Its present aim is to reach out to broader segments of the population, particularly mature adults and economically disadvantaged groups.[45]

Efforts to develop new goals reveal the aspirations of SGS to maintain its vitality as an entity within the orbit of a parent organization.

Notes

1. Philip Selznick, T. V. A. and the Grass Roots (University of California Press, 1953), p. 7-14; Amitai Etzioni, Modern Organizations (Prentice-Hall, Inc. , 1964), Ch. 2; Amitai Etzioni, ed. , Complex Organizations (Holt, Rinehart and Winston, 1965), Ch. 3.

2. Master Plan for the City University of New York, 1964, p. 13. These functions were originally stated in the Long Range Plan for the City University of New York, 1961-1967, p. 8-9. The Long Range Plan was prepared by Dr. Thomas C. Holy under the auspices of the Committee to Look to the Future, a Committee of the Board of Higher Education. Dr. Mary S. Ingraham was its Chairman. The Plan was prepared under a special grant of $75,000, appropriated by the City of New York.

3. Brooklyn College Bulletin, 1966-68, p. 61.

4. Men's Division Announcement, 1930-1931, p. 27 et seq.

5. Statement of School of General Studies to staff, January 16, 1950.

6. Board of Higher Education, City of New York, "Higher Education on the Offensive." Report of the Chairman 1943-1944, p. 25.

7. Board of Higher Education, City of New York, "A
   Broader Mandate for Higher Education." Report of
   the Chairman, 1946-1948, p. 32.

8. School of General Studies Announcement, 1950-1951, p.
   19.

9. Board of Higher Education, Minutes of Proceedings,
   April 17, 1950, p. 207-208.

10. "Annual Report of the Director," School of General Stud-
    ies, 1950-1951, p. 1.

11. Minutes of the Advisory Council, School of General Stud-
    ies, Brooklyn College, July 11, 1950, p. 1.

12. "Annual Report of the Director," School of General
    Studies, 1953-1954, p. 1.

13. The Police Science diploma program later developed in-
    to an Associate in Applied Science degree. A simi-
    lar program was also adopted at the Baruch School
    of Business at City College. A separate college of
    Police Science was ultimately instituted which replaced
    both the Brooklyn and the City programs. Food
    Service Administration, however, remained as a di-
    ploma program due to rather low student interest.

14. Brooklyn, Hunter and Queens acted jointly in endeavor-
    ing to introduce the B. S. in Accounting curriculum in
    their respective institutions.

15. Diploma in General Education Announcement, 1953.

16. Amitai Etzioni, Modern Organizations (Prentice-Hall,
    Inc., 1964).

17. Ernest E. McMahon, The Emerging Evening College
    (Bureau of Publications, Teachers' College, Colum-
    bia University, 1960), p. 46.

18. Two years later it was transferred once more and be-
    came an operating unit of the College Library.

19. Nicholas J. Demrath, Changing Character of the Uni-
    versity (Center for the Study of Liberal Education for
    Adults, 1959), p. 3.

20. Sol Jacobson, "Judicial Review of College-Admission Policies," Journal of Higher Education, Vol. XXXIV, p. 436-437, (November, 1963).

21. Ibid.

22. Minutes of Board of Higher Education, Calendar No. 8, May 7, 1954. This Board approval was on a proposal tendered by the Council of Directors of the Schools of General Studies, (emphasis added).

23. New York State Education Law, Sec. 6304 et seq.

24. "Annual Report of the Director," School of General Studies, 1954, p. 26-27.

25. Ibid.

26. Ibid.

27. "Annual Report of the Director," School of General Studies, 1960, p. 65-66.

28. See note 2.

29. "Report of the Directors of the Schools of General Studies" (November 28, 1961), p. 19 et seq.

30. Ibid. , p. 48.

31. Ibid. , p. 20.

32. Ibid., p. 49.

33. Ibid. , p. 50; (emphasis added).

34. Letter of transmittal to Board of Higher Education, Long Range Plan, p. ix.

35. Long Range Plan, p. 151.

36. Ibid. , p. 150.

37. 1964 Master Plan for the City University of New York, working copy incorporating November 1964, and June 1965 amendments (January 1966), p. 80.

38. Ibid., footnote 1 on p. 80; (emphasis added).   In 1965
    the total enrollment of the six community colleges
    was 10,482 students, the projected enrollment for
    1967 was 13,200 and for 1972, 23,000.

39. Ibid., p. 80.

40. Ibid., p. 80-81.   When the draft of the Master Plan was
    circulated to the colleges there was no section on the
    Schools of General Studies.   The only mention made
    was the statement and footnote quoted above under
    "Community Colleges."   The section on School of Gen-
    eral Studies was added after several draft proposals
    had been submitted by the Council of Directors.

41. Long Range Plan, p. 153.

42. Herbert Stroup, "Intellect Incorporated," 3 National
    Association of Student Personnel Administrators: The
    Journal of the Association of Deans and Administra-
    tors of Student Affairs (July, 1965), p. 27.

43. The Schools of General Studies in a Master Plan for the
    City University (January 1964), p. 1.

44. Ibid.

45. Myrtle S. Jacobson and Deborah Offenbacher.   Accent
    on Adults: the Small College Program at Brooklyn
    (Syracuse University, New York, 1970).

Chapter III

Innovation Through Cooptation

> "I hope you will all be maver-
> icks, willing to be stared at or
> even frowned down, willing to
> try and fall and pick yourselves
> up again, willing to take up the
> cudgels against obsolescent as-
> pects of so much of today's
> education."[1]

In the language of organizational theory,[2] goal
changes of SGS over the years may be seen as cases of
"goal displacement" or "goal succession" forced upon SGS by
the curtailment of ongoing programs and the concomitant desire to find new areas of activity. At the same time, however, many of its newly chosen goals were also innovations
made in response to community pressure and community
needs.

Innovation is, of course, a highly valued commodity
in our society--so long as the innovation advances goals consistent with the value system of the establishment. However,
when innovation involves not only a change in method or technique but also a significant departure from the existing goal
system, then adoption becomes much more difficult to attain.
This is especially true when the innovation necessarily demands critical reevaluation of existing priorities against
scarce resources. Change, if it is to occur, must then find
a point of integration within the system itself.

The Tensions With The Status Quo

The institutional ties that bind a sub-organization to its parent frequently act as a repressor of innovation planned by the sub-organization. Traditional values and priorities of the parent may inhibit introduction by the sub-organization of new goals as well as new methods and procedures. In the area of baccalaureate education, for example, the day college exercises the controlling influence and it prescribes the role of the evening college in that sphere. But in other spheres, too, such as vocational education, the development of new programs by the evening college must bear a burden of justification. Such programs, in the eyes of the parent, may be viewed as less "valuable" than the liberal arts baccalaureate program and, therefore, a possible dilution of the prestige level, not only of the sub-organization but more importantly of the parent itself.

Indeed, SGS over the years, was typed as "vocational" in orientation, a term which like "damnyankee" is often elided as "narrowvocationalism." Moreover, the School's commitment to a second chance philosophy further stigmatized it--even in liberal arts--as inferior in quality, for it was rather widely felt that these second chance students caused a deterioration of academic standards. [3]

In a democracy, the academic community is confronted with ambivalent value attitudes toward higher education. While cognizant of the American ideal of equality of educational opportunity for all who can profit from it, at the same time it seeks to serve the particular needs of superior students who will become the intellectual elite. The basic problem is how to achieve quantity education while preserving high quality. But these two may not be simultaneously

attainable by an individual institution.   Hence a choice has
to be made.   If institutional preeminence is the exclusive
choice, then quantity has to be sacrificed and only superior
students admitted.   For institutional prestige stems from the
success of graduates in the intellectual, professional and
commercial world after graduation.   All colleges and universities point with pride to the number of alumni who have a-
chieved the Ph. D. degree or who have become prominent in
the professions and in business.   And the glory reflects on
the individual faculty members.   High status of the faculty
member in his own discipline is, in large part, derived from
the status of the college or university with which he is associated.   Consequently, there is a faculty disposition to be
receptive only to those new programs and curricula which
will contribute to high status and which will not threaten
those achievements already institutionalized.

    In this respect, Brooklyn College does not differ from
other institutions of higher learning.   The high priority given
in recent years to scholars' and honors programs at the undergraduate level, quite apart from the introduction and expansion of graduate studies, including the relatively new
Ph. D. programs,[4] derives from the same concern for preeminence.

    Two significant examples of innovations introduced by
SGS are the subject of this chapter.   One novel experimental
program relates to the liberal arts area--the Special Baccalaureate Program for Adults.   The other relates to vocational or professional training--specifically the Nursing Science
Program.   How they were conceived, the resistances to their
birth, and the methods used to effect their adoption and con-
tinuance through organizational cooptation, are the central
theme here.

The methods used by SGS to gain acceptance of these
new organizational goals are reminiscent of Max Weber's
admonition that the particular methodology must be fitted to
the particular nature of the study. [5] Methodology obviously
cannot be divorced from the substantive data.   Otherwise,
the universe of discourse lacks coherence.   There was wide
difference in the methods used by SGS in introducing and developing each of these new programs, yet there was a dominant connecting thread in the methodological techniques.   In
both cases, the goal was to achieve legitimacy for the innovations so that they could grow and gain maturity.

Democratic and Bureaucratic Obstacles

It must not be inferred that resistance to curricular
change at Brooklyn College applies uniquely to those innovations undertaken by SGS.   Adoption of curricular changes,
regardless of their origin, is always a slow and arduous
process.   Both democratic and bureaucratic elements converge in a review procedure involving a vast network of committees that have initiating and review authority.   Starting
with the powers of individual instructional departments to initiate proposals, a proposed change must run the gamut of
faculty-selected and presidentially-appointed committees.   Administration plays a major role, too.   The Dean of the Faculties has among his specific responsibilities "advice and recommendations on curricular development and policies."[6]
Final approval rests with the elected Faculty Council and the
Board of Higher Education.

A proposal to add a course in statistics to the curriculum of the Mathematics Department, for example, starts
with the department's curriculum committee.   After approval
by a majority vote of the department, a document embodying

the proposal and its justification is submitted for review to
the Faculty Committee on Curriculum and Admission Requirements.   If approved, the proposal is submitted to Faculty
Council for ratification and then to the Board of Higher Education.   Almost always the latter's action is pro forma in
curricular matters.

Thus an elaborate system of legislative checks and
balances is built into the formal structure.   Informally, departmental vested interests come into play.   Proliferation of
courses in one department may impinge on the interests of
another.   In such circumstances the influence of the Dean of
Faculties and President may be decisive.   Frequently, jurisdictional disputes are difficult to mediate.   An example was
the proposal to "centralize" the teaching of statistics in the
Mathematics Department.   The Economics Department, which
already offered two statistics courses, maintained that the
courses should remain with it.   The departments of Sociology and Psychology each made counter-proposals for separate statistics courses within each discipline.   Apparently,
other departments were unwilling to rely entirely on statistics courses in mathematics.

Another example of a series of jurisdictional disputes
was evidenced when the single department of Anthropology
and Sociology was split into two separate departments.   Each
claimed jurisdiction over particular courses.   Is "Race and
Culture Contact" a course in Sociology or Anthropology?
Committees had to mediate the disputes.   Small wonder that
in his farewell address to the Faculty at Brooklyn College
(May, 1966), President Gideonse commented on the slow pace
of curricular change and warned the faculty against "the euphoria of entrenched inertia!"

The Principle of Organizational Cooptation

Philip Selznick defines cooptation as "the process of absorbing new elements into the leadership or policy-determining structure of an organization as a means of averting threats to its stability or existence."[7] The term cooptation may be applied to the case where a component unit absorbs into its policy-making structure key persons from the parent organization in order to gain legitimacy for new goals and implementing measures. This technique was utilized by SGS by inviting members of the day faculty to serve in both a consultative and a decision-making capacity in association with SGS staff in order to advance recognition of innovations.

Advantages flowed to both units of the organization from the cooptative process. In the first place, it avoided jurisdictional conflicts over the new area and maintained the sanctity of established spheres of authority. In the second place, it diffused the possible risks of failure that any innovation necessarily involves, while making experimentation and pioneering by the sub-organization possible. Thus mutual benefits inured to both. The disadvantages were in the unanticipated consequences. If the planners and initiators have a specific objective it may frequently be altered in the cooptative process. The new elements recruited may "waterdown" or substantially change the original idea. Thus the function of cooptation--to make a program possible--may have a negative impact on the resulting product in terms of the original goals of the participants.

If, in the view of the planners and innovators, the dysfunctions outweigh the eufunctions, the only alternative is to engage in conflict. This may or may not be desirable. It depends on how participants view their relative strength.

SGS administration rarely is willing to risk open conflict. Its philosophy is to avoid tests of strength and to rely chiefly on arts of persuasion and rational argument in the cooptative process, utilizing adaptive mechanisms as a major instrument for change.

The Special Baccalaureate Degree Program, as will appear later, illustrates how the program itself underwent a series of changes to make it acceptable and workable within the context of the total organization. However, the Nursing Science Program, which was a two-year degree program, attracted far less CLAS attention. For it was somewhat peripheral to what the College considered its major area of interest: the four year baccalaureate program. Nursing Science was, therefore, "outside the pale" of rigorous scrutiny. Nevertheless, for the program to come into existence, the active support and cooperation of members of science departments and committees had to be enlisted.

While the Special Baccalaureate Degree Program and the Nursing Science Program were quite different in substance, in student body, in faculty participation, in financing, etc., a common element unites them for organizational study. They were both innovative, and sufficiently different from accepted, traditional programs to encounter initial resistance by the governing faculty. While the types of cooptation that were utilized differed, in each case cooptation was still the method of developing legitimacy for the programs.

The Special Baccalaureate Degree Program for Adults

The story of the special baccalaureate program for adults begins with a dream.[8] But it is not a story of a dream come true. Rather it is the tale of a dream altered,

modified and tempered by the interplay of organizational
forces in the world of reality.

The idea of a planned course of study leading to the
baccalaureate degree embracing the interests, experiences
and aspirations of the mature adult had long intrigued some
of the SGS faculty. They wondered whether there were not
many serious-minded adults who, though not entirely satisfied with "piecemeal" courses in the usual adult education
programs, were still reluctant to commit themselves for
many years of study limited to evening hours. The prospect
of eight to ten years of college attendance, it was believed,
was too great a deterrent. It was also believed that the traditional sequence of courses was not sufficiently tempting or
challenging. Attendance in the same classes with much
younger, less worldly-wise and less sophisticated students
was believed to be another serious restraining influence.

These ruminations in search of a new approach to an
organized curriculum--designed for adults with intellectual
potential and high motivation--were brought to the attention
of the late John Schwertman, at that time (1953) Director of
the Center for the Study of Liberal Education for Adults.
Mr. Schwertman and his colleagues envisaged a program of
liberal arts studies for adults which would not be slavishly
bound by the well-established, traditional curricula, syllabi
and testing devices tailored for young, just-out-of high school
students. They boldly projected an educational experience
freed from the credit-counting procrustean bed of the traditional baccalaureate program yet one which achieved the essential objectives of a liberal arts degree. Perhaps admission standards, curriculum structure, instructional methods
and evaluation techniques could be modified in a manner
which would make them more appropriate for the adults who

were already leading responsible lives. Perhaps new vistas
in higher education could be opened by devising new roads
to reach the goals that a liberal arts degree is supposed to
accomplish. This was the dream which led to a unique experiment in higher education.

One basic assumption of the experimental conception
was that the crucial difference between adults and college
age youths, from an educational viewpoint, was "life experience," and that "life experience" could be evaluated in academic terms. The Research Associate of the Center for the
Study of Liberal Education for Adults framed the operative
question as follows: "Is it possible to set up an educational
program which systematically translates the cumulative edu-
cative effects of a life experience into credit for the liberal
arts degree?"[9] As a corollary, he inquired as to the purposes of a liberal arts degree. He argued that a person is
liberally educated if he "has knowledge within the great substantive fields of human experience; if he has developed well
his intellectual abilities; and if he has achieved sensitivity,
appreciation, and self-control in the areas of social, emotional and esthetic experience, then he is not likely to regard his education and his degree as coterminous and hence
can be considered liberally educated."[10]

In broad scope, then, the plan called for the selection
of adult students with rich life experiences and marked scholastic potential. Through counseling interviews, diagnostic
tests and other evaluation procedures the past achievements
of these students would be translated into academic equivalence. Additional study, as deemed desirable and necessary
for the student, would be prescribed in the form of class attendance, independent study, exemption examinations, the
writing of theses, or specially constructed tutorials and semi-

nars.   When the candidate had demonstrated to the faculty
committee that he had achieved a liberal education, he would
be recommended for the baccalaureate degree.

It was obvious, however, that the project could not
be launched without the support of the Brooklyn College faculty.   Support could not be taken for granted because the experimental plan not only significantly departed from traditional methods and procedures but, indeed, questioned the
hallowed pattern of course-credit accumulation.   To gain
such official support, the SGS Dean had to walk the precarious tight rope stretched between two pillars--from traditional academic value attitudes to novelty and innovation.   For-
tunately, a safety net had been woven to some extent in previous years in the sense that the faculty had become accus-
tomed to some of the techniques to be incorporated in the
experimental project. [11]   During the previous decade, for example, exemption examinations based on independent study
had been introduced and a system of waivers of prerequisites
and the granting of equivalent course credits had grown, particularly for returning war veterans and for foreign students.
The safety net, though, was minimal in view of the quite
substantial break with orthodox tradition which the project
contemplated.

Of course, the College faculty had to be satisfied that
the innovations would not dilute the quality standards of the
degree.   But it was equally important to satisfy the interests
of the Center, from whom financing of the project was sought.
The Center was not interested in a facsimile of the old curriculum and customary approaches; it was interested in new
trails, new experimental designs, new techniques.   Unless
these proved enticing, the Center would not invest in the project.   Funding was, as it practically always is, a decisive

consideration.   SGS was unable to finance the project out of
its own annual operating budget.   Existing programs consumed practically all available funds.   Moreover, SGS recognized that outside financing is a powerful impetus to the faculty's sympathetic consideration of the pioneering project.
The faith in the idea by a prestigious agency that is willing
to pay for its experimental adoption is an impressive factor
to any faculty.

     To be financed by a foundation was particularly im-
pressive in 1953 when financial support for experimental or
demonstration projects was difficult to secure.   Cooperative
research programs financed by the U. S. Office of Education
or other governmental agencies were at that time relatively
unknown.   Grants by the private foundations--Carnegie,
Rockefeller, Ford, etc.--were also relatively scarce at that
time.   With respect to grants, higher education had not as
yet grown to the affluent state it reached ten years later.
Thus the prospect of a grant from the Center represented a
prestigious prize.

The Cooptative Steps

     Involved in the core idea of the project was a major
question of educational policy.   Its principal design was to
introduce "a more flexible means" by which adults, with rich
life experiences, could achieve the baccalaureate degree. [12]
To pursue this objective, the support of both the President
and the Dean of the Faculties had to be first procured.   No
difficulties in obtaining their consent were anticipated, for
both were strong advocates of novel experiments in curriculum matters.   However, their blessings, though necessary,
were not sufficient.   The approval of faculty committees and
Faculty Council was also necessary.   Whether these bodies

would agree to such a radical break with tradition was not
at all certain.   To create the proper climate for at least
tentative approval--so that negotiations with the Center could
proceed with official sanction--the proposed program, with
deliberate subtlety, was named the "Experimental Degree
Project for Adults."   In academe, the word "experimental"
has a rather tantalizing charm.

Obtaining the Grant

        Armed with the blessings of the President and the
Dean of the Faculties, the proposal was then presented to
the powerful College Committee on Long Term Curriculum
Development for its endorsement.   For that purpose, the
SGS Dean wrote to the Committee:

> While we realize that even as an experimental pro-
> ject the plan represents some significant depar-
> tures from traditional academic procedures, we
> would not in any way suggest or countenance a re-
> duction in academic standards for the baccalaure-
> ate degree. [13]

        The rationale for the project was described by the
Dean as follows:

> We are convinced that there are considerable num-
> bers of mature students whose vocational and aca-
> demic experiences have placed them in a some-
> what different category from the usual undergradu-
> ate who comes to college directly from his high
> school training.   In some instances, these mature
> adults have had a wealth of experience in business,
> in the professions and possibly in academic studies
> abroad but do not have clear cut certification of
> academic qualifications that could be used for ac-
> creditation.   It is obvious, however, that while
> they lack formal requirements with respect either
> to admission or prescribed work at the college
> level, they nevertheless possess talent and show
> aptitude for unusual rapid progress in certain sub-
> ject matter areas.

With regard to the broad outlines of the experimental
design, he stated:

> It is felt that with adequate counseling, independ-
> ent reading and tutorial services many of these
> students might progress more rapidly toward a-
> chieving equivalent academic standing acceptable
> for ultimate accreditation toward the regular bac-
> calaureate degree. The basic need with respect
> to such students is not so much a new curriculum
> but rather a <u>sufficient flexibility</u> which would make
> possible a certain amount of independent study and
> special tutorial services as a substitute for regu-
> lar classroom hours and formal attendance.   This
> might be followed by comprehensive examinations
> that would enable the student to demonstrate his
> intellectual powers to the satisfaction of the col-
> lege faculty. [14]

Contrary to customary time-consuming deliberations,
the college committees acted promptly by endorsing the proposal "in principle" and recommending to Faculty Council
that it be adopted as a "proposed experimental project."
But to its endorsement, the Long Term Committee added
these precautionary words:

> It is understood that if the project is approved by
> the Ford Foundation, the Long Term Committee
> (of the College) will supervise the conduct of the
> study and will, at the earliest opportunity, bring
> to Faculty Council recommendations concerning the
> specific details of the project and any modifica-
> tions of present curricular policies and procedures
> which may be necessary to implement the study. [15]

Under these conditions, Faculty Council approved the project.

Now the problem was to secure the funds from the
Center.   Further communication with the officials of the
Center revealed additional hurdles.   Although they approved
the general concepts, they now wanted more evidence of
merit in the planned implementation.   They requested a con-

crete blueprint showing "how and what can be done." In addition, "what would happen to the program if no further outside help was forthcoming after the one year?" And finally and most crucially, they asked: "Is the project at all relevant to the Fund's greater concern with continuing liberal education for adults? That is, what wisdom is there in proving that adults can achieve a liberal arts degree in this way? What will this contribute to the question of how adults can be attracted and subsequently committed to the notion, that liberal education does not halt with a degree but is coterminous with life itself?"[16]

The Dean responded to these basic questions in a lengthy memorandum reiterating the objectives of the program, its financing and its research and evaluative aspects. Yet two more months elapsed and no definitive word was received. Further inquiry by the Dean brought word from Mr. Schwertman that: "I can only report that not a week has gone by without some action on my part to force the matter to a point where a green light can be given to you."[17] He added that though the officers of the Fund for Adult Education had approved the grant, final approval depended on the report of a special committee of the trustees to be submitted to the entire Board of Trustees. Finally, in February, 1954, the Board of Trustees approved the grant.

Developing the Operational Plan

The next set of problems was the type of organization, the character of personnel, the plan of operations and implementing techniques. Recruitment of students, criteria for admission, curriculum, and evaluations of "life experience" and kindred matters had to be developed. Not the least significant problem was the possible web of relationships within the existing college structure.

For a number of strategic reasons, the decision was made not to appoint a full-time administrative officer. The rationale for this decision was reported as follows:

> Neither the prospective size of the beginnings of the Experimental Degree Project for Adults nor the funds available appeared to justify assignment of a full-time administrative officer. In order to justify his time, a full-time head would probably have had to assume all of the functions associated with screening, counseling for admissions, evaluation and placement on the basis of previous academic training, curricular guidance, some aspects of the process of evaluating experience for college credit, visitation and appraisal of the teaching processes, and planning and development of appropriate courses and curricula. Such an organizational arrangement would, first, have placed a high premium upon the wisdom and general competence of such a person, and secondly, would have injected him into functional activities already specialized in the college and allocated to deans' offices, the registrar's office, the counseling office, departmental chairmen and their deputies, as well as several faculty committees. [18]

In order to avoid conflicts with existing functional offices, it was decided to appoint a Committee on Admission and Evaluation consisting of four faculty members, two drawn from SGS and two from CLAS. Thus the cooptative principle was built into the structure at the very outset. The Committee consisted of the Associate Dean of SGS as chairman who was also a professor of English in CLAS. A second member, from CLAS was a professor of psychology who "brought to the committee, in addition to her competence in the fields of test and measurements, experience as the administrative and policy leader in the Office of Exemption Examinations." The third member, also from CLAS, was a professor of biology who contributed "a comprehensive view of science in

education as well as extended experience with the work of
developing and teaching the integrated science course to
freshmen and sophomores." The fourth member was from
SGS, a professor of political science who "contributed experience from his position as Supervisor of the Division of
Counseling and Guidance in the School of General Studies
and work in the development and teaching of the integrated
social science course."

As a group, the Committee represented a cross section of the major divisional areas of the liberal arts branches, a number of specialized experiences particularly useful
to the Project, and extended acquaintance with the philosophy, rules, and practices that make up the daily features of
the college's operation. [19] Central to the selection of the
professors of psychology and biology from CLAS to serve on
the Committee was the fact that these two faculty members
enjoyed a high level of respect in their individual departments as well as in the college as a whole.

Student Recruitment

In view of the limited funds and the experimental nature of the project, the Committee on Admission and Evaluation first had to agree on the number of students to be admitted and the criteria for admission. An initial group of
about 30 students was agreed upon and the following criteria
for admission established:

1. Is the candidate over 30 years of age?

2. Is his background of life experience translatable
   into an academic level of achievement?

3. Is there evidence that he possesses academic
   promise?

4. How would a liberal education enlarge the
   scope of the candidate's contribution to the
   community and enhance his self realization?

Once these criteria were formulated, a lengthy, six-
page application form was devised to determine the extent
that a candidate satisfied the criteria.   Another central purpose was to determine how "truly liberal, non-vocational or
professional" was the candidate's motivation in seeking admission.

The Committee pointedly rejected vocational or professional aspirations, even though these might rest on a liberal arts foundation.   This bias was undoubtedly also consistent with the heavy liberal arts orientation of the donor of
the grant, the Center for the Study of Liberal Education for
Adults.   Professional or vocational goals presumably would
taint the purity of the liberal arts offerings.   In any event,
many candidates apparently detected the so-called liberal
arts bias, for they deliberately avoided indicating a professional or vocational interest and gave the "correct" answers
in the questionnaire. [20]

In order immediately to excite the interests of the
general faculty in the project and to involve them directly in
it, the Committee decided to request each faculty member to
recommend one outstanding candidate for consideration.   This
cooptative method had several advantages.   In the first place,
faculty members would then be serving as an initial screening instrument since they were limited to recommending not
many but only one outstanding candidate.   In the second
place, faculty members would presumably be serving unoffi-
cially as counselors to their respective candidates in the
preparation of the application, in preparing them for interviews and diagnostic tests and other preliminary evaluation
procedures.   Finally, those faculty members whose candi-

dates were accepted would have a high stake in the success
of the project.   That this procedure brought the results intended is evidenced by the fact that a total of 130 applications for admission were received through the activity of faculty members.

Of the 130 applicants, 57 were men and 73 were women; 96 were married and 34 were single.   Ages ranged from
21 to 66, but the majority were in their 40's.   Almost all
were in some vocation; there were artists, artisans, school
principals, social workers, lawyers, interior decorators and
housewives.   There were also . . . "a retired army colonel,
a police inspector, a director of religious education, several
rabbis, registered nurses, writers, an assistant post office
superintendent, an internal revenue specialist, an engineering
draftsman, a restauranteur, a rooming house operator, a
practicing chiropractor, a marine representative of a large
oil company, an assistant fire marshal and an expert on the
conservation of paintings in a museum."[21]

To determine scholastic promise, the candidates were
required to take the American Council on Education Psychological Examination.   Only 99 out of the 130 appeared for the
examination.   On the basis of the results, 50 were selected
and 49 rejected.   The successful 50 were then given a two-
hour screening and counseling interview.   Out of the 50, 32
were chosen and these were then subjected to the four-hour
area tests of the Educational Testing Service at Princeton.[22]

In light of this rigorous selection procedure, one is
reminded of a well-known psychiatric hospital in New York
which rigorously screens patients for admission and then
points with pride to its high ratio of success in restoring patients to mental health.   In comparison to State and City hospitals, this success rate is no doubt exceptionally high but

one might question the extent of the initial risk. Similarly
with the experimental project here. Candidates were so
carefully selected in terms of probable success that failure
became statistically improbable. But this selectivity was
crucial to the acceptance of the innovation and its break with
traditional patterns. Admission policies and procedures had
to be played "close to the chest."

Faculty Role in Student Evaluation

One of the basic, original concepts in the formulation
of the project was to confer the baccalaureate degree if the
student demonstrated to the satisfaction of the faculty that he
had absorbed, by a variety of means including life experience, the knowledge and competence essential to the purposes
of the degree. The idea was an evaluation of the quality and
depth of the educational wealth acquired by the student rather
than simply the use of an adding machine to total the number
of course credits completed for class room attendance only.
Such evaluation obviously involved very complex problems of
determining objective standards. Serious doubts were raised
as to whether too much diversity would be introduced into
broadly elastic criteria for granting the degree. It appeared
that the faculty was willing to evaluate "ability" and "achievement in life's experience" of each individual student but these
evaluations would have to be expressed in quantitative terms
of course credits. Furthermore, it was determined that no
change be made in the total number of credits required for
the degree and that it be held at 128. Practical necessity
pragmatically modified the dream.

In line with the policy of involving as many of the faculty as possible in the project, the Committee agreed to set
up panels of departmental representatives who would evaluate

the students' life experience in terms of course credit e-
quivalence in the department.   While the Committee prepared departmental lists of possible evaluators, these lists
were to serve solely as guides.   The individual chairman of
each academic department was given full authority to designate panel members to act as his representative on the evaluation team.   Grant of authority to panel members through
the department chairman was envisioned as a method of
minimizing criticism of the evaluation itself.

The task of equating a student's "life experience" with
academic credits was something entirely new and unprece-
dented.   The evaluator was, in effect, developing new standards of awarding course credit in lieu of the usual requirement of class attendance coupled with customary examinations.   The validity of the evaluations was thus of decisive
importance.   Objective standards and procedures for evaluation had to be formulated.

The essence of the evaluating procedure was sum-
marized in the following words:

> For the courses in his department the evaluator
> made up a check list of objectives, including fa-
> miliarity with subject content.   During the inter-
> view with each adult, his questions searched out
> the extent to which the candidate had achieved these
> objectives.   To confirm these findings, he assigned
> either a written examination, a performance test,
> or a paper to be prepared by the adult. [23]

Evaluators often denied credit.   Though the student
may have claimed such credit, evaluators discovered that the
student's "experience" was not sufficiently broad and systematic to be equated with the scope of the course objectives.
For example:

> A woman aged 53, who had had 15 years experi-
> ence as a purchasing supervisor and office man-

ager for a large shoe manufacturing company was
interviewed by the evaluator from the Department
of Economics, but his examination did not convince
him of the immediate creditability of her experience. "Formal economic analysis," he wrote,
"has constituted little or no part of her intellectual experience. She requires a period of reading
and independent study, concentrating on those
phases of business organization and operations in
which her practical experience has been most limited." [24]

In short, evaluators proceeded on the hypothesis that
"adults had already achieved a large measure of personal
and social maturity. Only when they gave evidence of having
already achieved the skills, habits, understandings . . .
could . . . adults . . . receive credit for (specific)
courses." [25]

The Committee on Admission and Evaluation clearly
had to proceed slowly and with the utmost caution lest it
tread on the toes of generally accepted academic respectabil-
ity. Carefully and laboriously the recommendations of the
evaluators were scrutinized and the supporting evidence
studied. If satisfied, these recommendations were submitted
to the Dean of the Faculties and the College Committee on
Course and Standing for approval. As reported by the program administrators:

The Dean checked the validity of the credits with
due attention to faculty policy and the Committee
on Course and Standing frequently called for even
more detailed explanation. Sometimes the Committee reduced the number of credits on such grounds
as overlapping between two departments or over-
specialization in certain types of courses. [26]

So that the floodgates not be opened too widely to the
attainment of course credits based on experience, the Committee on Course and Standing recommended that a student

may not be granted more than 32 credits for life experience, that is, the equivalent of one year's full-time study.
This recommendation was approved by Faculty Council.

Meanwhile, John Schertman wrote, with respect to
the technique of course-credit equivalence:

> I would like to point out why I think we can never
> achieve an exact equivalency with "a course." It
> is because no given non-academic experience is
> translatable exactly into academic terms. For ex-
> ample, ten years experience in the coffee export
> trade will not add up exactly to "International
> Trade 101," but in terms of a more comprehen-
> sive outcome the coffee exporting experience may
> well have produced outcomes which the course can-
> not--such things, for instance, as an intense un-
> derstanding of the culture, economy, geography and
> politics of Brazil. [27]

The Dean responded:

> You are correct in assuming that at the present
> time we are attempting to translate almost every-
> thing we do into exact course equivalents. The
> reasons for this procedure are twofold: 1) We are
> keenly aware of the necessity of going slowly in
> breaking away from academic traditions. Remem-
> ber, we have to keep our faculty sold on the pro-
> gram that they have endorsed. 2) The grant has
> thus far been provided for only one year. It be-
> hooves us therefore to make certain that whatever
> is done for the experimental group will be convert-
> ible into "legal tender" credits that will have full
> academic respectability in all quarters should the
> experiment come to a close before these candidates
> have achieved their degree. [28]

The element of "legal tender" was significant in quite
another sense. Students expressed concern that graduate
schools, committed as they were to the course-credit and
grade system, would not recognize credits based on life experience equivalence. In an early progress report of the
Committee, it was stated:

It might seem that, in an experimental project of
this kind, in which one of the goals is the determination of the validity of life experience, rather
than mere courses, as a means of liberal education, little attention would be given to the details
of exact course equivalency. In our dealings with
adults, however, we have observed that they are
extremely skeptical of a degree which on paper is
in any way "different" from the standard one.
Their distrust is matched by the attitude of graduate schools, which stress course equivalency for
admission and proper academic standing. [29]

While this progress report was issued in October

1954--a year after the program was instituted--the question

had been anticipated right from the beginning. That it had

been foreseen is evidenced by a letter addressed to the SGS

Dean in 1953 by Ewald B. Nyquist, at that time Assistant

Commissioner for Higher Education in New York State:

My fascination with the reading material you sent
me, as well as my disappointment, are bound up
in, I think, the development of the project. That
is to say, you start out with a perfectly good purpose and then at a particular point, you find out
that you are going to have to make this program
conform, in many respects, to your regular program. I am referring, of course, to the fact that
the adults turn out to be skeptical of a degree
which on paper is in any way different from the
standard one.

There was still another highly practical consideration.

The Center's commitment of funds was for only one year.

Whether the grant would be renewed was not known. If not

renewed after one year, it might be necessary for the stu-

dents to be absorbed into the regular college program at the

expiration of the grant since there was slight probability that

the College could continue the project without financial sup-

port. If the transfer were necessary, "courses" and "cred-

its" would be of significance to the students. Without such

course credits, they would lose a year's work toward the
degree.   As it turned out, the grant was renewed by the
Center, but this could not be anticipated.   In the view of
the Center and the Fund the visible "success" of the "experiment" was a prerequisite to the renewal of the grant.

Faculty Role in Courses and Curriculum

     In 1955, an additional grant made it possible to con-
tinue the project.   In addition, the Board of Higher Education authorized the establishment of fees for several special
courses and diagnostic tests.   This enabled the School of
General Studies to admit an additional 30 students who were
selected from over 200 applicants recommended by faculty
members.

     Experience in the first year of the program had dem-
onstrated that while some of these adult students were quite
proficient in certain specialized subject areas, many lacked
some of the basic preparation normally identified with freshman and sophomore course levels.   They frequently could be
granted credit for elective courses; but more often than not
they had inadequate knowledge in the areas of "basic preparation," that is, the "required course" level.   The Dean
wrote:

> To fill this gap by requiring such students to at-
> tend regular freshman and sophomore classes in
> these subjects, or even by setting up special pro-
> cedures for completing such course equivalents,
> does not seem to be the best procedure. [30]

A special grant was then made by the Center in order
to recruit a team of professors from the regular day faculty
to prepare a program of study especially tailored to the needs
of the adult students for the first two years of work.   The
selection of faculty on this team was to be so careful and

judicious "that the personnel . . . will command the respect of their colleagues and will do a piece of work that
will be likely to involve a minimum of revision and amendment by colleagues in the departments affected. "[31]   A study
in depth of the first two years of college work was to be
made so that there would be ". . . a sufficiently convincing
array of materials to persuade our Long Term Curriculum
Study Committee and, subsequently, our Faculty Council, of
the merits of this new approach. "[32]

A team of nine highly respected professors, faculty
members of the College, drawn from the four areas of the
Humanities, Social Sciences, Natural Sciences and Communications, was organized to work during the summer on a
document for the purpose of (1) formulating a clearcut statement of aims and objectives in a specific subject matter area
prescribed for the first two years of college work, (2) setting forth detailed outlines or reading materials relating to
these subject matter areas, and (3) constructing questions,
examinations and diagnostic tests for the purpose of determining progress and achievement in the respective disciplines.   The work of the team was to be coordinated by a
distinguished professor of education, a member of the College
staff, whose reputation in these areas was well-known to the
Center.

As a result of this team study, four integrated seminars were proposed, one in the Humanities, one in Social
Sciences, one in Natural Sciences-Mathematics and the fourth
in Communications.   Each seminar was to be of one year's
duration and was intended to cover the first two years of college work, equivalent to 64 credits.   Departmental acceptance
of this integrated package of seminars in the four fields of
learning was obtained and in April, 1956, the seminars were

approved by Faculty Council as "alternative equivalents" to
all prescribed courses for the baccalaureate degree.   The
resolution submitted to Faculty Council stated that:

> These seminar courses make it possible to capi-
> talize on adult experience by instruction in small
> tutorial groups supplementing considerable inde-
> pendent study.   The courses are sufficiently com-
> prehensive and integrated at a sufficiently high lev-
> el of scholarship to permit adults to build on what
> they have learned from life experience.

These integrated seminars specially established for a
distinctive group of students represented a remarkable innovation in the traditional curriculum for the baccalaureate degree.

Open Channels of Communication

Even though scores of faculty members were actually
involved in the project as sponsors of candidates, evaluators,
counselors, consultants, tutors, faculty representatives or
committee members, there were vast numbers of the faculty
who did not participate directly in the project.   Consequently,
every effort was made to keep the lines of communication
freely open.   When the second group of applicants was being
sought, letters again were sent to all members of the faculty
soliciting recommendations.   Progress reports of the Project
were circulated regularly in which were included detailed
studies giving specific information about students, courses,
testing devices, achievements and student interests.   Reports
also appeared periodically in the Staff Bulletin, a publication
issued monthly by the Dean of the Faculties.   Announcement
was made of the time and place of the weekly meeting of the
Committee on Admission and Evaluation and faculty members
were constantly invited to sit in on these meetings (a pro-

cedure rather uncommon to typical committees).   Faculty
members were also invited to write to the Committee expressing views, raising questions and offering criticisms.
The scope of the channels of communication were described
as follows:

> But there has been more to the process of com-
> munication than formal reports, correspondence,
> and invitations of one kind of faculty assistance or
> another.   The manner in which the Committee it-
> self has been located in the "middle" of the Col-
> lege administrative hierarchy has led inevitably to
> a variety of associations both formal and casual
> that have served to reveal to many colleagues the
> nature of its purpose and problems. [33]

Although systematic provision was made for checks
and balances in the formal structure, it was in the informal
relationships that many of the problems came to light.   For
example, in one academic department, where there was usually a split among members in matters of departmental policy, the evaluator (representing the Chairman) was accused
by the "other faction" of being "soft" and of allowing credits
for students beyond the point of "acceptability."   This allegation had to be quickly investigated and either refuted or
corrected since the scuttlebutt in the faculty dining room
could easily have been exaggerated beyond the actual facts
with great damage to the program.   Criticisms by some faculty members of students were also heard informally: the
students felt "privileged," they were being given undue attention in contrast to other SGS students, they were arrogant
and demanding, etc.   Here, again, the special status of an
adult student who held a responsible position in the work-a-
day world had to be explained.   Also the students themselves
had to be counselled about their proper relationship and de-
portment in their contacts with officers of administration,

counsellors and clerical personnel in offices of the Registrar, Bursar, etc.   Some of the sharpest criticism as well
as the highest praise was not manifested in writing nor expressed at committee meetings but was whispered in corri-
dors or exclaimed over a cup of coffee.   All SGS administrative officers, as well as the Committee on Admission and
Evaluation, were particularly sensitive to the informal
"grapevine" and responded with extreme alacrity to its message, whether based on gossip or rumor.

          The students in the project were also not diffident in
expressing their views.   SGS was most fortunate in having in
the Office of the Associate Dean, an administrative assistant
whose understanding personality and sympathetic manner encouraged students to communicate freely with her.   Frequently, many kinks were "ironed out" before they grew to serious proportions by the attentive and caring "listening" by administrative staff and counselors.

Breaking the Credit Barrier

          In 1957, the Committee on Admission and Evaluation
attempted another step toward broadening the area of faculty
discretion in granting credit for informal study by adult students.   They outlined thirteen cases of students who were
"typical of the exceptional quality of the adults enrolled in
our Project" and urged the desirability of crediting these
adults with "that part of the baccalaureate degree curriculum
which they have already mastered through life experience,
so that they may be able to concentrate on the broadly cultural academic studies that will fill the gaps in their knowledge and provide them with a liberal education."[34]

          The report indicated that after two years there was
sufficient evidence that under the present college require-

ments, some adults were required to take courses in areas
in which they are already competent, many were restricted
to a slower pace of learning than their capabilities warranted; and others were subjected to classroom experiences
that were inappropriate for adults.   For richly qualified
adults, the report continued, these features of the curriculum consumed unnecessary time and might, indeed, restrict
the level of educational achievement.

The report also reminded the faculty that "at Brooklyn College there have been for some time provisions for the
alleviation of such handicaps for younger undergraduates,
notably veterans who, through experience or background, have
already achieved some of the objectives of our course requirements.   These provisions authorize the use of tutorial
services, independent reading, exemption examinations, and
credit by examination for informal experience."[35]

The Committee on Course and Standing was, therefore,
requested to approve the following resolution and to support
its adoption by Faculty Council.

> Whereas on May 20, 1952 the Faculty Council
> adopted a resolution (Doc. 58, Item 11) authorizing,
> in exceptional cases at the discretion of the Dean
> of Faculty, students who have pursued academic
> study on an informal basis to be eligible for credit
> for courses on the basis of examinations up to a
> maximum of 32 credits;
>
> And whereas some mature adults have pursued in-
> formal study which is often equivalent to more
> than the number of credits specified in the above
> resolution:
>
> Now, therefore, be it resolved that upon recommen-
> dation of the Dean of Faculty, with the approval of
> the Committee on Course and Standing, "Mature
> adults who have pursued informal study be eligible
> for credit for courses on the basis of examination
> in excess of 32 credits.

The resolution was unanimously approved by Faculty
Council in April, 1957.   Though the resolution imposed no
ceiling, as a matter of practice the limit on the number of
credits for life experience was administratively increased to
54 by the Committee on Admissions and Evaluation.   The
average number of experience credits for which students
actually qualified was 32, some achieving as many as 46 and
others none.

Two Steps Forward and One Step Backward

By 1959, the word "experimental" to describe the
program was dropped and a more permanent title, the Special Baccalaureate Degree Program for Adults, was adopted
by Faculty Council.   Fifty adults, were added to the Program that year, bringing the total roster to 150 students.
The Program was now financed completely by special fees
paid by the students enrolled in it. [36]   The budget covered
not only expenditures for evaluative, counseling, instructional and administrative purposes, but also research and experimentation in curricular development.   Studies were being continued on the correlation between scores on diagnostic tests and achievement in college, and the relationships
of initial counseling interviews and subsequent abilities to
cope with personal and other problems.

In 1959, a special Research Committee was appointed
by the Dean, consisting of eminent faculty members in the
fields of humanities, social science and natural science to
formulate plans for adult seminars on the elective level and
to "provide the intellectual challenge and stimulation needed
by students with rich life experience."[37]   After briefly describing the introductory seminars and their success in dealing with subject matter on an adult level, the Research Com-

mittee proposed a series of capstone seminars. Its report
stated:

> After completing the introductory seminars, the
> students have been required to fulfill the require-
> ments for the degree in regular elective classes.
> After their preparation in the seminars, many of
> these students find that the elective classes do not
> offer them the integration, depth and enrichment
> to which they have grown accustomed. [38]

The committee requested comments and recommendations from Deans, Department Chairmen, Curriculum Committee members and others concerned. Many critical comments were received and many constructive suggestions were
made. After giving weight to these criticisms and suggestions, appropriate revisions were made. The proposed "senior seminars" were then submitted to the usual committee
channels. After being approved, they were finally ratified by
Faculty Council.

Many of the ingredients of the Special Baccalaureate
Degree Program had by this time become firmly institutionalized. It was no longer necessary for the program to check
every step. Reports of the success of students who had been
graduated from the program were widely circulated among
faculty, additional publicity was given at honors and senior
receptions. By 1960, there were thirty-eight graduates. Of
these, fourteen had been graduated cum laude, six magna
cum laude, and five summa cum laude. Almost all of the
graduates had continued studies in a variety of graduate and
professional schools. [39]

Nevertheless, procedural restrictions were introduced
by the new Dean of the Faculties on December 2, 1960 after
discussion with the Associate Dean of SGS. The aim was to
protect the Brooklyn College degree from any doubt of its

quality.   The Dean wrote:

> You will recall that Dean _____, you and I met
> in my office on December 1, 1960, in order to
> reach some agreements concerning policies to be
> applied in the Special Baccalaureate Degree Pro-
> gram for Adults. At the conclusion of our meet-
> ing, we were agreed that we would institute the
> following policies--
>
> 1. In the future, all recommendations for credit
>   in Economics courses which were handled by
>   Dr. _____ will be reconsidered and reevalu-
>   ated by Professor _____.
>
> 2. At no time will we authorize more than 15
>   credits in any one department.
>
> 3. We will not authorize more than 9 credits in the
>   areas of Voice and Diction and Rhetoric and
>   Public Address in the Speech Department. This
>   means that we will not grant more than 9 cred-
>   its in the following courses--Speech 10; 11; 18;
>   19. 1; 19. 2; 20; 21; 22; and 29.
>
> 4. Evaluators are not to recommend credit for any
>   Honors courses or for the old 81-82 courses.
>
> 5. We will no longer grant credit for any of the
>   performance courses in Music or for the follow-
>   ing courses--Music 5; 5. 1; 7; and 0. 71.
>
> 6. All teachers in the program for adults should be
>   furnished student evaluation forms each semester
>   and be urged to file them each semester. It
>   would be helpful if they are asked to comment
>   specifically with reference to the quality of the
>   work of the adult students.
>
> 7. When a student applies to an evaluator for cred-
>   it, he should submit to the evaluator his creden-
>   tials and, in written form, a statement of his
>   background and experience, on the basis of which
>   he hopes to have credit recommended.
>
> 8. The folder of each student in the program should
>   contain a completed plan of studies.

It may be desirable at some time in the future to
require written exemption examinations in elective
courses, in addition to the normal evaluation
which is now in use.

The Dean's memorandum, setting more precise guidelines and limiting the areas of permissible credit allowance,
served to make evaluators more cautious and more circum-
spect in granting credits.   In effect, the result was further
limitation on the flexibility of the evaluators and there was
a noticeable decrease in the average number of credits actually allowed to students.

The Success of the Innovation

Until 1965, only 25 students were admitted annually,
but in that year the enrollment was, with the approval of
the President, increased to 50 annually.   This approval was
cheerfully given for the statistics of student achievement
were quite impressive.   As of June 1965, there were 144
graduates of whom 85 were graduated with honors; 86 had
gone on to graduate study of whom 39 had already earned the
Master's Degree and 5 the Ph. D. degree and 8 more were
candidates for the doctoral degree.   Is it any wonder that
the SGS Dean proudly stated in his report to Middle States
Association with reference to the Special Baccalaureate Degree Project:

> It has (also) stimulated a liberalization of faculty
> attitudes and has influenced the regular college
> curriculum in the direction of greater integration,
> imagination and vigor. [40]

While the innovation had a rough road to travel, it
was finally accepted and accorded full legitimacy by the faculty and administration.   Obstacles existed at every stage of
the journey, but the principle of cooptation effectively served

as a dynamic force in clearing the road and making the
goals attainable.

The Associate Degree in Nursing Science

Though SGS enjoyed a high level of autonomy with respect to the two-year programs leading to the A. A. and
A. A. S. degrees, their introduction were not decisions autonomously made by the School.   Formal approval of the College administration and faculty was still necessary.   Administration and faculty of CLAS, whose primary concern was the
four-year baccalaureate degree, required that the need for
two-year programs be cogently demonstrated before acquies-
cing in their adoption.

The A. A. and A. A. S. programs stemmed from the
recognition on the part of SGS that for many high school
graduates unable to enter a four-year college an educational
void existed.   This inability to enter College was predicated
either on deficient high school average or subject units.

Consistent with its second chance philosophy, SGS administration believed that these students, ineligible at the
time for admission as matriculated students, were nevertheless entitled to another opportunity to show scholastic promise.   Furthermore, in a society constantly growing more
complex, there was an imperative need for a collegiate experience beyond the high school even if this experience were
limited to two years.   Thus a two-year Associate in Arts
program was conceived embracing both a terminal course of
study or alternatively a spur leading into the baccalaureate
track.   Students who did not initially qualify for admission to
the B. A. curriculum qualified for admission to the A. A. program on the basis of lower entrance requirements.

Career oriented curricula leading to the A. A. S. degree, while conceived mainly as terminal programs for students who wished a modicum of training in business or subprofessional areas, were primarily viewed as a necessary public service. They were, moreover, considered as an economically justified method by which the College could gain more intensive utilization of its space and facilties. Almost as a public utility applying for a franchise, the tests of public convenience and necessity were, in effect, the basis on which two-year programs were proposed and adopted.

Nursing Science as a two-year course of study on a college campus, rather than a three-year training period in a hospital school of nursing, clearly met the criteria of public convenience and necessity. In addition, a pioneering program in the health field reflected all the lustrous qualities of an innovative experiment, for it, too, involved a significant break with the traditional hospital school pattern of nursing education. However, such program had a rather attenuated relationship to a liberal arts college. Many factors of a nursing science curriculum just did not "fit" into a liberal arts curriculum. Consequently, there was sound justification for the amount of adaptation and improvisation that was needed to launch the program and to nurture it to maturity.

Significant is the fact that the active cooperation of instructional departments and members of the faculty, particularly those in the natural sciences, was essential. For that purpose, cooptation again was the guiding principle. While the public appeal of this program eased the cooptative process, its utilization was essential in order effectively to meet the multiplicity of problems presented.

The Historical Background

During World War II, the vast shortage of bedside nurses both for military and civilian functions became increasingly acute.   Efforts to deal with the shortage were reflected in part by the widespread utilization of greater numbers of practical nurses and nurses aides.   However, crash programs were obviously necessary to train more registered nurses.   As a beginning, a critical examination was made of the three-year traditional diploma programs in hospital schools of nursing.   Serious doubt was leveled at the considerable amount of housekeeping duties that student nurses customarily had to perform.   The critical question was whether, by placing the education of nurses on college campuses and eliminating the housekeeping duties, more nurses might not be prepared in a shorter period of time.

As early as 1951, SGS entered into contracts with the schools of nursing of the Prospect Heights Hospital and the Norwegian Lutheran Deaconesses' Home and Hospital to conduct classes for student nurses in the natural sciences and other basic academic subjects.   As a result of these contracts over a period of two years SGS gained intensive knowledge and experience in the area of nursing education.   At the same time, Brooklyn College initiated discussions with the New York City Department of Hospitals regarding the possibility of a cooperative venture in nursing science.   Thinking at that time centered almost exclusively around the four-year baccalaureate program.   Eventually Brooklyn College, Queens College and Hunter College developed plans for a curriculum leading to the Bachelor of Science in Nursing.   To avoid unnecessary duplication of curricula in the municipal colleges, the Board of Higher Education deemed it desirable

to offer this four-year program at only one institution.
Hunter College was selected for that purpose.

The experience in planning a four-year collegiate
nursing program constituted solid groundwork for the later
development of two-year programs.   First, it established
close cooperation between the Department of Hospitals and
the municipal colleges.   Second, it made abundantly clear
the desirability of collegiate programs for the education of
nurses.   Most important, it developed a group of informed
and sympathetic promoters of such programs in the municipal colleges.

Late in 1951, the Teachers College Cooperative Project for Junior College Nursing Education was announced.
This announcement immediately prompted SGS to request the
help of Teachers College in formulating an experimental two-
year program.   In February 1952, exploratory meetings
were held with representatives of the State Department of
Education, Teachers College and the Commissioner of the
Department of Hospitals to discuss collegiate nursing programs.   Representatives of Queens College and Hunter College participated in these discussions.   After the conclusion
of these meetings, a general outline of a two-year curriculum leading to the A. A. S. degree was prepared jointly by
Brooklyn College and Queens College.   The plan was presented
to the Board of Higher Education for ratification and on April
21, 1952 the project was approved "in principle."

Objectives of the Program

In essence, the objectives of the two-year on-campus
nursing science program were to:

    1. Eliminate repetitive service-centered hospital ex-
        perience and replace it by education-centered ex-
        perience carefully integrated with theory, thereby

shortening by one year the time required to prepare a bedside nurse.

2. Insure high educational standards by offering the
    program in college, employing college faculty ex-
    clusively, and using college laboratories and other
    facilities.

3. Enrich the standard nursing curriculum by includ-
    ing courses in general education.

4. Remove specific barriers to recruitment by award-
    ing the Associate in Applied Science degree. The
    aim was to attract more men and older women in
    addition to young people who would not want to
    give up the many advantages of college life for the
    sequestered period of training in the hospital
    school.

Part of the Brooklyn College proposal was predicated
on its nearness to Kings County Hospital. As a municipal
institution, Brooklyn College was in an excellent position to
work out cooperative arrangements for the conduct of appropriate nursing science courses at the hospital and integrate
them with clinical practice, particularly in view of the
staunch support of the Commissioner of Hospitals. Background sciences and academic subjects, however, would be
given on campus.

The shortage of nurses in New York City was so
acute that the Board of Higher Education looked with favor
upon a request for a municipally-supported operation. It
was, therefore, determined to request budget financing from
the City large enough to permit the program to be tuition-
free for qualified New York City residents. Finally, in the
Spring of 1954, a budget of $100,000 was appropriated for
the initiation in the fall semester of two experimental pro-
grams--one at Brooklyn College and the other at Queens College. A specific curriculum amplifying the general proposal

which had been approved "in principle" two years earlier
was submitted and it was approved by the Board of Higher
Education.   Course content, it was agreed, would be left
for the determination of the professional staff when engaged
for service.

Much had, indeed, been accomplished by this time.
But the plan was still a conceptional design recently pro-
duced on the drawing board.   Implementing measures now
had to be adopted.   The first critical step was the recruitment of professional staff.

Finding a Berth

Even before staff recruiting could begin, the first
problem was how to fit the nursing science program into the
College organizational structure.   One possibility was to constitute it a separate autonomous department.   Independent
department status, however, presented too many eccentric
elements.   First, the program was to be a 64-credit curriculum leading to the A. A. S. degree rather than a 128-
credit curriculum leading to the baccalaureate degree.   Second, nursing science as professional rather than liberal arts
education would undoubtedly not be considered on par with
instructional departments of learned disciplines in liberal
arts.   Finally, the qualifications for faculty ranks applicable
to liberal arts departments were inappropriate as criteria
for nursing science staff.   In view of the many adaptations
and exceptions that would have to be instituted, the idea of
nursing science as an autonomous instructional department
was abandoned.

The Division of Vocational Studies, a component of
SGS, offered an acceptable and viable pattern of organization.
By incorporating nursing science as a specialization under

the jurisdiction of this Division, a high degree of flexibility
in staff recruiting, curriculum planning, student admissions
and other operating procedures would be achieved. Nursing
science as a professional curriculum would then be, ceteris
paribus, within the general framework of the other career-
oriented curricula offered in the Division of Vocational Studies.

The table of organization of this Division, too, recommended the assignment of the nursing science program to
it. The Division was headed by a professor of mathematics
designated as the "Supervisor" (later the title was changed
to Assistant Dean), under the administrative authority of the
Dean of SGS. In addition to holding professorial rank, the
supervisor was a member both of the Advisory Council and
Policy Committee of the School of General Studies. These
links to official bodies were essential in establishing and ad-
vancing implementing measures for nursing science.

For each career subject area--like accounting, business management, industrial relations, etc. --as well as for
each general education area--like English, speech, history,
philosophy, etc. --"coordinators" in the Division of Vocational Studies had functions and responsibilities comparable to department deputy chairmen in the Division of Liberal Arts.
The "coordinator" function and title were clearly appropriate
for the nursing science program. From another point of
view, the placement of the program in the Division of Vocational Studies seemed eminently "natural": it was this Division that had conducted the "contract" courses for the two
Brooklyn hospitals and that had acquired a considerable a-
mount of knowledge and know-how in the nursing science area.

Recruiting a Co-Ordinator and Staff

Selection of the coordinator of Nursing Science, designed to obtain the best possible person for the post, involved the active participation of members of the faculty who
had engaged in the early planning of the four-year nursing
program.   A selection committee was formed which included
representatives of SGS administration, the departments of Biology, Chemistry, Education, Health and Physical Education,
the Office of the Dean of Students, as well as a representative from the New York City Department of Hospitals.   The
Selection Committee's task was an exceedingly difficult one
for, at that time, SGS had no tenure-bearing annual lines to
offer the candidates.   Appointment had to be on the basis of
an annual income expressed in terms of an hourly rate of
pay for a specified number of hours per year.   The rank
was that of "Lecturer," a rank which carried neither faculty
status, tenure, retirement rights, nor other faculty rights
and privileges.   The position, though full-time with responsibility for program development, administration and supervision of teaching staff as well as classroom teaching, was
thus one of low status and relatively low salary in terms of
the College hierarchy.

Colleges that had nursing curricula, schools of nursing and various teaching hospitals were contacted for recommendations of candidates.   Despite the obvious inferiority of
the "Lecturer" position vis-à-vis normal faculty status a
number of applications were received.   Interviews revealed
the reasons for the candidates' interest.   In the first place,
they were intrigued with the idea of an experimental two-year
program in nursing on a college campus.   In the second
place, the role of college administrator or teacher repre-

sented to them a much higher prestige level than that of being a school of nursing administrator or teacher.   While the
college rate of pay was to some extent higher and the hours
lower than that of the typical school of nursing, these considerations were not decisive.   The educational challenge
was the most significant element.

From all the applications filed, the Committee was
able to select a highly qualified, experienced and experi-
mentally-minded person.   She was a registered nurse holding a master's degree in nursing education from Teachers
College, Columbia University, and was a member of the staff
of the New York Hospital-Cornell University School of Nursing.

The next step was recruitment of competent teaching
staff.   For that purpose, an "Appointments Committee" to
parallel the structure and procedures of liberal arts departments had first to be formed.   With the approval of the
President, the SGS Dean designated the Supervisor of the Division of Vocational Studies, the Coordinator of Nursing Science and the Chairman of the College's Department of Biology as the Appointments Committee.   Its responsibility was
to interview candidates for teaching positions and to make
recommendations for appointment to the Dean.

Recruitment of teaching staff presented the same problems of "Lecturer" status: no tenure, no mandatory increments, no retirement rights, no sabbatical or sick leave
privileges, hourly rates of pay (no work, no pay), etc.
Nevertheless, well-qualified, capable young women with R. N.
and master's degrees and with extensive hospital experience
were attracted to the program.   The novel idea of a two-year
nursing program at a college rather than a traditional school
of nursing excited their imagination.   All were eager to par-

ticipate in what they regarded as a challenging experiment.
This eagerness also indicated their dissatisfaction with the
manner in which hospital programs of education were conducted.   They particularly resented the utilization of students for many menial housekeeping tasks as a "device to
cope with the shortage of chambermaids, washwomen and
other unskilled workers."[41]   In their opinion, this "down-
grading" process seriously interfered with the "upgrading"
of nursing students.   A significant number objected to housekeeping services by students on efficiency grounds; time and
energy that could be more constructively channeled to distinctly professional responsibilities were wasted on menial
chores.[42]

Curriculum

The curriculum in broad outline was initially approved
by the College Curriculum Committee, Faculty Council and
Board of Higher Education.   After the coordinator was selected, the specific details of the curriculum had to be
worked out.   Careful consideration was given to the professional requirements of the New York State Board of Nursing
in addition to the academic and science requirements for the
A. A. S. degree of the State Education Department.   The educational standards of the National League of Nursing were also observed.   Most important, clinical hospital practice,
unique to this course of study, had to be provided and properly integrated with basic science and academic subjects.

A special problem involved the natural sciences.   Separate courses in biology, chemistry and physics--as offered
in the liberal arts curriculum--were deemed inappropriate
for nursing students.   An integrated science course was
necessary.   Accordingly, a basic one-year course in general

science was organized with the cooperation of the Biology
Department. [43] This Department not only took the lead in
preparing the course outlines and syllabi; it also assisted in
recruiting departmental members to teach the integrated science courses.

A delicate balance between theory and practice was
maintained by the chairman of the Biology Department, who
was also named a coordinator in the nursing science program.   Course content and instruction had to merge theoretical science and practical application.   For one semester
he had the science instructors spend several hours each week
in the hospital observing the students in clinical practice activities in order to determine how scientific principles were
practically applied in the clinical situation.

Space

Since early 1950, Brooklyn College has suffered from
a shortage of space and facilities. [44]   Limitation of physical
space was, in general, a major deterrent to a more expan-
sive development of programs.   Solutions were not easy when
a program involved additional laboratory facilities.   Only new
construction could alleviate that shortage.   A science program
does not have the flexibility of the non-science areas.   In a
history course, for example, chairs could be added to accommodate 45 or even 50 students to a classroom typically
seating 40 students.   Laboratories, on the other hand, have
rigid limits of 25 to 30.   Benches, sinks, and other appli-
ances and equipment cannot be "stretched."

The laboratory space required for the nursing science
program proved to be a major problem area.   Were it not
for the interest and good-will of the Chairman of the Biology
Department, nursing science would have starved to death just

for want of laboratory space. He so arranged laboratory
schedules of the Department that nursing science was enabled to share laboratory facilities during periods not pre-
empted by the Department. While nursing science was a
residual claimant to this precious space, it was sufficently
accommodated to provide laboratory practice.

The consequences of the friendly interest of the Chairman of the Biology Department during this early period of
birth and struggle for survival cannot be expressed in quantitative terms. As liaison coordinator of the program, as
member of the staff appointments committee, as member of
the students' admissions committee, and as an influential
voice in most policy decisions, he performed vital roles. He
secured faculty support for the sharing of space, for curricular changes, and for manifold other adaptations and accommodations essential for the healthy growth of the program.

Student Admissions

When initial approval of the nursing science program
was sought from the Board of Higher Education, student admission requirements were intentionally stated somewhat
vaguely. It was proposed that "the professional nursing staff
should participate in the planning of the requirements as far
as possible . . ." since the nature of the potential student
body was as yet a great unknown. [45] To be sure, high school
graduation or possession of a high school equivalency diploma
would be required. But no numerical average or specific
equivalency test scores were as yet specified. In addition,
the admissions procedure would include psychological and aptitude testing but these, too, were not specifically identified.

Administrative authority for student admission to the
College rests with the Director of Admissions, who is respon-

sible to the Dean of Students of the College.   In the case of
nursing applicants, the Director of Admissions was requested (and consented) to have authority delegated to an admissions committee appointed by the SGS Dean and approved by
the President.   The committee consisted of the Chairman of
the Biology Department, the Supervisor and Assistant Supervisor of Vocational Studies and the Coordinator of the Nursing Science Program.   Counselors and clinical psychologists
served as resource consultants to the Committee.

In the beginning, "admissions standards were determined primarily by a series of educated guesses by the Admissions Committee" since no "authoritative predictors of
success" existed. [46]   As more experience developed in light
of student performance, it became possible for the Committee to formulate a series of objective criteria for admission.
Students were also given the Psychological Corporation test.
Standard scores were related to Brooklyn College norms and
the total battery score was calibrated with high school averages.   This permitted the construction of a combined score
(merging high school average and battery score) as an objective basis for admission.   The Committee also continued
to interview each applicant to evaluate such factors as motivation and personality.

During the first semester, forty-four students were
admitted.   The number admitted each semester thereafter
varied from twenty-four to forty, the number depending upon
the qualifications and potential of the candidates applying.   In
general, approximately one-third of those who applied were
admitted; two-thirds did not meet the admission requirements.   The Committee was intent on maintaining high standards: "it considers it better to admit few students than to
lower standards. "[47]

Nurse-Teachers in the College Community

Nursing education as a two-year associate degree program rather than a traditional four year baccalaureate program kept it separate from (but not equal to) the traditional
academic departments.   The greatest impact of this separation was on the employment conditions for members of the
nursing science staff.   Budgetary "lines" and appropriate
faculty status could not be provided for either the coordinator or members of the teaching staff.   In part, this was a
fiscal matter; the budget limited hourly paid staff to the
"Lecturer" title.   Customarily this form of compensation and
title are reserved for part-time staff not appointed, as is
full-time staff, in the ranks of Instructor, Assistant Professor, Associate Professor and Professor.   However, in the
case of the nurses, it was more than a budgetary matter.

For appointment to a regular line in an instructional
department, the Ph. D. degree is minimally required.[48]   The
nursing teachers, though they were all registered nurses and
professionally qualified, had only the Master's degree; none
had the Ph. D. degree.   In order to establish the program on
a permanent basis, and to provide the nursing faculty with
annual, tenure-bearing lines, special budgetary provisions
and special rank recognition had to be secured from the Board
of Higher Education.   In 1958, a joint proposal to that effect
was made by the Deans of Brooklyn and Queens College to
the Administrative Council of College Presidents.   The proposal pointed out that the nursing science programs at the
respective colleges, originally initiated as an experiment, had
demonstrated their effectiveness.   It pointed to the success
of these nursing graduates in the New York State License Examinations for Registered Nurses (99% passed the State

Boards on the first crack), and stated that they (the nursing graduates) had passed "the acid test of performance on the job . . . almost all of them are at work at hospitals in the City.. . . They have received high praise from their employers . . . hospitals strongly endorse our efforts in continuing this program and in extending the opportunity to increasing numbers of students. . . ." "Both colleges have demonstrated that bedside nurses can be prepared, and prepared well, in a two-year college program; and they have assisted in the alleviation of the critical shortage of nurses. . . . They have ensured high educational standards by offering the program in college, employing college faculty exclusively, and using college laboratories and other facilities."[49] Based on these representations, the Administrative Council submitted in November 1958, a resolution to the Board of Higher Education recommending:

1. That the Nursing Science Programs started experimentally at Brooklyn and Queens in 1954-55 be established on a permanent basis and the courses of study accepted provisionally by the Board of Higher Education be now adopted as permanent parts of the curricula at Brooklyn and Queens.

2. That the teaching staffs in the nursing science programs be appointed on regular annual lines with the amended salary schedules approved for community colleges (C. C. Associate Professor, C. C. Assistant Professor, C. C. Instructor).

3. That on each campus the coordinators in charge of this program be designated the department head with the first salary step in the community college schedule for that category.

The Board approved the resolution and the nursing programs at Brooklyn and Queens Colleges were granted legitimacy "on a permanent basis."[50] But the budget titles and positions suggested for the nursing staff were not approved by the Budget Director who exercised fiscal power equivalent to a veto. Hence the staff had to continue in the same inferior status position as before.

A year later, in order to improve the status of the Nursing Science Program not only in the college community but also in the eyes of the National League of Nursing, the President approved the proposal that the Nursing Science Program be separated from the Division of Vocational Studies and be organized as a new Division of Nursing Science. But the lack of faculty status of the coordinator of nursing science raised the question as to whether she could be named the divisional head. Additional improvisation was necessary. By placing the new Division "technically under the supervision of a Full Professor, even though an increasing degree of responsibility would be assumed by . . . the present coordinator," the problem was temporarily evaded. [51] It was understood that the Supervisor of the Division of Vocational Studies would continue to work very closely with the Nursing Science Coordinator until faculty rank for her was achieved. In the meantime, she was named the supervisor of the Division of Nursing Science.

Thereafter, a recommendation was made that the Nursing Science Supervisor be appointed to an annual line at the Instructor level. Procedurally, the only way that the recommendation could be implemented was to have such appointment made by an established department; however, the Division of Nursing Science had no status as an academic department. Consequently, the SGS Dean requested the Chairman of the Biology Department to secure the department Appointments Committee endorsement of the candidacy of the Nursing Science Supervisor and, at the same time, to obtain

a waiver of the Ph. D. requirement. The language of the
letter reflects the status of the program in the college community as well as the problems involved in the development
of programs "outside the pale" of "academic acceptability."
The Dean's letter stated:

> I am advised that for technical reasons it will be
> necessary to attach her (the coordinator) at the
> present time to one of the recognized academic
> departments on campus.   Should it be possible to
> obtain additional lines in this Division, in all like-
> lihood a separate teaching department would be
> created.   Meanwhile, it appears logical that the
> Biology Department should supply her with a tem-
> porary berth in order to legalize her appointment.
> We would greatly appreciate it if the Appointments
> Committee of the Biology Department could find it
> possible to make this magnificent gesture to a very
> fine lady. [52]

Interesting, indeed, are the categories of persuasion
mentioned in this letter: "technical reasons," "logic of a
temporary berth," "legalize the appointment," "appreciation" for gallantry.   Formal organization responded to these
persuasive categories and the requested appointment was
made by the Department of Biology.   It was then successively ratified by the Committee on Faculty Personnel and Budget and the Board of Higher Education.

But the hope that, if additional lines were obtained,
"a separate teaching department would be created" for nursing science never came to fruition.   Too many practical difficulties impeded this development.   When annual teaching
lines were included in the SGS budget (there were five included in 1960), additional improvisation had to be resorted
to for appointment of teaching staff to such lines.   Not being
a department, nursing science had no formal appointments
committee.   Therefore an ad hoc committee was formed for

this function. A three member committee was appointed
by the Dean with the approval of the President consisting of
the Supervisor of the Division of Vocational Studies, (a full
professor of Mathematics), the Chairman of the Biology Department and the Supervisor (formerly coordinator) of the
Division of Nursing Science. Recommendations by this Committee for appointment would technically be for "attachment
to" the Department of Biology as "Lecturer - Nursing."
This title was in lieu of the originally proposed community
college titles which the Budget Director refused to grant.
The salaries ranged from approximately $5,000 to $6,200.
The minimum salary for Instructor at the Senior colleges
in 1960 was $5,600.

To what extent approval by the Budget Director of
these specialized nursing science lines was in response to
community and political pressures is difficult to determine.
Nevertheless, the budgetary allocations after the establishment of the program in 1954, are revealing. After the initial budget of 1954, increases only for the expansion of student enrollment and for no other purposes were allowed.[53]

Budgetary Problems

In a letter addressed to the President accompanying
the 1960-61 budget request, the SGS Dean pointed out that the
nursing science budget was no longer adequate even to meet
the needs of the limited enrollment and that the program was
being subsidized by other SGS areas and sources. He en-
closed a dramatic clipping from the New York Times (October 3, 1959) reporting that the deaths of two babies in
Kings County Hospital were attributed to the shortage of
nurses. He reiterated his request for annual lines for teaching staff, to provide guaranteed annual increments, tenure

and pension rights.   By this time, approximately forty community colleges in New York State had established curricula
in nursing education and the Dean stressed the difficulty of
retaining experienced teaching staff.   Offers for positions
with higher salary, tenure rights and higher status were
threatening the stability of the staff.   The Dean also referred to a Kellogg Foundation press release and added:

> It is somewhat ironical that foundation funds total-
> ing $1, 795, 000. 00 are being made available to
> launch junior and community college education for
> Nursing in New York and other states, while ex-
> isting programs are virtually being starved to
> death. [54]

Letters deploring the sparse budget were also sent to
the New York City Budget Director by the Chairman of the
Nursing Committee of Kings County Medical Society, the Executive Director of Jewish Chronic Disease Hospital and the
Commissioner of the Department of Hospitals.   All of the
letters urged more adequate budget and applauded the quality
of the nursing science program at Brooklyn College, but they
were to no avail.

Teacher Status Problems

In 1961, when additional annual lines were provided
in the budget for nursing science, the question was again
raised with regard to the lecturer status of nursing science
teachers attached to the Biology Department.   The Chairman
of the Department wrote:[55]

> . . . . The nine people now on lecturer lines have
> a number of steps yet to be legalized before they
> become regular instructors, but these steps will un-
> doubtedly take place.   (They never did take place.)
> It should be clear that when and as they become
> instructors they become members of a sub-depart-
> ment and not voting members of the Department of

Biology.

> I think this important because I have to ask the
> departmental appointments committee to approve
> for reappointment and tenure people whom they do
> not know. They will approve such individuals on
> the basis of a recommendation of a sub-committee
> whose membership you have defined. This will
> safeguard any idea in anyone's mind that they are
> being asked to rubber-stamp an approval of tenure
> in the Biology Department. All of us recognize
> that none of these people are qualified or wish to
> become members of the Department of Biology,
> and that their appointments to this department
> would not be legal. I, nevertheless, feel a clari-
> fication on this point will eliminate any hesitancy
> on the part of the Biology Department Appoint-
> ments Committee members when asked to act in
> this capacity.

To this letter, the Dean replied that it was not the
intention to have these individuals "qualify as full-fledged
members of the Biology Department with all the rights and
privileges belonging to that status."[56] He added . . . "they
are simply to be construed as members of a sub-department
and not voting members of the Department of Biology."[57]
Formal structure again emphasized the need for temporizing
and improvising.

Though the classification "Lecturer - Nursing Science"
constituted an annual line, the nursing science teachers
nevertheless continued to be marginal in the college community. The fact that Nursing Science was never designated
as a "department" of the college no doubt contributed to the
marginal status. The teachers were "attached" to the Department of Biology but not voting members of it. Moreover, the "lecturer" title, although an annual position embracing tenure, pension, etc., was not included in the definition of "faculty" under the By-Laws of the Board.[58] Without faculty rank and as members of a "Division," not a bona

fide Department, Nursing Science lecturers were outside the
democratic and bureaucratic structure of the College.   For
example, these lecturers were not eligible to serve on col-
legewide or departmental committees; they had no representation on the Faculty Committee on Personnel and Budget or
on Faculty Council; they had no rights to vote for the election of a departmental chairman or an appointments committee.   They were hybrids not fully integrated into the College
culture.

Efforts to Integrate Staff

Aware of this hybrid character, SGS made special efforts wherever possible to include the Division of Nursing
Science supervisor and staff in administrative and operating
relationships.   The supervisor of Nursing Science was named
to the Policy Committee and the Advisory Council of the
School.   Nursing Science staff was included in general staff
conferences and other staff functions.   However, these as-
similative efforts were inadequate to instill in them a full
sense of participation in the college community.

When asked, Nursing Science staff spontaneously responded that they always feel as "outsiders," that the faculty
of other departments regard them as "from a different
world" and "not as equals."   At the annual SGS convocation
and conferences where the Nursing Science staff was treated
as equals they did not hesitate to verbalize their appreciation.   One staff member stated: "This is the only time I see
people from other departments."

In response to a request for reregistration of the program by the Division of Professional Education of the State
Education Department, an evaluation team visited the campus
for a critical review.   Its report struck at some of the ad-

ministrative and structural difficulties faced by a two-year
nursing program in a four-year liberal arts college.   Pointing out that "a basic requirement for appointment as an instructor in the College is the doctoral degree . . . and
that exceptions to this policy occur in the art and music departments," the report stated:

> Discussion was held with administrative persons
> regarding the position of the program in nursing
> within the college and the faculty rank.   It appears
> questionable whether an appropriate place for the
> nursing program and nursing faculty can be ob-
> tained within the present organizational structure
> of the college, although some progress has been
> made in securing certain faculty benefits for the
> nurse faculty members. . . .
>
> . . . the instructors . . . are appointed on annu-
> al salary lines and are awarded tenure privileges,
> but denied most other faculty privileges. . . .
> Participation in general faculty organization is not
> extended to the Nursing Science lecturers. [59]

The report characterized the program as "generally
successful" in meeting its objectives.   It especially referred
to the success of graduates in passing the State licensing examination.   However, some concern was expressed with regard to the breadth of clinical practice; and in order to better evaluate this aspect, it was recommended that further
study be made of the quality of performance by graduates.
With regard to staff status, the report stressed the obvious
weakness consistently pointed out by the administration:

> A major weakness in the program, which has been
> discussed on this and previous visits, relates to
> the status and function of the nurse faculty in the
> college. [60]

The Program's Phasing Out

With the adoption of the 1964 Master Plan of the
City University, the nursing science program was legislated
out of existence by the Board of Higher Education. The
eminently successful program was to go the way of all two-
year degree programs--out of the senior colleges and transferred to the community colleges. The phasing out process,
begun in 1965 ended in January 1967 when the last remaining students were graduated. Though the shortage of nurses
in the City of New York (as well as in the nation as a whole)
had grown even more acute--especially with the introduction
of Medicare and Medicaid--the Board of Higher Education
chose to eliminate these programs at the senior colleges and
to limit them to the community colleges.

The rationale for the transfer of two-year degree programs to the community colleges was to make room at the
senior colleges for additional baccalaureate students. On
May 29, 1964, the President of Brooklyn College wrote to
the President of Kingsborough Community College in Brooklyn:

> While "community and national needs for nurses"
> will predictably continue at a high level, the com-
> pelling pressures for space on our campus will al-
> so continue to build up, making the complete trans-
> fer of our nursing program a necessity as soon as
> Kingsborough Community College can develop such
> a program.

It is interesting to speculate why the faculty and the
Faculty Council and instructional departments participating in
the Nursing Science program did not oppose the transfer.
Only the School of General Studies protested the Master
Plan's decree. Inferences drawn from passive behavior are
no doubt difficult to pin down, but it is fair to say that the

marginal status of the program undermined strong dissent.
Surely if the Board had proposed the elimination of the Biology Department or of the Health Education Department,
vociferous faculty dissent would have been generated.   But
nursing science was never able to build vested interests that
could be valiantly defended.   The nursing science program
was viewed throughout its existence as "outside the social
system. "

A similar fate was in store for all two-year A. A. S.
and A. A. degree programs.   They, too, were gradually being transferred to the community colleges.   By 1969, the
phasing out process was completed.   But this transfer to
the community colleges was not an exclusively City University phenomenon.   The national trend is still the development of community and junior colleges for two-year terminal and transfer programs.   Given the major commitment
of Brooklyn College to four-year baccalaureate programs,
the extreme pressures upon space and facilities and the national trend to relegate two-year programs to the junior colleges, one might speculate whether anything could have been
done to retain the nursing science program in the School of
General Studies.   In view of the historical forces as well as
the internal pressures, it is highly doubtful that cooptation,
as an organizational mechanism, could have brooked the tide.

Variations on a Theme

A cherished part of the SGS self-image is that of in-
novator.   But SGS, as a sub-organization, may not choose
its goals unilaterally.   It is subject to the superior authority
of the parent organization.   To introduce innovations embracing new or different goals, SGS has to secure the approval and support of its parent.   Cooptation is a significant

means toward that end. Even though dysfunctional consequences may frequently result from giving positions of power
and responsibility to "outsiders," cooptation is, nevertheless,
a necessary instrument by which to increase the likelihood
that the two related organizations will in fact find compatible
aims in the innovation. By absorbing key members of the
CLAS faculty into the SGS policy-making and operational
structure, this likelihood is enhanced. Cooptation thus serves
the purpose of giving the parent organization a sense of full
participation both in the conception of the innovation and in
its implementation.

The two cases of innovation analyzed in this chapter
illustrate the manifold problems with which all SGS innovations have to grapple. These examples bring into sharp focus the subtle nuances of the cooptative process. Two different experimental programs, one in the area of liberal
arts and the other in professional education, were involved.
Each presented different problems and necessitated different
cooptative techniques. The ultimate aims were the same,
to gain legitimacy for the innovation.

The Special Baccalaureate Degree Program bore a
much closer relationship to the primary function of the parent organization as a liberal arts college than did the Nursing Science Program. But the experimental and innovative
features of the baccalaureate program involved such radical
departures from the status quo that acceptability had to be
secured. Cooptation was thus much more than a mere device
of expediency. It was the method by which to harmonize the
goals of sub-unit and parent organization.

In contrast to the Special Baccalaureate Program, the
Nursing Science Program, as a two-year professional curriculum, was far less intimately related to the parent's primary

function as a liberal arts college. While eyebrows were
raised as to whether scarce resources should be allocated
to this peripheral purpose, the pressures from the community were much too strong to invite serious resistance. The
grounds of public convenience and necessity elicited sympathetic faculty reception of this experimental program. But
its nature presented so many features eccentric to the College structure and procedures that improvisations and adaptations had to be constantly resorted to. To achieve some
degree of flexibility out of a bureaucratic structure bound by
time-honored and customary procedures, cooperation of the
relevant administrative mechanisms had to be enlisted. Imaginative improvisations and adaptations depended on a cooptative process.

While these two programs were quite distinguishable
from each other in curricula, instructional staff, student
body, financing and CLAS faculty participation, they nevertheless represented variations on the same theme. Both were
innovative and markedly different from traditional patterns.
Both had to gain legitimacy in the social system. Cooptation was the vehicle by which that result was accomplished
to a greater or lesser degree.

Notes

1. Samuel B. Gould, "Quality in Adult Education" an address to the Association of University Evening Colleges, Louisville, Kentucky. November 17, 1958.

2. See Amitai Etzioni, Modern Organizations.

3. See Chapter VI, "Image and Identity," for further discussion of this point.

4. Ph. D. programs were introduced in the City University
   in 1962.

5. As reported by Professor Albert Salomon, one of Max Weber's students.

6. Memorandum from President Harry D. Gideonse to Deans, Directors and Department Chairmen re: Administrative Responsibility, April 22, 1963.

7. Philip Selznick, TVA and the Grass Roots (University of California, 1949), p. 13.

8. SGS was the pioneer of a Special Baccalaureate Program for Adults. Other institutions which have since a-dopted similar programs are Boston University, Syracuse, Oklahoma, Queens College, Johns Hopkins, a-mong others.

9. Peter E. Siegle, in Introduction to: Bernard H. Stern, How Much Does Adult Experience Count? (Center for the Study of Liberal Education for Adults, 1955), p. 91. Siegle states that the suggestion was first fully developed in an article by John S. Diekhoff, "Time Off for Good Behavior," Journal of General Education, October, 1952.

10. Ibid., p. 2.

11. Edwin H. Spengler, "College Life Begins at 40" (unpublished, 1954), p. 4.

12. "Annual Report of the Director," School of General Studies, 1954-1955, p. 7.

13. Letter to Committee on Long Term Curriculum Development, October 8, 1953, (emphasis added).

14. Ibid., (emphasis added).

15. Document of transmittal to Faculty Council from Committee on Long Term Curriculum Development, October 22, 1953.

16. Letter dated November 9, 1953.

17. Letter dated January 20, 1954.

18. Bernard H. Stern and J. Ellswerth Missall, Adult Experience and College Degrees (Center for the Study of Liberal Education for Adults), p. 6.

19. Ibid., p. 7.

20. As reported by the Administrative Assistant who ana-
    lyzed the questionnaires.

21. Bernard H. Stern, "Degree Seeking Adults; a Prelimi-
    nary Report on an Experimental Project at Brooklyn
    College," (unpublished), April, 1954, p. 2.

22. Stern and Missall, op. cit., p. 35.

23. Ibid., p. 53.

24. Ibid., p. 56.

25. Ibid., p. 60.

26. Ibid., p. 55.

27. Letter dated July 15, 1954.

28. Letter dated August 2, 1954.

29. Committee on Admission and Evaluation, Adults as Col-
    lege Students (October 1954), p. 22.

30. Letter to Staff, dated December 28, 1955.

31. Letter of SGS Dean to John Schwertman dated May 23,
    1955.

32. Ibid.

33. Stern and Missal, op. cit., p. 15.

34. Brooklyn College, School of General Studies, "Experi-
    mental Degree Project for Adults, Accreditation of
    Informal Study for Adults," (Mimeo, January, 1957),
    p. 18, (emphasis added). It is interesting to note
    that no mention is made on reducing the time involved
    in obtaining the degree; emphasis is on broad cultural
    aspects of a liberal education!

35. Ibid., p. 1, 2.

36. Student fees were $15 per credit in 1955; $20 per credit
    beginning in the Fall 1958 Semester. As the program
    became more institutionalized, various developmental

costs diminished and SGS was able to cover operating and overhead costs out of student fees.

37. Memorandum to all Department Chairmen, Deputy
Chairmen, Department Curriculum Committees,
Deans, Directors and Members of the Long Term
Committee and Curriculum Committee from the Research Committee of the Special Baccalaureate Degree Program for Adults, November, 1960, p. 2.
The original seminars were only in the area of prescribed work and covered the first two years of
study.

38. Ibid. , p. 2.

39. Bernard H. Stern, Never Too Late for College (Center
for the Study of Liberal Education for Adults, 1963),
p. 27.

40. "Preliminary Report to the Middle States Association of
Colleges and Secondary Schools," 1966, p. 11.

41. Informal interviews with nursing science instructors.
Myrtle S. Jacobson, "Brooklyn College: A Study in
Social Structure," 1957, p. 10. (unpublished study).

42. Ibid. , p. 11.

43. Report on Brooklyn College Nursing Science Program
1954-1958.

44. This problem, critical in the development of SGS programs, will be discussed in Chapter V, "Stress and
Strain."

45. Report of Brooklyn College Nursing Science Program
1954-1958, p. 20.

46. Ibid. , p. 20.

47. Ibid. , p. 22.

48. Except in department of Music and Art where the degree
may be waived because of the special nature of the
subject matter.

49. Joint memorandum of Deans Edwin H. Spengler and
Glenn Howard, to the Administrative Council.

50. Minutes of the Board of Higher Education, December
    1958.

51. Memorandum to President Harry D. Gideonse from
    Dean Edwin H. Spengler, May 1, 1959.

52. Letter to Carroll W. Grant, Chairman, Department of
    Biology, May 22, 1959.

53. The amount of the budget was correlated with student
    enrollment

Year	Budget	# of Students
1954	$50,000	44
1955	70,119	83
1956	81,163	90
1957	80,997	111
1958	71,123	99
1959	71,123	113
1960	41,323 (+5 lines $25,000)	126

In addition to the increase in numbers of students in
the program, salary levels were going up in other
areas of the college. "Normal" increments were
still not adequately provided for existing nursing science staff.

54. Letter from Dean Edwin H. Spengler to President Harry
    Dc. Gideonse, October 4, 1959.

55. Letter from Chairman to SGS Dean, December 7, 1961.

56. Letter from SGS Dean to Biology Department Chairman,
    December 20, 1961.

57. Ibid.

58. Definition of Faculty Rank - Article VIII, Para. 8.1,
    p. 14, Board of Higher Education By-Laws. Only the
    Supervisor (in 1960 the title was changed to Assistant
    Director; in 1966 it was changed to Assistant Dean)
    became a member of the Faculty since she subse-
    quently attained the rank of Assistant Professor in the
    Biology Department as a matter of accommodation.

59. Report of Visit to Associate Degree Program in Nursing
    at Brooklyn College, School of General Studies, by

the University of the State of New York, The State
Education Department, Division of Professional Education, October 1 and 2, 1963, p. 2.

60. Ibid. , p. 8.

Chapter IV

Authority and Responsibility:

Internal Structure and Dynamics

> "Thirty spokes are made one
> by holes in a hub, by vacancies
> joining them for a wheel's use."
>
> Lao-tzu

Organization has been defined as "the arrangement of
personnel for facilitating the accomplishment of some agreed
purpose through the allocation of functions and responsibilities."[1] How functions and responsibilities are distributed
and articulated determines, in large measure, the effectiveness of the organization in achieving its goals.   Functions,
however, cannot be performed nor responsibilities carried
out without authority, the sanctioned and "legitimate" power
to act.[2]

In a complex organization, the areas of authority and
responsibility are formally defined in rules and regulations,
by-laws, directives, etc.   Graphically they are represented
by tables of organization which sketch the lines of authority
and responsibility as well as the internal communication system.   But, as noted earlier, formal rules, particularly in a
professional organization, do not necessarily preclude degrees of latitude in the performance of functions.[3]   After being established, rules and regulations are constantly being

interpreted by human beings acting out roles in an organizational setting. When individuals interpret, react and inter-
act with each other, they not only modify the means by
which to achieve objectives but even the objectives themselves.

     While the boundaries of organizational behavior are,
in fact, delimited by formal rules and procedures, it is well
known that informal patterns emerge. As men join each other at lunch or dinner, at cocktail parties, in clubs, and in
car-pools to and from work, informal groupings usually
emerge and gradually become established and patterned. Often, these patterns more subtly and profoundly influence the
formal job alignments. Sometimes the informal arrangements have negligible influence on the formal; sometimes
they serve to supplement or implement them; frequently, however, they frustrate or even counteract the formal organizational "law." In the final analysis, authority is made visible
by the behavior of the actors, by their choices of alternatives, their actions and their non-actions. These observable
patterns of human behavior frequently reveal the power structure of the organization much more cogently than the formal
hierarchy of authority. It is the day to day functioning of
individuals and groups within the milieu of the sanctioned authority which illuminates the mysteries of "who does what
and how."

Formal Academic Organization

     Though formal organization may be viewed as the
"structural expression of rational action,"[4] it takes a unique
form in the academic world. A college or university is a
special type of collectivity. It consists essentially of administration and a professional staff. The student body may be

viewed as the clientele.

The administrative controls necessary for rational
action relate to a great variety of material, human and fiscal resources and their efficient utilization.   But equally important for the attainment of academic objectives is responsible participation by the faculty in the institution's decision-
making processes especially when matters of professional
concern are involved. [5]   However, administrative controls
must and frequently do impinge on issues of professional
concern.   Thus a condition of tension may arise between the
decision-making claim of faculty in professional matters and
the managerial prerogatives exercised by administration.

SGS, as a sub-organization, has no independent faculty.   Whatever legislation is enacted by the college faculty
applies with equal force to SGS.   Moreover, to a very large
extent the administration of SGS is subject at many points to
the controls of the college-wide administration.   Since the
two organizational structures operate "under the same roof"
and central authority, their paths sometimes run parallel,
frequently converge, and on occasion overlap or intersect.

As each unit seeks zealously to guard its presumed
area of jurisdiction, the discernible patterns in the interrelationships are those of cooperation, competition and conflict.   While for some purposes lines of authority may be
clearly stated and precisely defined, for others they are
blurred.   At times, even when organizational lines of authority are clear-cut and unambiguous, solutions to concrete
problems may rest not so much on canons of interpretation
but rather on practical considerations of how authority should
be exercised.

Whether the authority and responsibility structure be
at times clear or blurred, explicit or implicit, it can, never-

theless, be analyzed from two vantage points:

1. Who has authority, i. e. , in which individuals or
   groups is the authority vested;

2. What is the authority for, i. e. , toward what end
   or purpose is the delegation of authority contemplated.

Authority Inter-Relationships

For the College as a total entity, the President delegates authority and responsibility, in addition to the SGS
Dean, to a number of college deans: Administration, Faculties, Graduate, Students, and Studies.   The functions of
these several deans, who are directly responsible to the
President, encompass the entire spectrum of college affairs.
But, significantly, their authority spills over into many aspects of the educational and administrative operations of SGS.
For example, one of the critical areas of "administrative
responsibility" of the Dean of the Faculties is that of curriculum.   Insofar as the same liberal arts curriculum is offered in both CLAS and in SGS, his authority extends to both.
The Dean of the Faculties also has "administrative responsibility" for "regular, full-time line" faculty positions and
personnel.   Here, too, the scope of the Dean's jurisdiction
extends into SGS with respect to many vital aspects of staff
appointment, tenure and promotion.

In the administrative hierarchy, the SGS Dean is directly responsible to the President.   As his deputy, the SGS
Dean has two functions:

1. He administers the School of General Studies and
   seeks to conserve and enhance its educational standards.

2. He initiates and develops appropriate programs of
   instruction within the framework of college regula-

While the SGS Dean has the authority and responsibility to administer the sub-unit and to conserve and enhance
its educational standards, his powers to initiate and develop
appropriate programs of instruction are explicitly circum-
scribed by the condition that they be "within the framework
of college regulations, procedures and policies. . . ."
What is the effect of this conditional limitation? Since the
other College deans have substantially similar authority in
their respective functional areas, the powers of the SGS
Dean are necessarily limited by their authority. Effectively
to administer SGS and "to conserve and enhance its educational standards" requires that the SGS Dean have at least a
concurrent voice in decision-making on matters affecting
SGS. Thus there is an inevitable criss-crossing of authority and responsibility between the SGS Dean and the other
deans.

This criss-crossing of authority and responsibility
pervades the total interactive process between parent organization and sub-unit. It extends to every area of concern:
curriculum, academic standards, student admission and retention standards, student activities, counseling and guidance,
faculty and staff appointments, promotions and retention, a-
mong many other areas.

A key point where the inter-twining of authority and
responsibility between parent and sub-unit is most sharply
revealed is that of faculty and other instructional staff appointments, promotions and retention. The nature of the
criss-crossing relationships and interactions emerge in bold-
est relief at this key point. Hence the mosaic of authority and
responsibility will here be principally illustrated by its most
typical and characteristic category, namely faculty and staff.

From the point of view of administrative authority
and responsibility with respect to SGS instructional staff, two
crucial questions may be propunded:

1. Who has power and authority to select, appoint and
   promote instructional staff?

2. What authority and responsibility does the staff itself possess?

Both of these questions will successively be analyzed
on three levels, for there are three categories of instructional staff in SGS, and the answers are somewhat different
for each.   The three categories of instructional staff are:

1. SGS "line" personnel who are permanent, full-time
   faculty members attached to college departments;

2. CLAS permanent faculty who teach in SGS on an
   overtime basis;

3. "Off-campus" temporary lecturers, essentially
   SGS part-time personnel.

As to each of these categories, there are differences
not only in selection and appointments but also in relative
rights, privileges and immunities.   Moreover, the jurisdiction actually exercised by the full-time, CLAS faculty and
deans also varies with the particular category of SGS staff
involved.   Parenthetically, the interrelationship with CLAS is
strongest and the latter's control greatest with respect to full-
time "line" faculty and least with respect to "off-campus"
temporary lecturers.

Annual Line Personnel

Brooklyn College has just one faculty.   No separate
group is defined as SGS "faculty."   Annual "line" personnel
for SGS are subject to the same formal requirements and

procedures for appointment, retention, tenure and promotion
as are CLAS personnel.   These functions are delegated to
the CLAS instructional departments and to the "college-wide"
Committee on Faculty Personnel and Budget.   The Faculty
thus exercises the power, subject to the approval of the
President, to determine its own membership.   This power
includes SGS annual line personnel, though the SGS Dean exercises concurrent authority with the Dean of the Faculties
in appointment, retention, tenure and promotion for faculty
assigned to SGS lines.   Personnel appointed to these lines
have all the rights, privileges, and immunities, including
tenure and retirement rights, applicable to faculty status generally.   They are members of the faculty with no theoretical
distinction as to the particular division, CLAS or SGS, to
which the individual's line is allocated.

The Small Ratio of Annual Lines

        Out of a total college-wide faculty of about 600, only
about 10% consists of SGS line personnel. [7]   In various instructional departments, the range varies from about 2% to 20%.
Relative ratios of CLAS and SGS faculty members in typical
departments are:

Annual Line Personnel

Department	Total	CLAS	SGS	SGS% [8]
Economics	20	16	4	20. 0
Education	95	93	2	1. 9
English	70	66	4	5. 7
Geology	10	8	2	20. 0

        A "minority" group is defined by sociologists as an
"underprivileged" group.   Underprivilege may stem simply
from the fact that a small group exists within a larger group
that holds the preponderance of power and authority.   This

condition of minority status is of special significance in
SGS.   To carry out its distinctive role as an evening college, SGS should presumably have a "faculty" of its own
that exercises authority independent of CLAS and which is
committed to unique SGS goals.   But SGS is not an autonomous unit; rather, it is a sub-unit with limited authority
that intersects with the superseding authority of the parent.

The minority status is also represented by the ratio
of annual lines to total instructional staff in SGS.   Of the
approximately 420 staff members in the SGS Division of Liberal Arts in the Fall 1967 semester, 58 or 13% were on annual lines; 112 or 27% were day session faculty members
teaching in the evening for additional compensation; 250 or
60% were off-campus, part-time lecturers.[9]

The small ratio of annual line positions is partly due
to the fact that it is a relatively new phenomenon in SGS.
It was not until 1957 that the first annual lines were provided in the SGS budget.[10]   Although only three annual lines
for administrative appointments exclusively were granted in
1957, SGS heralded this development as a significant break-
through from the traditional budgetary appropriations made
solely for hourly-paid lecturers.

The need for annual line positions for evening teach-
ing had been advocated even prior to the establishment of
SGS.   As early as 1948, Ordway Tead, then Chairman of the
Board, stated:

> As I have said in previous reports, unless and un-
> til the major group of the Evening instructional
> staff for matriculated students can be placed on the
> basis of annual salaries and be under close coop-
> erative relationships with the chairman of the day
> departments in the given subject, the quality of our
> Evening-session degree-granting instruction will
> suffer.[11]

Since 1952, almost every SGS budget document and
annual report included a request for annual line positions.
Typical was the following statement in the annual report of
1953-1954:

> The relatively slight attraction to professionally
> ambitious people of a part-time position paid on a
> modest hourly basis continues to be a great ob-
> stacle to the creation of a stable staff of teachers
> --too often in the end, the good teachers go else-
> where. [12]

The budget request for the same year pointed out:

> Existing inequities cannot be corrected all at once.
> However, . . . the city is obligated to provide
> the same standards of education for fully-matricu-
> lated students no matter what hour of the day their
> class may recite. [13]

Throughout the years, budget requests and annual reports
repeated the need for a SGS "faculty" to give responsible direction and leadership to the evening program.

From 1957 to 1960, only six annual lines were allocated for SGS. In 1960, a decade after the establishment
of SGS, twenty-five additional annual lines were provided in
the City budget; in 1961, eleven more and in 1965, sixteen
more were provided. Thus a total of fifty-two permanent
lines were created over the five-year period in relation to
a total staff of approximately 450. [14] These SGS lines varied
in rank from instructor to associate professor; in 1965, two
full professor lines were added. Quite significant from the
point of view of faculty status is the fact that each line was
set by the Budget Director at the minimum salary step for
the specific rank and not, as is common in CLAS, at a higher intermediate level between the minimum and maximum of
the rank.

SGS Line Appointments

Year	Professor	Associate Professor	Assistant Professor	Instructor	Total
Prior to 1957	1	2			3*
1957				3	3
1960		5	9	11	25
1961		2	4	5	11
1965	2	3	7	4	16
Total	3	12	20	23	58

* Transfers from CLAS to fill SGS administrative posts.

SGS, with the aid of the President, had fought long and hard for the establishment of annual lines. Their establishment represented a major victory to SGS. The vision was that annual line positions in SGS would provide a stable staff whose primary commitment would be to teaching the more adult and heterogeneous evening students. In addition, the hope was that this core staff of teachers with faculty rank and tenure would enable SGS administration to develop a nucleus of a "faculty" with authoritative powers to act on curriculum and other educational policies.

But the incipient development never matured further toward the vision of SGS greater autonomy. Authority and responsibility governing appointments, tenure and promotions continued to reside, under the by-laws of the Board, solely in the academic departments of the College. When the SGS line emerged as a new phenomenon, the old established departmental authority was not in any way modified but was fully preserved. While ultimate administrative responsibility regarding faculty appointments always rested with the President, he delegated it in part to the Dean of the Faculties in conjunction with the role of the individual departments to select the candidate.

Prior to the time that SGS lines were established, only the Dean of the Faculties had the administrative authority to recommend to the President faculty appointments suggested by the departments.   Now with SGS lines coming into the picture, the SGS Dean was included in this delegated power specifically with respect to SGS personnel.   Thus a situation of overlapping administrative authority was created: the area of concern of the Dean of the Faculties was defined to include all instructional positions in the College; overlapping it was the concurrent concern of the SGS Dean for its instructional staff.

In general terms, annual lines served to propel SGS further into the social system of the College itself.   For the first time, a part of SGS staff was not totally "lumpen-proletariat."   Annual line personnel in SGS became part of the total "ranking system" of the College.   As a result, SGS itself had to become more self-conscious about its authority and responsibility position in the total system.   Before the lines were established, the entire SGS staff consisted of hourly-paid temporary personnel who in every sense were in a "separate and unequal" position vis-a-vis the college "line" faculty.   SGS teachers knew it and the administration knew it!   It was an accepted fact of life.   Now a small segment of the staff was full-time faculty in a theoretical parity of position with day faculty.   While to the individuals on SGS lines and for SGS itself this theoretical parity represented a significant rise in status, it was, in reality, only a tiny step toward the vision.

The paucity of SGS full-time instructional positions was emphasized in an evaluation of Brooklyn College by Middle-States Association in 1966.   In the section dealing with

SGS, the evaluation team stated:

> Of greater concern than physical facilities is the
> limited institutional commitment by way of full-
> time faculty members . . . the visiting team
> questions the adequacy of 60 full-time faculty mem-
> bers[15] to provide the essential quality control of
> the academic program.   Considering the number
> of the offerings, the spread of full-timers must
> certainly be thin in places. [16]

The evaluation team thus echoed the continuing concern of SGS itself!   Not only is the "spread" of annual lines
"thin," but the small number of lines militates against the
probability of a SGS "faculty" functioning as a cohesive group
with a distinctive institutional commitment.

Allocation of Lines to Departments

How are SGS lines allocated among academic departments?   What centers of authority are involved in apportion-
ing faculty positions to twenty-five instructional departments?
The power to assign faculty lines to departments is administratively an exceedingly influential area of authority.

Before a substantial number of budget lines was allocated to SGS (prior to 1960), the power to distribute annual
lines in the college was vested exclusively in the Dean of
the Faculties.   The authority of the Dean was broadly stated
as follows:

> Whenever a tenure-bearing appointment seems to
> be indicated in a given department, the chairman
> will arrange to discuss the possibility with the
> Dean of the Faculties. [17]

In actual practice, the Dean first considers departmental
needs and then either assigns new lines or transfers old un-
encumbered ones to different departments based on his judgment of faculty balance and efficiency.   Final approval rests

with the President who usually ratifies the Dean's recommendations.   Departments may, of course, appeal the
Dean's decision but such appeal or reversal of his decision
is rather rare.

When in 1960 twenty-five positions were specifically
designated as SGS lines, a directive on "Appointments to
Annual Line in the School of General Studies" was issued by
the President.   With respect to such SGS positions, the
memorandum stated:

> 1. All annual lines in the School of General Studies
>   will be assigned for the staffing of courses in the
>   programs leading to degrees.   (This meant, in
>   essence, that they would be assigned to existing
>   academic departments.)
>
> 2. . . . . The Director (now Dean) will consult with
>   the respective department chairmen and the Dean
>   of the Faculties concerning staffing needs. . . .[18]

The implications of the language are plainly apparent.   The
words "will consult with" surely do not constitute an exclusive delegation of authority to the SGS Dean.   While the directive preserved the previous role of the Dean of the Faculties, a significant role was introduced for the SGS Dean with
respect to the allocation of SGS lines.

The apportionment of SGS lines to academic departments by the SGS Dean are determined on the basis of rational need such as student enrollment, number of courses,
variety of offerings, and areas of specialization to be covered.   Another determining factor is the ability of the department to fill the vacancy.   After the SGS Dean analyzes
the probable need of the department, he confers with the departmental deputy chairman regarding the department's willingness to accept the line and its ability to recruit.[19]   The
deputy chairman first obtains the views of the chairman and

then advises the SGS Dean as to whether there is a reasonable expectation that the department will fill the line.   If
there is, the SGS Dean consults with the Dean of the Faculties concerning allocation of the line to the department and
the appropriate rank for the appointment.   This is the operating relationship under conditions of concurrent authority.
There is joint agreement on the allocation and assignment of
lines and joint recommendations to the President.

Recruitment of SGS Line Personnel

SGS lines are a scarce resource, indeed.   They represent only 13% of the total SGS teaching staff.   As scarce
resources, it would appear that departments would actively
seek these line positions and would strongly compete to obtain them.   Curiously enough, the matter is not so simple.

While departments are, in general, interested in
building the representation of full-time faculty in SGS, there
are restraining factors.   In contrast to the appointment of
temporary "lecturers" to teach in SGS (a term-by-term contract renewal), appointment of a line person is potentially a
permanent commitment.   Line persons become eligible for
tenure and ultimately become voting members of the department.   Such an appointment, therefore, has far greater probability of affecting the composition of the department.   The
hiring of temporary "lecturers" does not have this effect.
Figuratively, the latter may be likened to making a "date"
in the sense that though the choice may be careful, considered and discriminating, there is no express commitment
for the future.   On the other hand, the appointment to a position involving potential faculty status is more akin to a
formal engagement where the bans are announced and, subject to a probationary period, the final intention for perma-

nent association is declared.   Hence departments are not always eager to request annual lines and are quite cautious in
committing themselves to filling them.   This caution is not
applied exclusively to SGS; there is a general tendency of
departments to move slowly and carefully in making appointments to tenure bearing positions.   However, the very small
number of total lines allocated to SGS makes every vacancy
loom large.   For example, sixteen lines allocated to SGS in
April 1965 were still unfilled by January 1966.   These lines
represented twenty-nine per cent of all SGS full time faculty
positions.

The power of the SGS Dean to allocate lines to a specific academic department, although requiring its consent,
nevertheless represents substantial control over the composition of staff.   By granting or withholding lines to a department, he necessarily shapes the composition of the staff.
All his actions, however, must be concurred in by the Dean
of the Faculties.

Another recruiting problem relates to the respective
vacancies for CLAS and SGS personnel in a given department
when the available ranks coincide.   Theoretically, the department should have an equal interest in recruiting for both positions.   In actual practice, however, the CLAS vacancy is
given priority of consideration.   If there is only one candidate, the CLAS position is staffed first; if there is a choice,
the "better" candidate is usually appointed to CLAS.   The
SGS Dean has slight affirmative power to change the order of
priority or the order of selection.   His power is merely to
reject a nominee.

A recent example illustrates the scope of the SGS
Dean's affirmative and negative powers.   A young man with
an outstanding "paper record," i.e., Ph.D. from Yale, re-

search and publications of notable value but with limited
teaching experience was interviewed by the Chairman and
the Appointments Committee of the department. At the time,
there were two identical assistant professor lines available,
one in CLAS and the other in SGS.   The SGS deputy chairman of the department, being impressed with the candidate's
qualifications, arranged for an interview with the SGS Dean.
The Dean was also impressed and he agreed to accept the
candidate for appointment in SGS.   However, the chairman
of the department wanted to be sure to secure the candidate
for CLAS.   He thus informed him that identical positions
were available and that he might choose either one.   The
candidate understandably preferred daytime hours and therefore accepted the CLAS appointment.

After one year of service, during which time the appointee was observed in the classroom by various colleagues,
the department Appointments Committee was of the opinion
that, despite his outstanding paper record, he was an ineffec-
tive teacher.   Usually when this is discovered during the
first year, efforts are made to improve teaching effectiveness through guidance and counseling by other more experienced faculty members.   But, in this case, the inadequacies
of the individual were apparently viewed as too grave to overcome and the department voted not to reappoint him.   The
Chairman then approached the SGS Deputy Chairman and inquired as to whether he would like to have him in SGS.   In
other words, he was not good enough for CLAS but apparently good enough for SGS!   He was not accepted by the SGS
Dean.

This case involved a bold and extraordinarily direct
approach by a department chairman which clearly reflected
a negative attitude toward SGS, one not restricted to a single

chairman.   If it were, it would not be significant for this
study.   The undercurrent of "first choice CLAS and second
choice SGS" exists in many departments.   This order of priority is usually far more subtle than the case cited, and
consequently, more difficult to discern.   The coincidence of
equal "line" vacancy in a department at the same level and
at the same time in both CLAS and SGS is not too frequent,
yet when it does occur it reveals the CLAS comparative advantage in the recruitment process.   This comparative advantage is possible simply because the department and not
the SGS Dean possesses the recruiting and appointing authority.

The contention is advanced that to recruit for the evening hours is far more difficult since most people prefer to
work during the day rather than in the evening.   There are
notable exceptions, of course.   For example, a person interested in research may prefer the daytime hours for this
activity and accept evening teaching.   However, recruitment
experience has consistently demonstrated that teaching during
evening hours is less desirable to most individuals than is
daytime teaching.   In light of this fact, the SGS Dean, when
interviewing candidates for appointment to SGS, makes every
effort to ascertain whether the candidate truly prefers and is
committed to evening teaching or whether he is merely agree-
ing to accept such appointment for the time being in order to
obtain a "back-door" entrance to the day college staff.   It is
most difficult to make judgments on such questions of motivation, but the marked trend of seeking transfers to CLAS constitutes suggestive evidence.

Transfers by SGS Line Personnel

Competition between CLAS and SGS for personnel is

not only evident when positions of equal rank in the same
department are available in both divisions; it is also revealed by the so-called "transfer tendency." For a variety
of reasons, SGS line personnel often become dissatisfied
with evening teaching and seek transfer from SGS to CLAS
by appealing to the SGS Dean after enlisting the support of
the Department and the Dean of the Faculties.

Transfer of line personnel out of SGS tends to under-
mine the stability of the staff; it also emphasizes the preferred status of CLAS. Consequently, it is a tendency
which the SGS Dean strives to restrain. Though he has the
power to frustrate a transfer, how extensive could his authority be in face of the realities confronting a sub-organization? Several examples will illuminate the nature of the
built-in competition between SGS and CLAS and the Dean's
theoretical power vis-a-vis its practical application.

Two young women were appointed to SGS annual lines
after they indicated a preference for evening teaching. One
had been an SGS lecturer for many years and stated that she
enjoyed teaching the more mature SGS students. The other
was engaged in psychological research with young children;
the research had to be done during daytime hours. Within
one year, the first woman married and then refused to continue in her evening assignment because she and her husband
"never saw each other." She obtained the consent of the
CLAS department for such transfer and the SGS Dean concurred after his efforts to persuade her to remain in SGS
proved fruitless. The second woman concluded her specific
research project with children and her interests turned to
other fields. No longer was there compelling reason to be
free during the day. In addition, she complained that her
social life and perhaps marriage opportunities were being

impaired by evening teaching.   On these social and personal grounds--quite appealing to compassionate gentlemen--she
obtained the support of the department for a transfer to
CLAS.   The department then brought pressure to bear on the
Dean to consent to the transfer.   Rather than resist the importunities and pressures of both the department and the
teacher, he acquiesced to the transfer.   She subsequently
married but the correlation between the marriage and the
transfer to CLAS has not been objectively established.

There are many other instances of SGS line personnel who requested and were granted transfers to CLAS.   Usually the reasons given to the SGS Dean for the requested
transfer are personal ones.   Professor A of the History Department, for example, stated that when he accepted the assignment in SGS he and his wife had no children but now they
had a two-year old child and another on its way.   His wife
was evidencing both anger and depression because of being
alone during the evenings so often.   Professor A stated that
his wife, despite her pregnant condition, threatened divorce.
To "save his marriage," he requested the department to ef-
fectuate a transfer to CLAS.   Again, both the teacher and
the department chairman implored the SGS Dean to grant the
transfer.   He complied.   Later, Professor A became deputy
chairman of the department.   Though he did not now work as
many evenings or as many hours per evening as before, he
still was doing evening work--but now for extra compensation.

Professor Y requested transfer to CLAS but the department did not initially grant his request because his services for certain courses scheduled during the evening hours
were needed.   His request was stated in terms of a preference to teach during the day for personal reasons which he

did not disclose.   Then Professor Y reported to the Department Chairman that he had received an offer of an attractive position at another college.   In order not to lose Professor Y, the Chairman requested the Dean to approve the
transfer to CLAS.   Faced with a possible "quit" unless the
approval for transfer was given, the Dean consented.

Professor Z had been an SGS lecturer for about fifteen years.   He frequently stated he enjoyed teaching at night
because he found the SGS student particularly challenging.
He completed his doctorate at about the time when SGS received its first series of annual lines and he was appointed
to the rank of Assistant Professor.   Three or four years
later, he was promoted to the rank of Associate Professor.
By this time, his children were grown.   In the meantime,
his wife returned to college as a student in SGS and completed her A. B. degree.   Professor Z told the writer: "I'm
getting older--I'm tired at night--I've had about twenty years
of evening teaching--I've had enough!   Now I'd like to be
like other people, work during the day and have evenings
off."   Professor Z requested transfer to CLAS but his application was, at first, denied by the SGS Dean because he was
beginning to be seriously concerned with the "transfer contagion."   Professor Z then appealed to the Dean on the
ground of ill health; he stated that he had very high blood
pressure and that his physician had recommended that he not
work late at night.   The Dean is a humane man.   He granted
the requested transfer on the ground that "he did not wish to
block the transfer of anyone who did not really want to stay
in SGS."   However, the Dean at the same time expressed
concern that the news of the transfer might be contagious.
It was!

A professor of economics expressed dissatisfaction

with his SGS assignments on the ground that elective courses, which he wished to teach, were only occasionally offered in SGS due to insufficiency of student demand. He claimed that SGS students are more vocationally oriented than are CLAS students and he did not enjoy teaching theory courses to the former group. He secured the active support of the department chairman who requested the Dean to approve the transfer. Again, not wishing to exercise his authority to block a transfer, he consented.

A member of the SGS Speech Department is a drama critic for a well-known literary magazine. Teaching three or four evenings a week interferes with his attendance at some plays he wishes to review. Though he has requested transfer several times from the Dean, the department has not acceded to his request. Under those circumstances, the Dean has no authority to grant the transfer.

When a requested transfer is endorsed by the department, the SGS Dean has always consented to it though he has the power, on agreement with the Dean of the Faculties, to refuse. His approvals have been based on the belief that a refusal would serve no useful purpose. A dissatisfied teacher is not a desirable faculty member. The SGS Dean has, however, insisted that the transfer not be effectuated until the department has recruited an acceptable SGS replacement at the same professorial rank. Nevertheless, the pressure for transfers seems to be increasing. To discourage departments from either encouraging or too easily accommodating transfers to CLAS, the SGS Dean is currently considering withdrawing the teaching line entirely from the particular department when a transfer is made. Whether this policy will have the desired effect is still an open question.

Tenure

Just as the academic departments have the power to recruit and to recommend an initial appointment, so do they have the initial power to recommend tenure. The procedures are identical for CLAS and SGS line personnel. Departmental recommendations for tenure are made to two college-wide sub-committees, one a presidential advisory committee and the other a Faculty Personnel and Budget committee. Each of these sub-committees reviews the qualifications of the candidates for tenure after a three-year probationary period. Similar sub-committees are designated to review the qualifications of candidates for promotion. The ultimate power to grant tenure or promotion resides jointly in Faculty Personnel and Budget and the President. Approval by the Board of Higher Education is also required but it is essentially pro forma.

Neither the Dean of the Faculties nor the SGS Dean have the authority to initiate recommendations for tenure. However, they are free to express their opinions to the department Appointments Committee, the two sub-committees, the Faculty Personnel and Budget Committee, and finally to the President. It is rather rare, however, either for Faculty Personnel and Budget or the President to overrule the recommendations of their respective sub-committees.

There were several instances where the SGS Dean disagreed with the departmental recommendations for or against tenure. In each case, the recommendations of the department prevailed. One particularly "tacky" case rather dramatically illustrated the SGS Dean's lack of power in this sphere.

In a certain academic department, it was generally

known that the department was "split" with respect to educational policies and practices; there were also marked personality clashes among members.   In the department there
was an assistant professor on an SGS line who also served
as deputy chairman of the department.   He had been appointed to the line by the Appointments Committee of the department and had been designated deputy chairman by the
Chairman.   During the first year of his assignment, the
deputy chairman found the aims and interests of the department (as represented by the Chairman) quite compatible with
SGS interests.   Later, however, departmental decisions with
respect to curriculum and, more important, SGS staffing,
seemed to him to be contrary to SGS interests.   He began
to express disagreement with the chairman and the "ruling"
majority of the department, charging that they were not acting in the interests of SGS.   He stated that he would be "un-
true" to his responsibility to SGS if he did not make his position clear to the chairman, the department and the SGS
Dean.   To the latter he reported that the chairman was attempting to heal the "split" in the department by yielding to
the "other" faction at the expense of SGS concerning curricular offerings and quality of staff.   When the time came for
him to be considered for tenure, the department Appointments Committee voted (on a split 3-2 vote) not to recommend him.   The chairman concurred in the majority decision.   Even though concerned with some aspects of the individual's overall performance, the SGS Dean urged that tenure
be granted, that the positive elements of his teaching ability,
administrative work, dedication and commitment to SGS made
him, on balance, a worthwhile member of the staff.   Nevertheless, Faculty Personnel and Budget and the President up-
held the decision of the departmental committee and chairman.

The "case" was widely discussed on campus and the
significance of the individual's "loyalty" to SGS as a factor
in the non-tenure decision was emphasized.   The fact that
the SGS Dean tried and failed to influence the department's
decision was underscored, it being interpreted as a lack of
power and influence on his part when a conflict arose between him and the department chairman.   In more diplomat-
ic language, the outcome was construed as one which "clari-
fied" the SGS Dean's limited authority to influence department decisions. [20]

Promotions

Power and authority for promotion reside primarily
in the faculty of the College.   Recommendations for promotion are first processed through departmental committees,
where a ranking order is voted and transmitted to appropriate sub-committees of Faculty Personnel and Budget.   The
sub-committees report their recommendations to Faculty
Personnel and Budget which then votes its recommendations
for final approval by the Board. [21]

Competition for promotion, as is true at most academic institutions, is keen.   Candidates compete with each
other not only within departments but also with colleagues
throughout the college for available scarce positions. [22]   Tension runs high on the college campus during the periods when
candidates appear before faculty promotional sub-committees
and again when the final vote is taken at Faculty Personnel
and Budget.   The disappointment of candidates for promotion
who have been eliminated in the competitive struggle is deep
and discernible.   On the day following the final voting, the
faculty dining room resounds with congratulations for those
who "made it;" it is difficult to meet the eyes of friends who

lost the round in the promotions battle.

Here again what is significant is not the general problem of promotion viewed against the backdrop of scarcity and selectivity but rather whether an individual's promotion opportunity is affected by the fact that he is in SGS. A statistical count of the percentage of SGS promotions in relation to all promotions to the rank of Assistant and Associate Professor[23] in the college is informative but does not provide any conclusive evidence because of the relatively small number of people involved. SGS represents ten per cent of the Assistant and Associate Professor lines at the College. Of 145 Associate Professors, 12 are in SGS; of 253 Assistant Professors, approximately 25 are in SGS.[24]

Faculty Promotions
Comparison of SGS With CLAS

Year	Rank Promoted to	Total College Promotions	SGS Promotions	SGS Per Cent of Total
1966	Ass't. Prof.	26	2	8
	Assoc. Prof.	20	4	20
1967	Ass't. Prof.	30	6	20
	Assoc. Prof.	31	0	0

Many variables enter into the considerations for promotion. Apart from the individual's qualifications (including publications, and the evaluation of these by promotions committees), length of service and salary level in the rank are also significant factors considered. Thus the fact that SGS lines are relatively recent may be a decisive factor in reducing promotional opportunity in many cases.

However, it is the opinion of many staff members, -- even by those who have been promoted--that being on an SGS

line is an impediment to advancement.   Staff members who
were interviewed made several points on this question.
Typical arguments are the following:

> The committees responsible for decisions are col-
> lege and not SGS committees; therefore,
> the candidate is not sufficiently known to the com-
> mittees and the committees are not familiar with
> the work the candidate does specifically for SGS.
>
> Also, the difference in the hours of work, i. e. ,
> day or evening, precludes getting to know many of
> the committee members responsible for decisions.
>
> Many SGS staff members were hired at one level
> lower than they should have been.   In other words,
> the individual accepted a position at one rank less
> than his qualifications should have produced simply
> because it was all that was available at the time
> and he "settled" for less.   (Note--this is undoubt-
> edly also true of many people in CLAS.)   There-
> fore, the promotion which shows up in the statis-
> tics is not so significant--it is merely an overdue
> "adjustment. "
>
> SGS faculty members who were promoted had to do
> much more than CLAS faculty or "prove" them-
> selves, including spending long hours, both day and
> evening, at the college. [26]

Disappointed staff members who were not successful
in gaining promotion frequently placed the blame on the fact
that they are on SGS lines.   Typical statements were:

> I'm not around enough during the day and don't
> know the people on the promotion committees.
>
> SGS faculty are low on the totem pole and are not
> granted equal consideration.
>
> They (the college committees) are not aware of the
> quality of my work because it's done in the eve-
> ning.
>
> It's because I can't hang around here all day--

and evening too.[26]

How valid these assertions are is most difficult to
ascertain.   The record of success in SGS promotions seems
to cast doubt on the reasons assigned for not achieving a
promotion.   Whether the reasons are true or not, however,
is not so relevant as is the fact that they are perceived as
the responsible reasons.

That authority is vested in college-wide committees,
that SGS is a sub-unit in the dominant parent organization,
that it does not have its own independent faculty and its own
decision-making bodies, evokes grave concern and even anxiety when individuals find themselves both in a position of
dual responsibility and in competition with CLAS colleagues.
These relationships pose serious organizational and morale
problems.   Where and in whom authority is vested is clearly
of immense importance in psychological terms to the individual within the organization.   Necessarily, the attitudes,
perceptions, concerns and anxieties filter down to all levels
of the organization.

Dual responsibilities and loyalties of SGS line personnel are most keenly felt in tenure and promotion situations.
In fact, immediately upon induction on a line, the duality of
divided authority between CLAS and SGS is sensed and the
future risks with respect to tenure and promotion envisioned.

Shortly after appointment of the new staff member, he
is called to an orientation meeting with the Dean of the Faculties.   This meeting is in accordance with authority delegated by a presidential memorandum.[27]   The new appointee
is informed that he is a member of the staff of the college
and also a member of his academic department and is oriented by the Dean of the Faculties as to his responsibilities
to the college and the department.   In addition, he is oriented

by the chairman of his department with regard to rights, privileges and responsibilities there.

The orientation procedures apply to all new appointees. But then the SGS appointee is also oriented by the SGS deputy chairman and by the SGS Dean with respect to additional responsibilities toward that unit of the college. The SGS faculty member finds that he is expected to participate in the work of the college committees,[28] departmental committees,[29] and also special SGS committees.[30] Retention, tenure and promotion depend upon the individual's participation in at least a few of these committees. He will be expected to participate both in Faculty Day, a CLAS function, and Staff Conferences, an SGS function. As a full member of the department, he will be invited to attend honors ceremonies and senior receptions during the day and similar honors ceremonies and senior receptions separately for SGS students in the evening. He will be invited to march in academic processionals at the College commencement but also at Convocation, an exclusively SGS ceremony. He will be requested to join the Faculty Club (Day) and if he is married, his wife will be recruited for the Faculty Wives' Club. But he will also be invited to join the SGS Faculty Club!

Since tenure and promotions stem from the academic department which consists of predominantly day faculty, it is necessary for the new staff member to become well acquainted with other members of his department. Most of the day faculty are not present during evening hours. Committee meetings are almost always held during daytime hours. Consequently, an SGS person may find himself on campus from 12:00 noon until 10:40 P. M. at various times. One of the most frequent complaints of SGS line faculty is centered on the duality of responsibility coupled with the time incon-

venience arising from the fact that most of the academic
and educational "business" of the college takes place during
daytime hours.   It might reasonably be conjectured that the
transfer contagion, too, is to an appreciable degree related
to this condition of dual responsibilities and dual demands.

Deputy Chairmen and SGS Administration

The SGS deputy chairmanship is a post of significant
responsibility.   The deputy is responsible for advising students on selection of courses, counseling of department majors, planning curriculum offerings and staffing of courses
with qualified personnel.   Most important, however, is the
crucial role of the deputy chairman as the administrative
link between the day department and its evening segment.

From what source does the deputy chairman derive
the authority to carry out his functions?   The deputy is
fundamentally the appointee of the chairman of the department although the approval of both the SGS Dean and the
President is required.   In the formal administrative jargon
of the college, it is stated that the deputy is "recommended
to the SGS Dean," who in turn "recommends to the President."   The authority of the deputy chairman as the departmental representative in SGS stems from the department
chairman, the administrative head of the entire department
which embraces both CLAS and SGS.   Authority to act for
the department in SGS is delegated by the chairman.   But
the authority to act on SGS administrative matters concerning the department is delegated by the SGS Dean.   Hence
authority stems from two different sources, the chairman
and the SGS Dean, and the deputy chairman is responsible to
both.

Account is taken of this duality of authority and re-

sponsibility in the selection of a deputy chairman.   Usually
the chairman consults with the SGS Dean before making his
recommendation.   Not infrequently the Dean is given the
choice of one among two or possibly three candidates.   Once
appointed, the deputy enjoys a type of tenure: he cannot be
removed from his position except for cause shown and upon
charges filed.   However, when a new chairman is elected
by the department, it is his prerogative to recommend a new
deputy chairman.

The deputy chairman as a member of the college faculty may be either on a CLAS or SGS line.   However, SGS
has drawn heavily on day personnel for the filling of this important administrative position.   Of the twenty-five deputy
chairmen, twenty-two are day faculty; only three are on SGS
lines.   The small number of deputy chairman positions filled
by SGS line personnel is predicated on two main reasons.
First, the introduction of SGS lines is relatively recent and
the turnover in the position of deputy is quite slow.   Consequently, most CLAS faculty incumbents who were appointed
prior to the period when SGS lines were instituted have re-
mained.   Second, even when a post is vacated by a resignation or because of the election of a new department chairman,
there may be no "appropriate" SGS person in the department
to fill the vacancy.   There are so few SGS people in any one
department that there may either be a dearth of administrative talent and/or a reluctance on the part of an individual
to assume an administrative assignment.   Of seven replace-
ments made within the past six years, two are SGS personnel.   The other five were selected from CLAS because, in
the judgment of both the chairman and the SGS Dean, the individuals chosen were the best suited for the job.

The twenty-two deputy chairmen on day lines serve in

SGS on an "overload" basis for extra compensation; the rate
of compensation varies with the size of the department and
the individual's academic rank.   Until about 1956, it was
possible to pay deputies on an hourly basis for all their
work in SGS.   However, as departments grew in size and
complexity and the work of the deputies expanded, multiple
position regulations limited the number of hours of "overtime work"; this prevented increases in the hours granted
to deputies representing some of the larger departments.
To avoid the impact of the regulations, arrangements were
made with the Dean of the Faculties, and concurred in by
the department chairmen, to allocate a portion of the deputy's day assignment to his work in the evening.   (SGS reimburses the day college for these services in an elaborate
fund "exchange" system.)   For example, if the size of the
department required ten weekly hours of time in SGS, the
deputy was "released" from his CLAS load for four hours
and paid by SGS for six hours, the maximum number allowed by Board multiple position regulations.

   The post of deputy chairman in the evening is perceived by most as a prestigious and desirable one.   Not only
does it confer authority but it also provides additional compensation.   On the negative side, the deputy may find himself in an ambivalent position should there be conditions of
stress between policies and decisions of the day department
vis-a-vis SGS.

   The deputy chairman's role illustrates, perhaps better
than any other, the varieties of ties between the parent organization and its sub-unit.   To summarize:

1. The deputy is appointed jointly by the day chairman and the SGS Dean.

2. The deputy's authority stems from two sources,

the chairman and the SGS Dean.

3. The deputy is usually a day faculty member responsible for administering evening policies and goals.

A review of just one area of his functions--that of staffing and supervising--will demonstrate the limited scope of his authority arising out of the inter-relationship of subunit and parent organization. The deputy chairman usually recruits personnel for evening teaching but appointments are made by the departmental Committee on Appointments. After approval of a candidate by the departmental committee, the deputy has the responsibility of recommending a rate of pay to the SGS Dean, of assigning specific classes, or observing class teaching and of generally ascertaining whether the teacher is effectively doing his job. However, the deputy chairman is not always a member of the departmental committee empowered to appoint and to review the individual's competence to teach. In only eight of the twenty-five instructional departments, is the deputy a member of the appointments committee. To be sure, the deputies have the responsibility for assignment, supervision and evaluation but theoretically they lack the formal authority to share in decisions on appointments, retention, and dismissals if not members of the committee. De facto, however, the deputies are free to express their opinions to the departmental committee and, in the absence of unusual circumstances, their opinions are given great weight. Thus the theoretical lack of authority realistically works out as almost tantamount to the possession of authority.

Frequently, also, the department may have a policy of giving priority of assignments to day staff personnel who wish to teach in the evening. Unless the department is expanding this may mean that a good part-time teacher is not reappointed. Here the deputy has little choice but to abide by the department choice. Another example where problems of interlacing of day and evening policies exist is the case of a day instructor whose course in the daytime is cancelled for insufficient registration. The chairman, with the concurrence of the Dean of the Faculties, may "fill out" the individual's program by requesting the deputy to schedule him for a course in the evening. This may happen at the last moment--at registration time--and yet the deputy is obliged to comply even though this "reluctant" acceptance may curtail or even eliminate the schedule of a preferred part-time teacher in the evening.

This dual role and responsibility of the deputy--as the chairman's representative in SGS and as SGS' representative in the department--can be viewed as a gestalt. Sometimes one aspect is in the foreground and another in the background; at other times, it is the reverse. Role integration is, however, attainable. In most cases the probability is high that administrative kinks will be "ironed out" along the way. When there is irreconcilable conflict, the duality of the role presents a dilemma and the deputy may find himself sitting on the proverbial picket fence--a rather painful posture!

One particular example of conflict will be recounted here even though it is not too common. While this case exemplifies the authority of the deputy, it also reflects the limitations upon such authority. It also illustrates the interactions arising out of duality of interests and possible conflict of those interests between the CLAS department and SGS.

The department chairman requested the dismissal of
a deputy chairman who, he contended, was functioning a-
gainst the best interests of the department.   The chairman
charged that the deputy was making choices of courses to
be offered and teaching staff to be assigned of which he did
not approve.   The SGS Dean did not accept the recommended dismissal.   The inter-organizational dynamics were not
purely an example of administrative struggle on rational
grounds.   Affective elements also played a part.   First, the
department itself was divided; the chairman held his office
by a slim majority.   The Appointments Committee was similarly "split."   In addition, the personalities of both the
chairman and the deputy were volatile and fiery.   Many of
their arguments had questionable rational or logical foundations.   It appeared that the arguments were as much based
on an emotional clash of personalities as on differences of
point of view regarding the substantive issues of courses and
staffing.   To begin, the department was in trouble with respect to a declining student enrollment in SGS courses; it
had few "majors" and these were steadily diminishing.   The
first difference of opinion related to the courses that should
be offered in the evening to attract more students.   Unless
more students were attracted, there would not only be loss
of jobs for department members but also continued diminu-
tion of the department's prestige and position in the college.
The chairman had one idea about which courses should be offered, the deputy had another.

The particular courses that are offered are quite intimately related to staff and staffing.   While it is true that
the Appointments Committee of a department must approve
all new appointments to SGS, once approved the deputy has

the power to arrange assignments. He may schedule more courses for those he believes to be capable teachers and fewer courses or none at all for those whom he believes less capable or inadequate for the job. Further, most departments give priority of consideration to existing day faculty to teach in the evening for additional compensation if they so desire. In the case at issue, the deputy refused to accept the services of several day faculty members, contending that some of the part-time evening people were substantially superior as teachers and as "scholars." The deputy further argued that the decrease in course offerings plus utilization of some day faculty, would preclude reappointment of some of the temporary part-time staff members who had served the department well over many years. The chairman, nevertheless, insisted on the assignment of several day faculty members. He won this first round but not without an exchange of several vitriolic letters back and forth.

Additional clashes occurred when the deputy recommended the non-reappointment of a part-time evening lecturer; the SGS Dean fully supported the deputy's decision. The chairman disagreed and attempted to retain the individual. There was a bitter struggle and the individual was not reappointed in SGS.

After a period of time with intermittent disagreements, the chairman of the department informed the SGS Dean that the deputy no longer represented him or the department, that the deputy did not have his confidence and would have to be dismissed from his assignment as deputy.[31] When the Dean pointed out that "formal" charges would have to be instituted for that purpose, the chairman indicated that he was ready to take such a step. However, the Dean then decided that a hearing on formal charges would mean open conflict that might be damaging to the deputy, the department, SGS and the College. He, therefore, attempted to reach a compromise solution. He proposed that the deputy be permitted to continue his assignment until the end of the spring semester; beginning in the fall term, a new deputy would be chosen. The Dean believed he could persuade the present deputy to step out gracefully in order to avoid the stigma of hostile accusations in support of formal charges. The Dean was ready at the same time to offer the deputy, whom he believed to be a person of good-will and faithful to SGS, another administrative position in SGS dissociated from his own department. In his attempt to negotiate a settlement of the dispute, the Dean went so far as to indicate to the chairman which new deputy would be acceptable to him--a choice with which the chairman would have agreed--provided that the chairman would agree to the postponement of the dismissal and its conversion to a graceful resignation.

The Dean sought the assistance of the President in support of the proposal. The President, concurring in the Dean's desire to avoid open conflict, called the chairman to a conference in order to "iron out" the difficulties. But the antagonism had apparently gone too far and tempers had reached too high a pitch. The chairman insisted that the deputy resign or be dismissed within the week, otherwise he himself would resign. The President accepted the ultimatum. He accepted the resignation of the chairman. [32]

Thus the authority of the SGS Dean to concur in the choice of a deputy chairman, or in his dismissal, was sustained. This authority to designate the deputy is shared with the department chairman. While shared authority always has the seeds of disagreement and conflict, the relationship of the SGS Dean and the department chairmen has been eminently

amiable.   Only in a rare case, such as the one described,
does real conflict arise.

Roles of CLAS Faculty in SGS

Regular day faculty members may teach part-time in
SGS for additional compensation up to the limits allowed by
the multiple position regulations of the Board of Higher Education. [33]   It is assumed that faculty status in the college
ipso facto qualifies an individual to teach in SGS.   The flow
of CLAS personnel into and out of SGS depends on the individual's choice and on department policy; almost all departments give higher priority for assignments in SGS to permanent faculty members than to temporary "lecturers."   In
this matter, the SGS Dean has limited control.

SGS administration generally welcomes CLAS teachers
and, indeed, points with pride to the number of faculty members of professorial rank on its part-time staff.   Visiting
evaluation teams, such as Middle States Association, though
concerned with maximum limits of "overtime" hours, favorably evaluated the association of this faculty group with SGS.
A school with relatively few annual lines of its own and a
large and varied part-time "lecturer" population gains institutional and outside prestige through this segment of its instructional staff, for CLAS faculty members have the recognized symbol of professional qualification, the Ph. D. degree,
coupled with professorial rank.

Compensation for these faculty members was, until
1965, at an hourly rate directly related to their CLAS rank
and annual salary.   The formula of hourly rate varied over
the years from 1/1000 of the annual salary in 1950 to 1/750
by 1964. [34]   In 1965, the hourly rate was converted to a semester-hour compensation plan.   While the formula was ex-

pressed in "semester-hour" terms rather than in hourly
terms, the amount of compensation was approximately the
same.   Whatever the formula, payment per course for
teaching in SGS is still significantly lower than for the e-
quivalent teaching time on an annual basis.   In general,
SGS rates of pay are 60% of the annual line equivalent.
This disparity is a matter of historical fact not only at
Brooklyn College.   It is a reality that has plagued practically all evening colleges throughout the country since their
inception.   Protests against "discriminatory pay practices"
appeared in the early 1940's in teacher-union documents; the
same protests, worded differently, continue to appear in
statements by both the Legislative Conference of the City
University of New York and the United Federation of College
Teachers.   The Deans of the Schools of General Studies have
fought vigorously for a pay structure for part-time teachers
proportionately equivalent to that of full-time teachers. While
some progress has been made over the years, (the change in
formula from 1/1000 to 1/750 for instance), SGS pay scales
nevertheless continue to lag substantially behind those of the
day colleges.

The disparity in compensation for teaching a course
on an annual line compared to teaching on a part-time SGS
assignment has been defended by budget officers on the ground
that an annual line carries with it many responsibilities outside the classroom, that the faculty member's salary cannot
be reckoned "by the course" but rather as a total job.   Participation in extra-curricular activities, counseling of students, departmental meetings, committee assignments, curricular planning, etc. are all considered as part of "the
job" in addition to classroom teaching.

Many of these functions, such as in the area of cur-

ricular planning, are just not open to SGS personnel because
such planning is exclusively the authority of the CLAS faculty. While many of these activities inure to the benefit of
SGS and are essential to its effective functioning, its authority and responsibility do not extend to them. It is the position of SGS administration, moreover, that the dispropor-
tionately lower rates of pay discourage fuller participation
in such SGS affairs that come within its authority and responsibility. While never tested, it is entirely conceivable
that if the salary structure more closely approximated the
full-time salary equivalent, there would be a greater willingness on the part of staff to participate as well as further
ground for demanding and greater probability of getting such
participation.

A recent administrative decision to allocate one additional paid hour for student conferences in certain courses
in selected departments for part-time SGS students was a
step in this direction. Special conferences with students are
thus secured because they are compensable services. [35] But
it must be added that regardless of compensation, there are
always dedicated individuals who give freely of their time
and energy in informal counseling of students, acting as faculty advisors to student organizations, writing letters of
recommendation, participating in committee work and, in
general, serving the students and the school more than could
be officially required of them.

Until about 1958, teaching and administrative assignments in SGS for additional compensation was in high demand
by CLAS faculty. For many, relatively low academic salaries made "moonlighting" a necessity. The need for supplementary earnings created competition among faculty members
for overtime assignments. However, limited SGS budgets

precluded accommodating all applicants since hourly rates
for CLAS personnel were usually higher than those for
equivalent "off-campus" teachers.   Thus in any one department during one semester not more than one full professor
from CLAS might usually be engaged to teach in SGS.
Limitations also had to be imposed on the employment of
persons in the other professorial ranks.   In short, the
budget allocated by the SGS Dean to each department had to
be "spread" to cover the instructional costs of the courses
to be offered.   It was at this budget point that the SGS
Dean was able to exercise control of the teaching assignments.   Personnel had to be distributed in such a way as to
make the most effective use of available money.   This distribution of teaching assignments, the province of the deputy
chairman, was always difficult, for it is hard to resist requests from senior members of one's own department.   Frequently, deputy chairmen made choices to include a few faculty members from CLAS of high rank and salary; to "balance" the cost they hired a few inexperienced graduate students at substantially lower rates to teach introductory
courses.

        The percentage of CLAS faculty teaching in SGS has
declined markedly over the years.   In 1958, there were approximately 129 CLAS faculty members teaching in SGS;
this constituted 37% of the total SGS teaching staff.   By 1966,
there were approximately 110 CLAS teachers, representing
about 27% of the total SGS teaching staff.   This decline in
ten percentage points reflects only the number of teachers;
if calculated on the basis of course credits taught, the percentage decline is much greater.[36]

        There are several reasons for this decline:

1. The rise in the level of salaries of annual faculty members which made "moonlighting" less necessary.

2. The widening dollar gap between the hourly rates paid in SGS and the higher annual salaries equated to rate per hour.

3. Higher salary levels in the Graduate Division and greater prestige gained by part-time teaching in that division and at other colleges and universities in the New York metropolitan area.

4. The growth in research and consulting opportunities on a part-time basis in private industry which provided more attractive opportunities for supplementary earnings.

5. Increase in federal research grants which provided additional alternatives.

6. Social Security coverage instituted in 1956 for annual faculty members.   In 1952, only part-time teaching assignments were included in social security coverage; the law excluded full-time annual line personnel on the ground that they were covered by the retirement system.   Many CLAS faculty taught in SGS to acquire sufficient quarters of coverage for social security benefits.   In 1956, however, the law was amended to extend coverage to annual line faculty members.   It was, therefore, not necessary to teach in SGS to acquire social security coverage.

The CLAS faculty member who teaches in SGS provides yet another link between the sub-organization and the parent college.   This link with CLAS is particularly important to SGS.   A larger percentage of CLAS faculty who do not have a connecting role in SGS are only vaguely aware of its nature and objectives.   For these CLAS personnel, the SGS administration, teaching staff and students are known only through official publications like the college bulletin, newsletters and routine memoranda that are circulated.   Deluged by paper as

are all faculties in large universities, most of the staff
read such literature superficially and, therefore, continue
to be only remotely aware of the special programs, admission standards, student body, staff and operations of SGS.
They become aware and interested only when there are overlapping concerns such as courses to be offered, proposed
curricular changes, space and room distribution, access to
secretarial services and other facilities.   The lack of full
communication is understandable in view of the size of the
institution.   It is even difficult to keep track of what is hap-
pening in one's own department.   In the Education Department alone, for instance, there are over 100 faculty members in the day and an additional 25 in SGS; in addition to
about 42 different courses offered, there are special units
like the Educational Clinic, the Early Childhood Center, and
a variety of specialized institutes and workshops.   The Education Department is only one of twenty-six academic departments.   Small wonder that it is difficult for individual faculty members to be acquainted with areas in which they do
not actively participate!

By teaching in SGS, the CLAS staff member gets
first-hand knowledge of SGS, its students, courses, part-
time staff as well as understanding of its problems.   Formal
meetings and informal contacts between CLAS faculty and off-
campus evening personnel have frequently been advantageous
to the individual, SGS and the College as a whole.   For example, when SGS colleagues meet at scheduled evening meetings or informally in staff rooms or at dinner, ideas on curricular development may be exchanged though the area is
basically a CLAS function.   Many times, the off-campus
part-time teacher has been invited to suggest new courses,
plan syllabi and participate in construction of study guides

and examinations.   Formal and informal contacts between
the two groups broaden professional concerns and diminish
the social distance.

It must, however, be pointed out that this close contact does not necessarily improve relationships.   "To know
them is to love them" is not always an inexorable fact.
Sometimes the reverse is true.   There have been many ex-
pressions of criticism from CLAS staff not only with regard
to SGS students but also of part-time staff employed.   The
negative criticism of SGS usually centers upon characteristics that deviate from the norm of day session practices,
procedures and personnel.   In those cases, CLAS customary
means and ends are always assumed to be the only valid
standard of comparison.

This inter-connectedness of teaching staff is not a
one-way street.   Not only does the CLAS staff member carry
information, ideas and problems of SGS back to the department in the day but he also acts as a carrier of CLAS "culture" to SGS.   He brings to SGS both the experience and the
standards of the day college.   Since the large majority of
part-time evening lecturers have other commitments during
daytime hours, they are not on campus during the time when
the academic department engages in its major functions.   The
presence of CLAS faculty members is a major communication apparatus for these part-time evening lecturers.   The
exchange of ideas and problems which would simply be impossible because of the barrier of different working periods
is thus somewhat bridged if not surmounted.   The principle
of cross-fertilization of ideas and problems is not, of course,
the manifest reason for the employment of CLAS staff at
night.   Their employment is primarily to round out a qualified teaching staff.   However, the latent functions which

emerge from the various contacts are nonetheless significant.

The SGS Majority Group: Lecturers

Historically and traditionally, part-time students have
been substantially taught by part-time staff. When SGS came
into existence in 1950, it inherited from its predecessor, the
"Evening Session," an instructional staff of 180 part-time
"lecturers" in addition to 85 day session faculty members. [37]
Thus from its earliest history SGS has relied on its corps
of part-time lecturers for the major portion of its instructional function.

The category "lecturer" includes all members of the
teaching staff in SGS not on annual lines. The term commonly used to describe this teacher is "off-campus lecturer,"
connoting that he is recruited from the "outside" and except
for his part-time instructional position in SGS he has no official connection with the college.

The "off-campus lecturer" category now comprises
approximately 60% of the SGS teaching staff and is, therefore,
of great significance in the staff's composition and functioning. To understand the social role performed by this category of teachers, it is necessary to identify who they are,
their backgrounds, qualifications, functions and responsibilities. Their involvement in the job is ultimately related not
only to the role expectations harbored by administration but
also to the role perceptions of the individual lecturer himself.

Identity and Source

Utilization of part-time personnel who wish to teach
in the evening makes it possible to recruit staff with a wide

diversity of experience in full-time day employment.   Part-
time teachers consist of business or professional people,
teachers from other schools and colleges or graduate students in doctoral programs.   In the business or professional classification, the staff includes persons from a variety
of walks of life like accountants, lawyers, mathematicians,
research and applied scientists, artists, musicians, writers,
statisticians, entrepreneurs in small businesses of their own,
industrial and labor relations men among many others.   This
business and professional group is motivated to teach in the
evening as a "second job" for various professional and personal reasons.   While none denies that the supplementary
income is a factor in the desire to teach in the evening,
most indicate that it is not the primary reason.   Many state
that the teaching experience provides a welcome change of
pace from a day in business or professional activity; others
refer mainly to the stimulating exchange of ideas with colleagues and students; still others frankly point to the prestige value which is carried back to their day position.   The
lawyer or accountant whose clients know him also as a "college teacher" or the practicing clinical psychologist whose
patients look with great respect at his college affiliation are
a few of the examples cited.   One such evening teacher
writes:

> 'After a hard day's work at the office, more work?'
> some people ask me.   I tell them it is not more
> work; it is something else again.   Let me try to
> explain what I mean. . . .
>
> Before class, I have time to wrap my feet around
> a restaurant counter stool and wolf down a ham-
> burger.   Sitting beside me will be two or three
> other convertible businessmen who become teachers
> by night, my colleagues in the College.   One chap
> is a personnel man for a big life insurance com-

pany; another is an industrial relations consultant.
An accountant is usually the wing back during our
Ketchup huddles.   I am an advertising agency man
myself.   Management, marketing, accounting, fi-
nance--you will find representatives of many walks
of business life on our owl shift. . . . Most businessmen relish the chance to talk to men outside
of their own specialities, to josh them a little, to
try to gain some insight into their worlds; we are
no exceptions. . . . We are welded by the common bond of our common interest in education.

For the businessman who can teach night school,
the classroom exchanges and the preparatory reading are of real value.   No two classes attack a
problem in the same way.   The case, as approached one year by a group, will take on entirely new dimensions and colorations with another
class another year.   The instructor is forced out
of the narrow specialization of his own job, forced
to refine his own experience and to draw upon it,
and forced to orient himself in the broad world
before he can orient his students. . . .

Here is the chance for the all-day businessman to
remind himself of the foolishness of that once-
popular slogan, 'those who can't, teach.' [38]

Of the off-campus lecturers, the business or professional group makes up approximately 38%, teachers from
other schools or colleges make up approximately 42% and
graduate students constitute approximately 20%.   In recent
years, an increasing number of graduate students either com-
pleting course work for the Ph. D. or working on doctoral
dissertations have been appointed.   For them, SGS represents
an opportunity for part-time employment while studying and
often it provides the only source of income.   Salary level is,
therefore, of considerable importance. [39]   Once they earn the
Ph. D. degree, the low income of the lecturer position coupled with absence of tenure or promotional possibilities becomes critical and they leave for greener fields.   The conse-

quence is high turnover in this category.   To them SGS is
just the first rung of the academic ladder providing income
and experience during an apprenticeship period.   Interesting-
ly, many of these graduate students have served in SGS for
ten or more years while continuing work toward the doctorate; some have given up the quest for the degree but remain
as part-time lecturers.

The lot of the evening lecturer, particularly the
graduate student, is expressed humorously in a parody on
a Gilbert & Sullivan song from The Pirates of Penzance.
It was written by an SGS teacher and sung by a staff group
at a recent SGS Faculty Club party.

Evening Lecturer's Song

I am the very pattern of a model evening lecturer.
I haven't seen my wife so long I cannot even pic-
    ture her.
I'm dedicated to the lot of students with maturity,
Which is equivalent to vows of poverty and purity.
I haven't had time to do the work upon my doctor-
    ate,
Because when there's a make-up test, I get twelve
    bucks to proctor it.

When people ask if I regret my choice I holler,
    "No siree."
Between ourselves, I wish I'd gone into my father's
    grocery.
I've great contempt for daytime kids--I nod my
    head judicially;
"Of course," I say, "they're very bright but do
    things superficially."
And if some colleague doubts my word I cheerfully
    will fracture her.
I am the very pattern of a model evening lecturer.[40]

Authority to Appoint

Authority to appoint part-time lecturers and responsibility for their quality are shared among the appointments

committee of the academic department, the deputy chairman
for SGS and the Dean.[41] The deputy chairman usually recruits, the appointments committee selects and then recommends jointly with the deputy chairman, who also proposes
the rate of compensation for the approval of the Dean.   No
provision in the by-laws of the Board expressly delegates
authority to the appointments committees for this appointive
function; on the other hand, its authority with respect to appointments of full-time faculty is explicitly stated.   Despite
the absence of a specific delegation of authority, the accepted and long-established college practice has accorded
legitimacy to the authority of this committee to evaluate, select, and recommend candidates for part-time teaching assignments in SGS.

In the total area of instructional staffing, it is with
respect to the part-time, off-campus lecturer that SGS administration has the greatest degree of power.   Delegated
to the Dean is the authority "to approve and transmit to the
President, recommendations for appointment of part-time
personnel."[42]   While the Dean has no authority to initiate
appointments, he has the specifically stated authority to "approve" (or disapprove).   For example, if a department finds
recruitment difficult (recent cases abound in the sciences
and mathematics) the committee on appointments may recommend several young, graduate students for teaching assignments.   Because many of the evening students are older and
more mature and also because the student body itself is a
heterogenous one, it is the view of the Dean that the graduate "trainee" may not be the best choice.   He may wish,
therefore, to limit the numbers of graduate students appointed to teach.

How potent is the power to disapprove?   Suppose, for

example, that the Dean disapproves the department committee recommendations.   The committee may then make other
choices.   But if the committee refuses to substitute other
candidates, neither the Dean nor the deputy has the power
to initiate an appointment without the approval of the appointments committee.   Thus the divided authority may lead to
an impasse situation.

Fully cognizant of this possibility and seeking to avoid
such contingency, the Dean has consistently utilized informal means to reconcile any differences and to maintain effective working relations with academic departments.   He may,
for example, confer with the deputy chairman to discover
whether a determined effort has been made to recruit more
mature experienced personnel from other colleges or universities or from professional groups or industry.   He may also offer additional budget to the department to obtain a
higher-ranking person whose services could then be substi-
tuted for a neophyte.   If he is convinced that the deputy and
the department have "done their best," he will usually accept the recommendation for that semester with a request
that renewed effort be made for the following semester.   If,
however, there is still substantial doubt after consultation
with the deputy, the Dean has several indirect courses of
action available to him with which to apply pressure.   He
may, at registration time, eliminate a course or courses
with marginal registration, which he might otherwise have
permitted to remain, thereby making a shift in staff necessary.   He may also, in planning for the following semester,
reduce the number of classes scheduled in that department.
Usually a department will do its best to recruit "acceptable"
personnel rather than face reduction in its offerings.

But even indirect pressures have their practical limi-

tations.   Student need and demand for courses must be given
due weight along with staff and budgetary considerations.
Here the Dean must make choices among competing values.
Is it better to leave a course in the schedule even though
the teacher may not be totally "acceptable" if the student
demand is great?   In the case of offering more budget for
a higher-ranking person, is it better to spend the limited
funds this way or to schedule yet another course in that department or some other department where student need is
pressing?   The decision-making process is part of the complex of administrative authority and responsibility.   Wherever
authority to make choices exists it must be prudently exercised in the context of the responsibility to students, to staff,
to the School and to the College.

Staff Turnover

Appointments to the rank of lecturer are made each
semester and continuity of service is achieved only by successive reappointment.   Neither promotion, tenure, nor retirement rights are attached to this title. [43]   It is interesting
to note that the by-laws of the Board of Higher Education describe in detail the qualifications for appointment to full-time
instructional ranks from the lowest level of Fellow and Research Assistant to the highest rank of full Professor.   For
example,

> Instructor--For appointment as an Instructor, the
> candidate must have demonstrated satisfactory quali-
> ties of personality and character, ability to teach
> successfully, interest in productive relationship or
> creative achievement. . . . [44]

In the same article of the by-laws, the section on "Lecturer"
simply states:

> Lectureships are temporary. [45]

How temporary is temporary? The following table indicates that the modal number of years of service in SGS of off-campus lecturers is one year or less; the median is between one and three years:

Length of Service--Part-time Off-Campus Lecturers
SGS Division of Liberal Arts--Fall 1965

No. of Years	No. of Lecturers	Percent of Total
1 year or less	60	27
1 - 3	54	25
3 - 5	50	23
5 - 7	24	11
More than 7	30	14
Total	218	100%

These figures are for the Division of Liberal Arts only. Since the Division of Vocational Studies will be completely phased out as of 1968, it has not been included either in the analysis or the statistics previously cited in this chapter. However, the statistics for comparative length of service in Vocational Studies are significant and are, therefore, set forth in the following table which shows a mode of more than seven years and a median of three to five years:

Length of Service--Part-time Off-Campus Lecturers
SGS Division of Vocational Studies--Fall 1965

No. of Years	No. of Lecturers	Percent of Total
1 year or less	20	18
1 - 3	22	20
3 - 5	17	16
5 - 7	19	17
More than 7	32	29
Total	110	100%

In the Division of Liberal Arts, only 25% have served for five years or more; in Vocational Studies, 46% have

served for five years or more.   Since both divisions have
the same salary levels and conditions of employment, it
seems clear that the contrast can be explained basically by
the compositions of the staff.   Vocational Studies has a far
higher proportion of business and professional men serving
as lecturers; to them teaching is a supplementary activity
and not a career aim.   On the other hand, Liberal Arts
draws more heavily on graduate students who aspire to a
teaching career.

As far back as the first annual report for the Evening Session in 1949, the Dean identified the root causes for
the high rate of turnover in the Division of Liberal Arts as
follows:

> The general calibre of the Evening staff, both in
> academic preparation and teaching skill, needs
> strengthening.   It is a truism that, because of the
> heterogeneous character of the student body and
> their special problems, a higher level of teaching
> skill and attention to individual needs is required
> than in the Day Session.   Yet, because of the still
> relatively low rates of remuneration for more
> challenging teaching problems, we have not suc-
> ceeded in attracting more competent off-campus
> teachers.   Some departments openly declare that
> they regard the Evening Session as a 'proving
> ground' for instructors considered as candidates
> for Day Session positions.   Until the Evening Ses-
> sion can offer positions on regular annual lines with
> full tenure rights and annual increments it will have
> to expect a high rate of turnover of its staff. [46]

The fact that SGS is a sub-organization in the total
College complex serves to underscore the temporary character of the lecturer position.   A group without rank and tenure
working in a community where positions are defined by rank
and supported by tenure is necessarily a transient one.
Surely they do not constitute a stable permanent "faculty."

Salary Levels and Responsibility

Salaries for part-time lecturers have consistently been considerably lower than those in the day college.   A statement made by the Chairman of the Board in 1944 is still valid today.   He said:

> The most serious shortcoming in our evening session work has to do with the method of compensation for evening teachers which has grown and for which scant defense can be offered beyond the fact that it has become a customary practice. [47]

The scale of salaries is based primarily on degrees already held, additional work toward higher degrees, and professional experience related to the subject area taught by the individual.   As previously stated, lecturer salaries based on a semester-hour formula is approximately 60% of the full-time line equivalent.   The fact that evening employment is supplementary income for some and considered a "trainee" assignment by others makes it possible to recruit reasonably competent staff.   In addition, the prestige value inherent in college teaching, even though part-time, further enhances the ability to recruit capable professional and business people.   For the individual, therefore, the part-time lecturer positions provide supplementary income, prestige, or training and experience in teaching at the college level.   For SGS, the part-time "off-campus" teacher provides instructional staff at low-cost.

Perhaps these factors of low salary level, temporary nature of the assignment, and the subtle separation and status distinction between day and evening staff led David Boroff, a former lecturer in SGS at Brooklyn College to characterize this teacher as:

A marginal man without tenure and perquisites
paid by the hour and virtually unknown to his day
session colleagues, he is the exploited coolie of
New York's academe, doing a difficult job with
rare skill. [48]

Stability Versus Flexibility

Organizational management recognizes that organizational stability rests, to a large extent, on the foundation of staff stability. Thus the great interest in the employment of full-time personnel whose primary work commitment is to the organization itself. SGS administration has continuously stressed the need for a full-time faculty in order to achieve a degree of staff and organizational stability. But it lives with the reality of a part-time staff which comprises about sixty per cent of the total work force. In the absence of a full-time faculty, SGS has to function within the orbit of the parent organization in the formulation of programs and curricula, staff appointments, counseling, student activities and other educational facets of an academic institution.

How much responsibility for educational policy, curricular development, student relations, staff appointments, among other operational matters, can or should a part-time staff be expected to assume? For example, can the professional or businessman who has a full-time responsible position in business, industry or the professions be expected to participate in functions ancillary to the teaching of his classes? Or can the part-time teacher who is a graduate student working on a dissertation reasonably be expected to participate in those functions? The role prescriptions of part-time lecturer realistically cannot include the vast array of functions and responsibilities which are now ancillary to the teaching commitment.

Not to be overlooked is the fact that the lecturer position makes possible for SGS a flexibility not enjoyed by any other degree-granting unit of the college. New programs, new curricula, experimentation in teaching techniques, and adaptation to the changing interests of a changing student body in particular subject areas can readily be accommodated by shifts in the composition of this non-tenured instructional staff. The strength of SGS in the college community is, in part, derived from its reputation as an experimental center in the midst of a relatively stable college community. Experimentation requires a high degree of staff flexibility. But this functional aspect of staff flexibility has its dysfunctional counterpart. A flexible and changing staff impairs a coherent continuity of educational goal setting and implementation.

Summary: Reverbations of Limited Authority

The extent of policy-making and managerial authority exercised by a sub-unit of a larger organization has far-reaching significance. SGS is not autonomous but is more or less subject to the controls of the parent's centers of power and authority.

At the key point of instructional staff, the mixed nature of the work force and the diversity of rights and privileges pertaining to the different categories, strongly influence the capacity of the staff to work toward common goals. The very fact that SGS instructional staff lacks sufficient participating powers as an organized faculty in the decision-making processes creates an exceptional challenge for SGS when threats to its organizational integrity occur. Likewise, the capacity of SGS administration more effectively to attain its unique goals is considerably weakened because of the limited policy-making and administrative powers granted to it.

The discrepancy between the responsibilities of the
SGS Dean and his authority, especially in matters concerning appointment, promotion and tenure of faculty, are a
source of strain which decisively affect the character of the
evening college.[49] In the next chapter, we shall see how
these strains are intensified by pressures arising not out of
the internal structure and dynamics of the parent/sub-unit
relationship but from sources outside their mutual relationship.

Notes

1. John M. Gaus, "A Theory of Organization in Public Administration," in The Frontiers of Public Administration (University of Chicago Press, 1936), p. 66.

2. Authority is defined by Max Weber as "the probability
   that certain specific commands (or all commands)
   from a given source will be obeyed by a given group
   of persons." The Theory of Social and Economic
   Organization, Talcott Parsons, ed.   (Free Press,
   Glencoe, Illinois, 1947), p. 152.

3. Howard S. Becker, "The Teacher in the Authority System of the Public School" in Amitai Etzioni, Complex
   Organizations (Holt, Rinehart, Winston, 1965), p.
   243-257.   See also, Chapter I "Organizational Structure," p. 11.

4. Philip Selznick. "Foundations of the Theory of Organization," American Sociological Review (1948) Vol. 13,
   p. 25.

5. Robert MacIver. Academic Freedom in our Time, (1955);
   Russell Kirk. Academic Freedom (1955).

6. Memorandum from President Harry D. Gideonse to Deans,
   Directors, Department Chairmen, Deputy Chairmen,
   "Responsibilities of the Director," School of General
   Studies, September 1, 1959, (emphasis added).

7. In terms of "full-time equivalent" students, SGS is approximately one-half the size of CLAS.

8. This variation among departments reflects idiosyncratic conditions such as departmental needs, level of lines available, willingness of department to fill a vacancy at the time, available candidates, etc.

9. These are raw, unadjusted figures. They should be adjusted on the basis of teaching load equivalence since the average teaching load of SGS annual line staff is about 1.5 times that of either a day-session person teaching in SGS on an "overload" basis or the off-campus, part-time lecturer.

10. There were three budget lines provided to the Evening Session in 1948 but these were utilized exclusively to transfer three faculty members from the day-session to fill the administrative positions of Director, Associate and Assistant Director.

11. Board of Higher Education, City of New York, A Broader Mandate for Higher Education, Report of the Chairman, 1956-1948, p. 35.

12. Annual Report of the SGS Dean, 1953-1954, p. 3.

13. Budget request of the SGS Dean to President, 1953-1954.

14. Exclusive of Nursing Science where a total of twelve "lecturer" lines were provided.

15. Actually only 58.

16. Middle-States Association of Colleges and Secondary Schools, "A Report of the Evaluation Team of the Committee on Institutions of Higher Education," October 30 - November 2, 1966, p. 22.

17. Memorandum from President Gideonse to Department Chairmen, "Appointments on Instructional Lines," May 27, 1967.

18. Memorandum from President Gideonse to Deans, Directors, etc., June 9, 1960.

19. The deputy chairman is the chairman's representative in

SGS (see next section for a description of the role of
the deputy chairman in SGS).

20. In another contest with the same department, however,
the results were reversed.   See p. 181-185, this
chapter.

21. The President is granted power under the by-laws to
recommend promotions independently to the Board,
Article IX, Sec. 9-4, p. 23.

22. The City University operating on a "line" budget has a
limited number of non-convertible "lines" available.

23. The rank of Professor is excluded because length of
service precludes eligibility for promotion to this rank
for SGS faculty at this time.

24. 1967 Statistics.

25. Interviews with faculty members, May - November, 1966.

26. Interviews with staff, December, 1966.

27. Memorandum of President Gideonse to Deans, Directors,
Chairmen of Departments, "Appointments to Annual
Lines in the School of General Studies," June 9, 1960,
provides:

> The Dean of the Faculties will interview and orient
> new appointees to the School of General Studies as
> he does currently for new appointees to the staff of
> the College of Liberal Arts and Sciences.   The Di-
> rector (Dean) will orient new appointees in matters
> exclusive to the School of General Studies.

28. There are ten committees of the faculty and fifteen presidential committees.

29. Curriculum, student affairs, appointments, promotions,
among others.

30. There are approximately ten of these, i. e. , Effective
Teaching, Scholarships and Awards, Aims and Programs, among others.

31. This would not affect either his rank or tenure as a faculty member of the department, solely his assignment

as deputy chairman in SGS.

32. It is interesting to note that the chairman was replaced
    by the man whom the Dean had hoped would be the
    next deputy chairman.   This man was acceptable to
    the President, too.

33. Prior to 1965, the maximum number of teaching hours
    permitted on an "overload" basis was twelve per an-
    num; in 1965, the number was reduced to ten and in
    1966, further reduced to eight.

34. Practices with respect to ceiling rates at each rank
    level varied among the colleges; Brooklyn College ad-
    hered to a graduated scale of ceiling rates related to
    instructional ranks.

35. An additional reason for the establishment of the confer-
    ence hour was the increase in class size in some de-
    partments. Unfortunately, there was not sufficient
    budget to achieve this added hour in more than a few
    departments.

36. Since permissible teaching load declined from 12 hours
    per year to 8 hours per year (see footnote 34).

37. These day session faculty members served in SGS on
    an "overtime" basis for additional compensation.

38. Richard J. Thain.   "Teaching on the Swing Shift," (un-
    published report) in On Teaching Adults, Center for
    the Study of Liberal Education for Adults, (Chicago,
    1958).

39. Series of informal interviews with about 100 SGS staff
    members, October, 1966 to April, 1967.

40. Lyrics by Edward Spingarn, Assistant Professor, Depart-
    ment of English.   Professor Spingarn was a lecturer
    in SGS for approximately 15 years before appointment
    to a "line" position.

41. The Board of Higher Education has official appointive
    power.   All "appointments" which emanate from the
    colleges are officially "recommendations" to the
    Board.   Except in rare cases, action of the Board in
    approving appointments is pro forma.   We will, there-

fore, avoid the cumbersome repetition of the word
"recommended."

42. Memorandum of President to Deans, Directors and De-
    partment Chairmen, "Responsibilities of the Direc-
    tor (Dean), School of General Studies," October 1,
    1959, p. 2 (emphasis added).

43. Until 1952, when enabling legislation was passed by the
    New York State Legislature, lecturers did not even
    have social security coverage.

44. By-laws of the Board of Higher Education, Article XV,
    "Conditions and Qualifications for Appointment and
    Promotion," Sec. 15. 7, p. 45.

45. Ibid. , Sec. 15. 12, p. 47.

46. "Annual Report," Evening Session 1948 - 1949, p. 9-10,
    (emphasis added).

47. Report of the Chairman, Board of Higher Education,
    City of New York, "Higher Education on the Offen-
    sive," 1943-1944, p. 27.

48. David Boroff. "A Kind of Proletariat Harvard," New
    York Times, March 28, 1965.

49. For a similar distinction between "actual" and "expected"
    authority as a source of conflict, see Victor A.
    Thompson, Modern Organization (New York, 1965),
    passim.

Chapter V

Stress and Strain

The Effects of Environmental Pressures

> "The rivalry of the patterns is
> the history of the world."
>
> William James

Probing the subtleties of the relationships of educational institutions to the society at large, one college president raised the challenging question: "We wonder, and increasingly, just who calls the shots in higher education."[1]
He then pointed out that "no institution is immune from
forces beyond its campus." Institutional response to external pressures, he added, involves "a responsibility of awe-
some proportions" for institutions cannot avoid the "responsibility to distinguish need from demand, the important from
the unimportant."[2]

In more concrete terms, Phillip H. Coombs identified some of the external forces as the growing complexity
of the world in which we live, the "enormously expanded demand upon the universities for research," the "prospective
increase in customers," and the "expansion of government
expenditures for research and development in the colleges
and universities."[3] Other pressing demands upon universities "both serious and frivolous" which he noted were:

> The demands for special services to special
> groups in the community, the pressures of pro-
> fessional societies to expand and upgrade offerings,
> and the pressures of non-professional occupational
> groups to lift themselves to professional status and
> respectability by establishing a special school and
> a special degree at the university. There are
> other important pressures, less evident to the pub-
> lic, but acutely felt by the university, to maintain
> or achieve a respectable rank in the academic
> pecking order, through expanding curriculum offer-
> ings, developing new graduate programs, building
> strong departments, attracting and turning out good
> students, and by elaborating certain academic
> forms and rituals best understood by anthropolo-
> gists. [4]

While confronting this myriad of pressures, colleges
and universities are simultaneously responding to on-campus
pressures stemming from intra-organizational relationships.
The latter pressures are simply part of the inevitable process of dynamic vitality and growth-surges of any organization. However, if these pressures challenge the essential
value system of the organization or any sub-organization,
they will be met with strenuous efforts to prevent "en-
croachment" on established organizational and value structures. As in any other social system, once traditions and
values are established by the organization or any of its components, the imperative to "stay alive" with all one's structural and functional attributes intact becomes paramount.
Thus resistance to pressures, whether they emanate from
on-campus or off-campus factors, precipitates organizational
stress and strain.

Maintenance of a formal organization as a going social system constantly requires development of appropriate
means of self-defense. [5] "The security of the organization
as a whole in relation to social forces in its environment
. . . requires continuous attention to the possibilities of en-

croachment and to the forestalling of threatened aggression
or deleterious (though perhaps unintended) consequences
from the action of others. "[6]

The term "organizational life" has frequently been
employed by sociologists in the examination of social interaction within formal organizations.   In organizational life,
as in the life of an individual, "the process of living is the
process of reacting to stress. "[7]   The special interest in the
patterns of organizational stress and strain is not a morbid
concern with a pathology of organizations but rather a focus
on "normal" interactive processes.   As Simmel so clearly
saw, conflict is a social process "designed to resolve diver-
gent dualisms--a way of achieving some kind of unity--(re-
solving) the tension between contrasts. "[8]

Although stress and strain are inevitable "facts of
life, " and are, indeed, often potent stimuli to growth, they
nevertheless evoke irksome discomfort in those charged with
the maintenance of the organization.   During the rain storm,
it is often a bit difficult to feel the full impact of the knowledge that the grass will be greener and the flowers brighter
as life-giving moisture is absorbed into the soil.   The emphasis on stress and strain obviously does not preclude the
dynamics of cooperation and integration coexisting in organizational life.   These behavioral categories, too, are threads
that consistently run through the tapestry of organizational
analysis.

Since the elements of stress and strain are frequently
enmeshed at the same time in elements of cooperation and
integration, causal connections may be elusive.[9]   Organizational "change" does not always emerge despite the existence
of pressures.   Nevertheless, the inference can be made that
when change does occur, it is in response to pressures orig-

inating either from within or outside the organization, i.e.,
to a tension resulting from forces which exerted a push or
pull against resistance.

The Focus on SGS

The focus here is on pressures exerted upon SGS by
the broader environment which surrounds both it and its
parent: these are, the City of New York, the City University and finally the Board of Higher Education. In some instances, the pressures affected SGS directly; in other instances, there was a "two step flow" of stress which developed through and with CLAS. Most clearly is this reflected
in the brief historical period, 1960-1967, when the operational scope of SGS, more than in any other period, bobbed
like a cork on a turbulent sea. Social and economic forces
in the City of New York converged upon the City University
and were transmitted, in turn, to the senior and community
colleges. Specifically, the enormous increase in demand by
recent high school graduates for admission to college, the
growth of community colleges, the increase in size and scope
of graduate programs, the City's concern with higher education for socially and economically disadvantaged groups--all
linked to an acute scarcity of space and other facilities at
the senior colleges--exerted a severe impact on all the
Schools of General Studies.

No doubt pressures from the "outside" will be experienced in varying degrees by the organization's component
units. Neither parent nor component units is impervious to
external pressures. The 1967 budget difficulty of the City of
New York, for example, was the occasion for a severe reduction in the City University's budget. Brooklyn College as
a whole was required to pare $1 million, of which $200,000

were allocated as the SGS retrenchment share. This fiscal
stringency applied to the parent is an obvious example of
consequential effects upon the sub-unit. The impact of other pressures on SGS is less direct and, therefore, more
subtle. An instance is the effort of the City of New York
to provide higher education for larger numbers of its youth
while providing expanded opportunity to a larger proportion
of Negro and Puerto Rican students.[10] While this effort
challenged the policies of the Board of Higher Education and
the City University, the consequential shock waves were
transmitted to all the senior colleges.

Plainly the impact of external pressures upon the different units varies according to their position in the hierarchy. If space and other resources are desperately scarce,
priority choices must be made. When a liquid flows through
a funnel, the total pressures do not diminish in magnitude
as the liquid approaches the narrower appertures; the flow
just gains force and velocity. Metaphorically, sub-unit is
that part of the funnel with the smallest circumference and
consequently is subjected to the greater impact.

It must again be emphasized that frequently the goals
of the sub-unit do not wholly coincide with these of the parent organization. In that case, the priority choices will
most probably give precedence to those activities which directly further the goals of the larger and more influential
sector of the organization. For example, one of the major
goals of SGS is to provide a "second chance" for higher education to working adults who do not have the conventionally-
accepted requirements for admission to the day college.[11]
Would there be room for these adults in SGS in face of pressures to increase the proportion of the City's youth to be admitted to college? A severe shortage of existing space and

facilities coupled with increased pressure for student admission to the day school might require a "spill-over" into the
evening hours by these matriculated, full-time students.
Clearly, an inferior priority position for SGS for "second
chance" SGS students would drastically affect its goals. This
peril actually exists and does not represent a case of goal
displacement. [12] It is rather a threat of a radical change in
the essential quality, jurisdiction and structure of SGS. Indeed, the threat actually challenges the existence of SGS in
its entirety as a separate organizational entity.

Pressure from the City University

The period between 1960 and 1967 was critical in the
life of SGS, for during that period the scope of its functions
was drastically curtailed.   This was the period when the
first Master Plan (1964) made clear the intention of the
Board to have all two-year programs transferred from the
schools of general studies to the community colleges as soon
as their facilities permitted such transfer.   It was, therefore,
a time of transition, a time for redefinition of function and
realignment of areas of authority and responsibility.
It will be recalled[13] that the original mandate by the
Board establishing the Schools of General Studies defined
their powers in two terms.   First, they were granted jurisdiction over all courses leading to diplomas and certificates,
over all other non-degree work, including adult-education
courses, and over all non-matriculated students. [14] But by
1963, there were no longer any diploma, certificate or non-
degree programs in the School of General Studies at Brooklyn College.   Of the original non-degree areas of jurisdiction the only group remaining was that of the non-matriculated students.   Second, the Board assigned responsibility for

administrative supervision to the Schools of General Studies
over all course work leading to degrees. [15]   SGS was thus
to function in the area of all degree work in an administrative capacity within the limits set by the faculty of the College which had exclusive jurisdiction over all degree programs. [16]

Even the extent of responsibility for degree work varied among sister institutions.   The Board's language was
broad and it therefore allowed room for institutional interpretation.   At the same time, it conserved and guarded the
degree-granting powers of the faculty.   In the practical application of the Board's directive at Brooklyn College, the
extent of faculty interest and control ranged from high to low
on a continuum: greatest in the areas of the four-year baccalaureate program, less in the two-year liberal arts degree (A. A.) and least in the two-year vocational studies and
nursing degrees (A. A. S.).   The faculty's major concern was
with the baccalaureate program including courses and areas
creditable toward the A. B. degree.

As the two-year programs phased out, the only area
remaining in SGS was the one leading to the baccalaureate degree.   Over this area, SGS had least control and autonomy.
Its greatest degree of autonomy was over students classified
as non-matriculated.   With respect to them, it still had the
jurisdiction granted by the Board in 1950.

SGS jurisdiction over non-matriculated students was,
at this point in its history, most important.   SGS sought to
utilize the non-matriculated category to encourage adults who
lacked either the qualitative or quantitative requirements for
admission as matriculants to enroll as baccalaureate aspir-
ants on a part-time basis.   These students would be given
special counseling and encouraged to strive to attain matricu-

lated status through scholastic accomplishment in college
courses.

A consideration of not negligible importance was the
fact that non-matriculated students pay fees ($18 per cred-
it) and these fee funds constitute a significant source of
revenue for the College.   The importance of these revenues
is not solely the amount they represent; equally significant
is the degree of budget flexibility they provide.   Operating
on a "line" budget with positions rigidly prescribed by the
budget director, the College eagerly welcomes a flexible
source of "cash" revenue. [17]   Since SGS has the power to
determine admission and retention standards and the numbers of students to be admitted as non-matriculants, its role
as the revenue producing agency contributed rather strategic
elements to otherwise limited powers. [18]

A Threatening Proposal

As pressures mounted for increased admissions of
recent high school graduates to the day college, questions
were raised as to the educational validity of providing facilities for non-matriculated students (despite the financial resources that they contributed).   In a "Working Paper," issued in October, 1963, the Dean of Studies of the City University described the nature and extent of the "enrollment
crisis" in the City's colleges and advocated a "painstaking
reappraisal" and a reassessment by the City University of
"the priority which it will assign to each program in its effort to make the best possible use of the intellectual and
physical resources at its disposal."[19]

The Working Paper recounted the pressures for increased admissions currently being felt by the City University.   Part of the pressure stemmed from the post World

War II population bulge: the high school graduating class of
1964 in New York City was expected to be 14.5% larger
than that of 1963; the class of 1965 was anticipated to be
7.7% still larger than 1964.   Concomitantly, the social and
political climate of the City was strongly in the direction of
admitting socially and economically disadvantaged students
to the City University's colleges.   This pressure further
added to the potential growth figures.

The City University's goal was to admit more students than reflected by the increase in high school graduates
for the plan also envisaged reduction of the high school average necessary for admission.   The high school average required for admission to the senior colleges was raised to
85% by 1963; back in 1953, it had been about 82% of 83%.
The average required for admission had been increased over
the years to maintain an uneasy balance between limited
space and facilities and the increased demand for admissions
based upon the teen-age population bulge.   Moreover, there
had been a steady rise in the ratio of high school graduates
who sought entrance to college.   Now the object was to readjust the high school average for admission back to the levels of a decade before.[20]

What impact would this proposal have on SGS and particularly on the non-matriculated student category?   The
Dean of Studies posed the alternative choices in the following question:

> Is it better practice to admit widely and to weed
> out the sub-standard students on the basis of their
> actual achievement in college, than to shut the
> gates to a great many who have attained grades
> which a decade ago would have gained them admis-
> sion?[21]

The form of the question in an "either-or" alternative

is revealing. It assumes that there is no room for <u>both</u>
the non-matriculated student and all those who could "qualify" for matriculated status. Put on an "either-or" basis,
an exclusionary choice would necessarily have to be made.
The Dean's answer on the priority choice he set up was to
make "our main target, the degree candidate in our undergraduate and graduate programs. "[22]

The Dean, of course, recognized that the decrease
in the numbers of non-matriculated fee-paying students
would affect the University's budgetary flexibility. He acknowledged that financing out of fee funds rather than out of
tax levy monies had provided many services to all students.
Without these funds, services may have to be curtailed.
Cognizant of this loss, he urged that "a total revision of
these (budgetary) procedures, long promised, is long over-
due. "

But the Dean's memorandum implied consequences far
beyond the mere validity of retaining non-matriculated students. While the paramount concern was the current high
school graduates seeking admission to the day program, the
necessary effect would be to place the present fully matriculated part-time student attending SGS during evening hours
in an inferior position with respect to opportunities for admission and class enrollments. Concerning "our prime obligation to our degree candidates," the Dean significantly
asked:

> What increase in student capacity can be antici-
> pated if, during the fall and spring semesters, we
> wipe out the dividing line between day and evening
> sessions for matriculated students and run the col-
> leges from 8 A. M. until as late in the evening as
> is necessary and practicable?

The implication was quite clear. Although alternative

suggestions were made for more intensive use of existing facilities[23] which would increase the capacity of the senior colleges by an estimated 20 percent, it was implied that these alternatives would not provide enough help. It was also implied by the Dean's question that an increase in student capacity (for full-time degree candidates) could be achieved by running the colleges "from 8 A. M. until as late in the evening as is necessary and practicable." Adoption of such practice would have practically spelled the annihilation of SGS.

Opposition to the Threat

The Brooklyn College evening newspaper KEN quoted the section of the Working Paper on eliminating "the dividing line between day and evening" and added that the matriculated evening students would be at a disadvantage in this arrangement. It quoted a Brooklyn College spokesman as saying that ". . . such a solution would not be acceptable here . . . our evening session fully matrics, with their limited amount of free time, must be given first preference to all students--bar none." It further reported that at Brooklyn College both "President Harry D. Gideonse and SGS Director (Dean) Edwin Spengler had labored hard and long to help insure SGS' record of accomplishment and leadership . . ." and that neither the President nor the Dean "view favorably" the suggestion to erase the day-night dividing line. [24]

This was a rather mild understatement of the views of the Dean and other SGS administrators. The two parts of the working paper that were of major concern to the Schools of General Studies; i. e. , (1) the "dawn-to-dark" proposal which would eliminate the separation of the "Day" from the "Evening" college and, (2) the low priority to be assigned to

non-matriculants which would drastically curtail or eliminate
this group meant a solar plexus blow to SGS' total being and
sphere of operations.   In the perceptions of the schools of
general studies, the line dividing the day and evening sessions is not only a demarcation of time; it is also a differentiation of goals and educational philosophy.   Indeed, it was
in recognition of this very difference of function and purpose
that the schools of general studies were established as separate organizations.   A denial of the need for the functions
performed or a relegation of these functions to secondary or
tertiary significance at a time when space was available only
for "top priority" goals implied serious doubts as to any
need at all for the Schools of General Studies as distinct organizational entities.

Logistics of Self-Defense

The SGS Council of Directors (now Deans and Directors) responded to the working paper by issuing, in November, 1963, a document addressed to the Administrative Council and to the "Committee to Look to the Future" of the
Board.   The document was entitled "The Schools of General
Studies Look to the Future."   While the SGS Deans made no
explicit reference to the working paper,[25] they indicated that
they were attempting to reevaluate SGS practices and procedures because of the "anticipated effect on the role of the
Schools of General Studies of the sharp increase in the number of applicants for admission to the City University foreseen for 1964-1965."   Recognizing that the Schools of General Studies and their students would necessarily be affected by
increased pressures for daytime baccalaureate admissions as
well as by the growth of community colleges, the Deans centered their attention on redefining the "sphere of education"

in SGS.   They proposed the following three broad categories
of students to define the future role and functions of the
schools:

1) Baccalaureate Degree Candidates. [26]

2) Pre-Matriculants: This category would include
   students whose record of achievement was only
   slightly below those qualified for baccalaureate matriculation and who were considered to be "potentially" comparable to baccalaureate candidates.

3) Non-Matriculants:[27] This category was described
   as intended to provide opportunities for persons
   with irregular or interrupted educational backgrounds . . . "designed for many persons who
   have limited educational opportunities due to a lack
   of facilities in the areas in which they spent the
   formative years of their lives." With regard to
   non-matriculants, the Deans also said:

> These groups include persons with high school edu-
> cation minimally as well as many others with par-
> tial college training, whose needs cannot be met by
> the community college in many cases.   Many, if
> not most, could not afford the fees charged at pri-
> vate colleges.   Higher education would be closed to
> them if not for the School of General Studies. [28]

Throughout the Deans' document ran the theme emphasizing the qualities and characteristics of the Schools of General Studies which set them apart as organizations distinct
from the day college.   Of the non-matriculated category it
pointed out that here was ". . . one of the features which
most differentiates it (SGS) from the day college." In sweeping terms, the document stressed that the Schools of General Studies ". . . serve a wide variety of needs and much of
the time, in ways which a day program could not be expected

to initiate and carry on. "[29]

The report concluded with a broadly encompassing
statement, later incorporated into the Master Plan, 1964:

> We believe that these varied educational purposes
> of the schools of general studies are of singular
> significance to the City of New York, as they have
> been for more than half a century when the eve-
> ning sessions of the City College first began.   In
> planning the future of the City University at this
> time, we should bear these purposes in mind and
> continue to make every effort to achieve them as
> effectively as possible using space and time to the
> maximum. [30]

This statement reflected the strategy of "self-defense"
employed by the sub-organizations against proposals which
threatened their very life.

The Real Reasons for Retreat

The proposals of the working paper to abolish the dividing line between day and evening sessions and to accord
low priority for admission of non-matriculants were not
adopted for a number of reasons.   With regard to "dawn-to-
dark" scheduling of classes, there was substantial faculty disapproval. [31]   Day session faculty objected to being required
to work during late afternoon or evening hours.   Their willingness to work during these hours, in their view, should
remain a matter of choice and subject to additional compensation, as now practiced.   With respect to the non-matriculated category, the substitution of City funds for tuition fees
collected from this group of students did not appear to have
an early chance of adoption when the City's fiscal position was
a precarious one.   Though legislation was proposed to provide
State aid to generate additional funds, this legislative proposal seemed to have little chance of adoption in the foreseeable

future.

The Quest for a Plateau

Despite the failure of adoption of the working paper's proposals the continuing accent on youth by the City University deeply concerned the SGS Deans.   They continuously sought to obtain a more explicit recognition of a place for adults in the blueprint for higher education.   The Master Plan, 1964, included no reference to the proposed pre-matriculant category suggested by the Deans. [32]   Instead, the Master Plan emphasized upper-division work in the Schools of General Studies "as the community college graduates seek to further their education in the junior and senior years. "[33] No special mention was made of mature adults and continuing education.   Subsequent revisions of the Master Plan-- more particularly the Plan of 1966--perpetuated this omission.   It included three categories of students for the schools of general studies as: 1) Baccalaureate Matriculants; 2) Post-Baccalaureate enrollees;   3) Non-matriculants.

A New Salient

On July 2, 1966, the New York Times reported that an expansion program to include 30, 000 additional students by 1972 had been projected by the City University which was then operating at 125% of capacity. [34]   Legislation setting up a $400 million City University Construction Fund, to be financed jointly by the City and the State, was designed to make the expansion program possible.   The University's plan was to build two additional senior colleges, expand community colleges and add structures to the existing senior colleges.   At Brooklyn, two new buildings and two additions to existing buildings were projected involving a $33. 7 million expansion program to increase plant capacity to 12, 000 students.

It is interesting to note that there were two separate
"titles" or "headings" in the 3.5 column <u>New York Times</u>
article. The first was "Operating Over Capacity," and the
second was "Aid to Evening Students." The only meagre
reference to evening students under that heading was the
first, one-sentence paragraph, which read:

> The provision of new facilities for full-time day
> students will also give the University more space
> for part-time evening students.

Not mentioned in the article was the provision that
all fee funds (now) held at the senior colleges would be
turned over to the City University and ultimately to the City
of New York to be used as security for bond issues floated
by the City to cover its share of capital outlay for new
building construction. [35] The fee funds accumulated by the
senior colleges (largely from fees paid by two-year degree
and non-matriculated students) were thus pledged as collater-
al security for the City's share of interest and amortization
payments on bonded indebtedness incurred to finance the
building expansion program.

The construction fund coupled with separate monies
made available to rent temporary space in anticipation of increased admissions during the 1966-67 academic year served
to some extent to relieve the pressures on the Schools of
General Studies. At Brooklyn College, there was still visible (though not ample) classroom space to maintain enrollment at the 1965-1966 levels. In part, viability was a-
chieved by CLAS increasing class size, by starting classes
at 8 A.M. instead of 9 A.M. and by the Graduate Division
utilizing Saturday mornings for some classes. Thus the existing categories of SGS students--baccalaureate matriculant,
non-matriculant (including post-baccalaureate)--were, for the

time being, maintained.   No immediate change, therefore,
occurred either in SGS policy, goals, student population, or
organizational structure as a result of the events leading to
the working paper or the events which followed in its wake.

Reverberations of the Threat

Why, then, describe the total situation as one of
stress and strain?   First, the proposal to "eliminate the dividing line," expressed by an influential spokesman of the
City University, conveyed the strong impression that the City
University's recognition of the avowed purposes and commitments of the Schools of General Studies enjoyed relatively
low priority in the University's hierarchy of values.   Second,
although the plan was not effectuated, its abandonment apparently did not squarely rest on a positive affirmation of
the roles of the Schools of General Studies; rather, it was
not adopted chiefly on the basis of non-acceptability by the
day faculties and new construction plans.   It was obviously
discouraging to administration and instructional staff of an
educational unit to learn that they are wanted principally for
their money; the fee funds were a major issue.   Third, and
most important, following the publicity given to the working
paper, both instructional staff and students expressed great
insecurity for months thereafter.   The students viewed the
threat as serious; they literally besieged administrative officers with queries about the future of their education.   SGS
"line" faculty with tenure raised anxious questions whether,
if SGS were eliminated, (although this had never been stated
or even suggested) their positions would be automatically
transferable to CLAS.   Other "line" faculty, without tenure,
more anxiously inquired whether their positions would be
eliminated entirely.   Hourly paid lecturers openly and frankly

spoke of seeking other jobs; indeed, many asked for letters
of recommendation "just in case." How can the full effect
on morale, on turnover rates and continued vitality of an organization be assessed in the light of a threat, real or implied, to its very existence? Fourth was a reverberation
most difficult to assess. What was the conscious or sub-
conscious effect on CLAS committees responsible for the allocation of space and other facilities? How did the questions
raised on SGS' area of jurisdiction and sphere of influence
affect the priority judgments of committee members in considering future space allocations for SGS? Decisions in such
critical areas are, to a large extent, the product of implant-
ed attitudes.

Transmitted Pressures from the College

Ironically, modern man seeks to conquer outer space but
man in academe still has to cope with shortage of space here
on earth. The extent of the problem at Brooklyn College was
dramatically expressed by President Gideonse in a Convocation address.[36] He pointed out that the average coop space
required as the minimum to raise five Rhode Island Rock
hens, according to standards formulated by the Department of
Agriculture, is 25 square feet. At Brooklyn College, he
added, the average staff room space allocated for an individual faculty member is 26 square feet! When five chickens are
equal to one professor there is a problem!

The college administration, with the assistance of the
Presidential Advisory Committee on Space and Facilities, has
utilized many devices to stretch existing building facilities to
their utmost capacity. The scheduling of early morning and
some Saturday classes has already been mentioned. Increased use of large lecture sections instead of small reci-

tation classes in a variety of disciplines has also been employed as a stretching technique. The expansion of exemption examinations, requiring no class attendance, and increased credit allowances for independent study, also not requiring class attendance, though not instituted for the express purpose of saving space have, in fact, achieved this unanticipated benefit. On a much smaller scale, use of T. V. and other teaching devices in large sections have also contributed to the conservation of classroom space. Off-campus classroom and office space has been rented for adult education (non-credit) programs and some auxiliary services. But these are a drop in the bucket in light of the pressures to accommodate existing students as well as substantially to expand daytime enrollments. Several instances arose where inadequate classroom space during daytime hours resulted in pressure on SGS to relinquish classrooms during evening hours for CLAS courses to be scheduled in the evening.

Severities of Contraction

As has been stated, the period, 1960-1967 was one of transition for SGS. The two year programs were rapidly being phased out and transferred to the community colleges. A slight decrease in the qualitative requirements for admission (combined SAT score and high school average) to CLAS, created a further decline in enrollments in SGS. [37] Although it is not the policy of SGS to keep enrollments at high levels merely for the sake of maintaining numbers per se, there are several cogent, practical reasons for a policy geared to the maintenance of existing enrollments:

1. Any decline in enrollment is reflected in decreased tax-levy budget allocations for the following academic year.

2. Once a decline occurs, there is a two-year lag
in the restitution of budgetary allocations even
though the decline may be later "corrected."

3. Decline in enrollment also results in a decrease
of fee fund income (from non-matriculated students).

4. Past experience has demonstrated that when space
is relinquished, it is exceedingly difficult (or impossible) to retrieve it.

A period of transition for an organization is usually
also a period of critical reexamination of goals and reasons
for being. Apart from considerations of budget and space,
SGS saw the transition period as an opportunity to reinforce
and reemphasize its primary purpose--the continuing education of adults in the community. [38] It did not conceive its
role as passively responding to "demands" of the adult community. Rather, it made the distinction between "demand"
and "need" and conceived its role as that of stimulating the
"demand" for higher education by developing the awareness
of "need." If SGS were to continue as a separate organization with distinctive purpose and function, it would have to
resolve to reorganize its material and human resources for
the purpose of embarking on a comprehensive campaign to
stimulate interest of prospective students whose backgrounds
and needs come within the ambit of its domain.

Equally important to its commitment to a principle in
higher education, SGS had a deeply felt commitment to itself
as an organizational unit. As Philip Selznick points out in
his Foundations of the Theory of Organizations, the "need of
an organization to perpetuate itself" is profoundly an integral
part of the picture. Implicit in this "need" for self-perpetu-
ation is the commitment to existing students to continue their

education and a commitment to faculty and staff to continue
their job opportunities.   These are all facets of the need
for self-preservation.

A vital condition precedent to the continued existence
of SGS was the ability to preserve its budgetary and space
resources.   If these were permitted to contract or diminish, SGS would effectively be precluded from growth and development in the area of continuing education for adults.   Or,
to put it another way, diminishing student enrollment   had
to be simultaneously restored by new groups in order to
safeguard present budget and, no less significant, allocated
classroom space.   The maintenance of the status quo in budget and space was not, to be sure, an explicitly stated intention. [39]   Nevertheless, the objectives were quite clear.
To achieve the "stated" and "real" intention of expanding
the numbers of adult clientele which constituted its primary
educational concerns, as well as to maintain its own organizational identity, SGS had to, as necessary conditions, assure
the essential fiscal and space resources.

Within the sub-organization, then, there existed a
compelling drive for maintenance.   But within the College,
there was the countervailing pressure upon SGS to contract.
How did the countervailing pressure manifest itself?   What
was the reaction to the pressure?

Action and Reaction

During the 1965-66 academic year, the SGS Policy
Committee continuously included on its agenda as "unfinished
business" the problem of expansion in the area of baccalaureate education for adults, both in the matriculated and non-
matriculated categories.   Alpha Sigma Lambda (the evening
honor society) was encouraged to develop means by which to

alert the adult community to the educational opportunities
available in SGS.   For this purpose the honor society
formed a "Committee on New Students. "   This Committee
wrote press releases and other informational literature and
distributed them to parent-teachers associations, libraries,
religious organizations and other community agencies where
it believed an interested public existed.   The public relations officer of SGS prepared various brochures describing
the nature of existing programs for adults and these were
widely circulated.   Indeed, SGS established a separate Division of Program Development to conceive programs and to
develop implementing measures for attracting prospective
students.

The Policy Committee reviewed the liberal arts curriculum and decided that a streamlined and "packaged" program of studies constructed out of the existing courses would
be more appealing to adults who were indecisive about starting or returning to college.   Entitled the "Basic Program
for Adults, " the aim was to formalize a sequence of studies
within the core curriculum.   As much as possible, related
courses would be integrated, (such as political science and
history), and conducted in small seminar type classes at a
sophisticated adult level.   It was the view of the Policy Committee that specification of a sequence of courses out of the
core curriculum supplemented by integration of related disciplines and supported by seminar techniques did not represent a major change from "the present structure" but "an
approach to the liberal arts curriculum that would be more
meaningful for adults. "[40]   However, the Dean of the Faculties did not so regard the proposal.   Instead, he informed
the SGS Dean that the proposed "Basic Program for Adults"
would be submitted to the Long Term Committee. [41]   Such

referral actually meant that no steps could be taken to develop or to implement it. While the Policy Committee fundamentally disagreed with the Dean of the Faculties, it had no choice but reluctantly to accept his decision.   This adoption of a program designed to expand the adult student enrollment met a road block.   Referral to the Long Term Committee realistically viewed involves a long-term quest in the labyrinth of academic red tape.

A similar experience also involved a proposed program entitled CLEAR (Community Leadership through Education and Responsibility).   The project was conceived and formulated in terms of obtaining a grant of funds under Title I of the Higher Education Act of 1965.   New York State Department of Education officials, in preliminary discussions, evidenced enthusiastic interest in this project.

The central idea was to adapt the existing courses and curriculum in relation to a set of ultimate objectives. These were:

1. To educate adults with leadership potential for responsible community leadership, and

2. To put them on the matriculated track toward the B. A. degree.

Time was of the essence.   The filing of applications for grants to the State under Title I had an early expiration date in February, 1967.   However, the Dean of the Faculties questioned the educational legitimacy of the plan to adapt existing courses to the stated objectives.   The filing deadline expired and regrettably no application could be filed.

The significance of the CLEAR project, as pointed out by SGS, directly related to the question of the role that a university should play in the urban community, especially with respect to the disadvantaged.   Training for Community

Leadership with Education and Responsibility--so that the
disadvantaged can develop the indigenous leadership to help
themselves--was urged as a vital social obligation of the university.   This social obligation, SGS maintained, is not adequately being fulfilled at present.   Awareness of this educational philosophy has since won wide acceptance by deans
and faculties throughout the country.   Brooklyn College's
SGS, while frustrated in developing this significant project,
is nevertheless proud that it was one of its imaginative conceptions.

         To establish a new program is a long and arduous
task. [42]   Quite apart from the necessary committee approvals,
it was the view of the SGS Policy Committee that at the time
the college climate was not favorable to "new" programs in
SGS.   For this was, as has been stated, a period of severe
hardship with respect to space.   Any development which
seemed "expansionist" would undoubtedly, the Policy Committee believed, meet with parent resistance. [43]

         However, SGS administration did not entirely abandon
its objectives.   Rather than invite a direct confrontation with
the Dean of the Faculties and a long, hard struggle with a
variety of college committees, the Policy Committee decided
to utilize existing mechanisms and facilities to make current
programs more attractive to adult students.   It dropped the
title "Basic Program for Adults" and, instead, emphasized
in its printed literature the scope and variety of curricula
available to adults.   It planned extensively to utilize the counseling services to help adults achieve a "sense of direction."
In addition, it emphasized exemption and proficiency examinations as means of accelerating the time within which to a-
chieve the degree.   Further, it planned to create smaller
classes and seminars, wherever possible, specially geared to

groups of adult students.   As described in <u>Accent on Adults</u>
(see note 38), fruit finally began to grow in 1968 on the
SGS tree in Brooklyn.

Pushes and Pulls

The college attitude toward expansion[44] in SGS is
further illustrated in another exchange with the Committee
on Space and Facilities.

In September, 1965, the following item appeared in
the Policy Committee Minutes:

> Discussion was continued on the changing popula-
> tion in SGS and the need to attract the adults in
> the community.   It was also pointed out that the
> SGS at Brooklyn College is the only evening unit
> in the City University that doesn't advertise in the
> newspapers.[45]

In November, 1965, the Minutes of the President's Advisory
Committee on Space and Facilities included this challenging
statement:

> Dean G. opened discussion on the implications of
> the planning in progress by the Policy Committee
> of the School of General Studies regarding "the
> need to attract the adults in the community."   The
> fact that such a move is made without consulting
> with this Committee raises problems of space al-
> locations affecting other programs in the College.
> Following a general discussion of this topic by
> this Committee it was the consensus of the mem-
> bership that Dean G. should consult with President
> Gideonse on this problem.[46]

In its Minutes of December 9, 1965 the Policy Committee
responded:

> It is not yet determined whether <u>additional</u> space
> will be required for the School of General Studies.
> Meanwhile, members of the Policy Committee will
> continue to implement the objectives stated in the
> Master Plan for the City University, which are

strongly supported by President Gideonse in his
Biennial Report, 1963-1965. New programs, as
well as policy decisions to supplement them, have
consistently been cleared with the President. Requests for new space, predicted on expansion in
enrollment will, of course, be cleared with the
Committee on Space and Facilities. [47]

The following excerpts from the President's Biennial
Report, 1963-1965 were appended to the minutes:

There is a large, untapped reservoir of potential
students who are eager to participate in an expanded program designed especially for adults
. . . this is a profitable investment in human
capital and one that will richly repay society . . .
We must, therefore, open our doors to mature
persons--particularly those with potential to score
in the upper percentile of academic performance--
who wish to undertake serious study in college-
level work . . . . Every effort must be made to
improve and enlarge the educational opportunities
for such students. [48]

After quoting from the Master Plan as to the varied educational purposes of SGS and their significance to the community, the President's Biennial Report emphasized the role of
SGS to:

(1) Accommodate a larger number of qualified
candidates in the now well-established Special Degree Program for Adults; (2) Construct a series
of liberal arts credit programs for the continuing
education of women, designed primarily for self-
enrichment, intellectual activity and the cultivation
of critical thinking. (Pages 38, 39.)

The President pointed out that:

The planned withdrawal from the two-year programs
coupled with the growth of upper-division work will
enable our School of General Studies to serve ever
larger numbers of urban residents . . . the school
can function as an important instrument of self-
fulfillment and personal growth for large segments
of the population, and thereby can play a vital role

in strengthening and preserving our national philosophy of equality of opportunity. (Page 39.)

What did not unambiguously appear in the official
documents was that the Space Committee was contemplating
transfer of the classroom, staff and office space used by
SGS to other areas of the College as SGS phased out its two-
year programs.   SGS administration obviously intended to
retain this space for expansion of those programs remaining
and for new programs to be introduced.   It sought particularly to expand its non-matriculant enrollment for those
adults who would, hopefully, be guided, counseled and assisted toward the baccalaureate matriculated track.   To be
sure, many of the adult students whom it sought would, based
on their earlier high school performance, be qualified to
enter at once into fully matriculated status.   Many more,
however, would not have the necessary requirements for admission and would have to enter as non-matriculants.

With this goal in mind, the SGS Dean sought the further support of the President.   In May, 1966, President
Gideonse issued a memorandum addressed to the SGS Dean,
with copies circulated to the Deans of Administration, Faculties, and Studies and to the Business Manager.

> The gradual phasing out of the Associate Degree
> Programs is reflected in the current enrollment
> statistics for Brooklyn College.   Understandably
> these figures will show further decline as matricu-
> lants for the A. A. and A. A. S. degrees complete
> their respective courses of study.   Some of these
> students will be replaced by candidates for the bac-
> calaureate degree.   The Master Plan (Second revi-
> sion, 1966, p. 15) provides that: 'The unique func-
> tion performed by the Schools of General Studies is
> that they offer higher education to citizens worthy of
> the opportunity but unable to meet the conditions un-
> der which the normally qualified day-session en-
> rollee studies. '

To the extent that classroom space and other facilities are available, you are authorized to proceed at once with plans for augmenting SGS enrollment by encouraging qualified non-matriculated
students to enroll in liberal arts credit programs.
In moving in this direction every effort should, of
course, be made to preserve the high standards
of academic performance with which Brooklyn College is identified.

The mandate from the President to "proceed at once
with plans for augmenting SGS enrollment" cleared the air.
But gossip and rumor still had it that the President's action
was based primarily on the College's need for non-matriculated fees and that the aim of SGS to "offer higher education
to citizens worthy of the opportunity" was a secondary consideration.

Once again, pressures had left their mark. SGS
strained under the blow to its pride and status. In contrast
to General Motors, it is embarassing for a sub-organization
in academe to be loved principally for its money!

Pressure from the Board

The multiple position regulations of the Board of Higher Education are an example of a pressure on SGS which is,
in a sense, derivative. Though not primarily aimed at SGS,
its impact is, nevertheless, directly and clearly felt. These
regulations are rules adopted by the Board which apply uni-
formly to all the colleges in the City University. They limit the amount of compensated work which a full-time faculty
member may perform in addition to his primary "regular"
assignment.

While the dominant purpose of the multiple position
regulations is to limit the activities of faculty with respect
to "overtime" work, the unintended consequence is to impose
staffing restrictions upon SGS. For, as has been stated, ap-

proximately 27% of the total teaching in SGS is performed
by personnel from CLAS on an overtime pay basis.   In addition, approximately 80%[49] of the administration of SGS is
performed by CLAS faculty either on a reassigned (or released) time arrangement or on an overtime pay basis or a
combination of both.   There is little doubt that most of
these individuals would not accept the assignments unless
they were coupled with additional compensation.

No comparable arrangement exists in CLAS.   Administrative assignments there, including the elective office
of chairman of an academic department, are an integral
part of the individual's schedule.[50]   From its beginning, SGS
recruited many of its teachers and most of its administrative officers from CLAS ranks and compensated them on an
overtime pay basis.   This practice evolved partly because
there were no SGS faculty lines and partly because the work
was to be done during evening hours.   Evening work is traditionally regarded as "overtime" work in institutions of
higher education except where the major business of the college or university takes place during evening hours.[51]   Since
SGS is dependent on CLAS personnel for part of its teaching
staff and a larger part of its administrative staff, it plainly
has a substantial interest in the regulatory policies and procedures affecting the activities and economic position of
CLAS personnel.

Although the Board had adopted regulations with regard to maximum multiple position hours as early as 1949,[52]
additional impetus was generated for further reduction by a
number of new factors.   The teaching load of the regular assignment was directly linked to the permissible overtime allowance.   On a national level, institutions of higher learning
were generally reducing teaching schedules.   Brooklyn Col-

lege's teaching load was 15 hours per week, a work schedule considered to be high compared with the national norm.
It was argued that the goal of reducing the regular teaching
load was inconsistent with the policy of permitting as many
as 12 hours per week annually as a compensable overload.
Reduction of the regular teaching load, therefore, was tied
in with a reduction in the permissible overtime hours.

Outside Pressures

The Middle States Association of Colleges and Secondary Schools selected the faculty teaching load question for
special comment in 1955.   The Association pointed out:

> The standard teaching . . . is 15 semester hours
> although various devices are used to reduce this
> load for administrative assignments and in some
> instances for research and counseling. We believe
> the teaching load to be too heavy for an institution
> which expects research or creative productivity and
> which offers work of graduate level. . . .[53]

The report continued to state that one of the most
difficult problems faced by the institution was the total load
carried by members of the faculty; that under existing policy
a faculty member could teach 12 additional semester hours
per year (15 with special permission).   The report also
cited "equally liberal" policies with respect to other paid
"outside" (professional, teaching and consulting) employment.

In its recommendations for action at Brooklyn College,
the Association strongly urged ". . . that this matter (teaching load) engage the immediate attention of the College and
of the Board of Higher Education. . . . We believe that the
present 15 hour schedule should be reduced.   It is clear,
however, that any effort to reduce it will have to be accompanied by measures restricting permissible outside employ-

ment.[54]   Otherwise the <u>present imbalance</u> between regularly assigned full-time duties and permissible spare time activities will be increased."[55]

The Long Range Plan

The Long Range Plan for the City University of New
York 1961-1975 endorsed the recommendation made by the
Middle States Association as follows:

> In view of the newly created University status
> which will bring . . . extension of graduate work
> to the doctorate and increased emphasis on re-
> search, it is believed that the future development
> of the University is best served by a gradual re-
> duction in the amount of outside employment by
> the University's teaching staff.

The Long Range Plan for the City University openly
recognized that a reduction in permissible overtime hours
would create considerable strain on SGS.   The Plan, therefore, took cognizance of the relationship between reductions
in multiple position hours and staffing in SGS.   Adjustments
should be gradual, it stated, and be extended over a three-
year period.   The recommendation was that:

> The Board of Higher Education continue its vigorous
> efforts to secure additional lines for the Schools of
> General Studies which will:
>
> a. starting September 1, 1963, permit a maximum of
>   ten (10) hours of multiple job employment* per
>   year to teachers on annual salary in Day Session;
>
> b. starting September 1, 1964, permit a maximum of
>   eight (8) hours of multiple job employment per year
>   to teachers on annual salary in Day Session;
>
> c. starting September 1, 1965, permit a maximum of
>   six (6) hours of multiple job employment per year
>   to teachers on annual salary in Day Session.
>
> d. In some exceptional cases where the educational

needs of the schools of general studies demanded
it, the limit may be extended to twelve (12) hours
of multiple job employment per year for teachers
on annual salaries in the Day Session; furthermore, a full report be submitted by the individual president to the Administrative Council each
semester indicating the names, hours, and reasons for such multiple job employment.

*An hour of multiple job work means one classroom
period per week for a term. For the purposes of
this recommendation, two administrative hours will
be deemed equivalent to one classroom period.

The introductory statement "The Board of Higher
Education continue its vigorous efforts to secure additional
lines for the Schools of General Studies . . ." and the statement in paragraph (d) that "In some exceptional cases where
the educational needs of the School of General Studies demand it . . ." were inserts made after strong representations by the SGS Council of Deans and Directors. The
troublesome impact of the gradual reduction in permissible
multiple position hours on the composition of SGS' staffs was
persistently pointed out by the Council of Deans and Directors in a variety of documents and letters transmitted to Professor Thomas C. Holy, Chief Consultant to the Board, in
connection with the preparation of the "Long Range Plan."

The Complicating Consequences

The Board of Higher Education adopted the multiple
position regulations as proposed in the Long Range Plan.
However, there was strong resistance to the suggested reductions, both in SGS and among those faculty members of CLAS
who had been teaching in SGS. The original twelve hours
per year made it possible for CLAS staff to teach two courses
in SGS each semester, each course consisting of three credit
hours. Since three hour classes in SGS met twice a week,

CLAS faculty members stated that it would not be financially worthwhile to teach just one course each semester. They
could, of course, teach two classes in one semester and
none in the next; but this would complicate department
scheduling; it would moreover require an even greater elas-
ticity of part-time personnel.

An "in one semester--out the next" would create the
need to recruit part-time personnel to work only as replace-
ments for CLAS personnel in those semesters they were
precluded from teaching.   The problem was further compli-
cated by the fact that many departments were changing curricula in the direction of developing four-hour, four-credit
courses instead of three-hour, three-credit courses.   Under
the 12 hour rule a CLAS person could teach two three-hour
classes each term.   Under the 10 hour rule he could teach
two three-hour classes one term and only one three-hour
class the following semester, thus giving him a total of 9
hours of teaching time.   However, he would have to be at
the college during two evenings a week in both semesters.
Under the 8 hour rule he could teach only two three-credit
courses aggregating 6 hours; whether he could do this in one
term or two semesters would be contingent on the department's scheduling possibilities.   In those departments which
had changed to four-hour, four-credit courses, the maximum
he could teach would be two courses a year.   The reduction
in permissible hours, therefore, gave impetus to the staff to
look elsewhere for other opportunities to earn additional
money.   In the sciences particularly, many preferred to--and
did--accept consultant positions at other institutions outside
the city system, preferably in graduate schools, where, although the hours of employment were limited by the regulations, the rates of compensation were considerably higher.

Pressure from the staffs and particularly from the
Schools of General Studies led to the review of the regula-
tions by the Administrative Council and in May, 1964, the
Board of Higher Education adopted the following resolution:

> RESOLVED, that in view of the fact that no new
> full-time positions in the schools of general stud-
> ies became available during the years 1962-63 or
> 1963-64, and none has been allowed for 1964-65,
> the planned year-by-year reduction in maximum
> extra part-time instructional service be frozen at
> the present level of ten hours for one year and
> that the matter then be reviewed annually. [56]

As a partial solution of the staffing problem, additional lines were allocated in September, 1965, to the
Schools of General Studies. In December, 1965, a Board
resolution was adopted reducing the number of permissible
multiple position hours to eight.

Apparently there still seemed to be the need, in the
view of the Administrative Council, for additional confirma-
tion of the policy principle relating to multiple positions. In
part, it stated:

> Primary Commitment. Appointment to a college or
> university faculty position is a full-time assign-
> ment. In addition to classroom teaching, the ap-
> pointee is presumed to engage in committee work,
> conferences, and writing and research, as well as
> other academic and institutional pursuits and serv-
> ices. It is therefore expected that no staff mem-
> ber will engage in any occupation or employment,
> whether for extra compensation or not, which will
> impair the services rendered to the institution or
> interfere with the normal schedule of duty hours
> or unduly burden the working week and year. Each
> member of a faculty has a responsibility to observe
> professional standards of behavior in becoming in-
> volved in supplementary activities. [57]

The policy statement again reiterated that "research, writing
and occasional consulting and lecturing" are considered "ap-

propriate" activities for members of the faculty. In addition, "full-time faculty participating in the doctoral program" are expected not to engage in additional teaching."[58]

As far as SGS was concerned, the most significant portion of the memorandum was the following:

> It is the policy of the university and its colleges to achieve exchanges of services, wherever possible, by budgetary interchange or the balancing of interchanged services, with no additional academic load or extra renumeration for the individuals concerned.[59]

While the general policy was thus stated, the maximum allotment of eight hours (per week) per year, as formulated in 1965 continues in effect. However, the rigors of the rule were considerably relaxed in exceptional hardship cases by liberal interpretations by the Dean of Administration and by the President.

The story of multiple position regulations, their impact on SGS and on the relationship between SGS and CLAS also serves to illustrate how rules designed to achieve a specific purpose in one part of an institutional structure have a different impact on another part. Like a pebble thrown into a pool, the ripples become wider circles as the distance from the center increases. With growing needs for staff coupled with a general scarcity of teachers and administrators, competition for qualified personnel is keen. Limitations imposed on the extent of overtime work for CLAS faculty aggravates an already difficult situation for SGS. The limitation to four hours each semester (or eight hours per year) militates against the incentives to work in the evening. It is rather difficult to persuade a man who teaches during daytime hours to remain on campus for two evenings per week just for a three or four hour course. The alternative is to

recruit personnel from other colleges and universities. But
this alternative is less desirable; CLAS faculty members
provide a connecting link with the day college faculty and administration.

But the greatest difficulty is with faculty in administrative positions. Administrative posts require individuals
with specific types of experience. The remuneration has to
be sufficient to attract such competent and qualified personnel regardless of whether the administrative experience was
gained in CLAS or SGS. When, for example, the multiple
position hours permitted under the regulations were reduced
from 12 to 10, many deputy chairmen threatened to resign.
Some of the departments are so large that at least ten hours
(per week) per semester[60] are required to do the necessary
work of recruiting staff, scheduling of classes, observing new
teachers, planning programs, counseling students, etc. To
some extent, SGS solved this problem by arranging, with
presidential approval, to have four of the ten hours per semester on an "exchange" basis with CLAS. This means that
the individual is "released" from his CLAS assignment for
these hours and SGS reimburses CLAS for this time. The
additional six hours are then compensated on an overtime
basis. When multiple position hours were reduced from
twelve to ten, the SGS Dean requested that the President permit these hours to be prorated over a twenty-week period
and thereby be equated to a somewhat lower overload figure
per week. [61] This equation was based on the fact that administrators do, indeed, start work earlier and finish later in
the semester than do the teaching faculty. The cooperation
of the Dean of Administration and the President in approving
this principle "saved the day"; deputy chairmen, coordinators,
and other administrators continued their assignments in SGS.

Although the number of multiple position hours has since
been reduced to eight, these administrators have been permitted to continue on the revised formula of twenty weeks.

Nevertheless, SGS feels that it is on "borrowed
time," for it must continuously seek Board approval of exceptions for an established policy.   The original theory was
that SGS line personnel would replace CLAS faculty doing
administrative work.   This has not happened for a number
of reasons.   First, there are relatively few SGS lines.   Second, there is a superior need for line faculty to provide a
corps of teachers, not administrators, for SGS students.
Third, perhaps SGS "line" faculty are more capable as teachers than as administrators; or perhaps the department chairmen have simply not chosen SGS personnel as deputies.
Whatever the reason, there are still only three out of a total of twenty-five SGS staff holding the posts of department
deputy chairmen!   This ratio is fairly typical of administrative assignments granted to SGS personnel.

Successive efforts to limit the reduction in multiple
position hours has thus far failed.   Once again what appeared
to be in the best interests of the day college was not necessarily in the best interests of SGS.   While cooperation from
the President and the Dean of Administration averted crisis
in SGS, the stress and strain from the multiple position rule
remain.

The Varieties of Organizational Interaction

It is interesting to speculate as to why conflict or direct confrontation was not the method chosen by the deans
and directors of the Schools of General Studies to nullify the
threat to a large segment of their teaching and administrative
personnel.   Perhaps it was the belief that conflict would re-

sult in defeat, that they could not win this battle in face of the attitude of the accrediting agencies.   Perhaps open conflict is a method only of very last resort in academe.   Perhaps the issue of overtime work limitation is too complex and its relationship to reduced CLAS teaching loads too intimate.   Perhaps the national trend is too strong and the evening college too weak.   The events are reminiscent of Weber's observation that the stream of history goes on "behind the backs of the actors."

Stress and strain are normal conditions in any organization, whether academic, industrial or commercial. One needs only to allude to departmental rivalries and conflicts in the same firm to discern the inevitability of stress and strain.   For example, the quest of an advertising department for a more liberal budget frequently encounters the resistance of the comptroller's office.   Or the wish of a research and development department to engage in certain experimental activities may meet the opposition of the engineering department.   Stresses such as these become magnified when an organization consists of a number of component divisions each of which builds up its own mystique, traditions and aspirations.   The examples cited in this chapter illustrate the realities of stress and strain in an academic sub-unit vis-à-vis its external environment.   These examples are but historical incidents composing a continuous process which, in broad scope, may be characterized as typical in formal organizations.

The several incidents described are illustrative of the interactive process of competition (rivalry for scarce space and personnel resources), contravention (blocking of innovative projects) and conflict (proposed merger of day and evening sessions).   Competition is a process accorded high so-

cial value since Adam Smith's <u>Wealth of Nations</u>. Moreover, competition is so intimately related to a system's
needs for achievement incentives that it is usually accepted
as the norm of risk-taking and efficiency drives.   Contravention usually leads to frustration, but if it is not experienced too frequently or too intensively, it may even create
a constructive fighting spirit.   Conflict, as pointed out by
Coser, often has the effect of inducing and intensifying internal solidarity.   However, if conflict is too threatening to
survival or if success is too remote or too infrequent, it
may have the opposite effect; it may shatter morale and cohesiveness.   Viability depends on the intensity and frequency
of any and all of these processes.

The stresses and strains described in this chapter,
which highlighted the weaknesses of the SGS position vis-à-
vis the parent organization, did not go unnoticed by those on
whose loyalty and morale the success of SGS depends: its
instructional staff.   The theme of the following chapter,
therefore, is the attempt of SGS administration to project a
favorable image to counteract its alleged "second-class citizenship" and the reactions of those for whom the projection
is intended.

Notes

1. Homer D. Babbidge, President, University of Connecticut,
   "The Outsiders; Some Thoughts on External Forces
   Affecting American Higher Education," paper delivered
   at a conference at Syracuse University on <u>Dynamics
   of Change in the Modern University</u>, June 15, 1965,
   p. 1.

2. <u>Ibid.</u>, p. 9.

3. Phillip H. Coombs, Secretary, Fund for the Advancement
   of Education, New York, "The University and its External Environment." (Minico - 1960), p. 3-5.

4. Ibid., p. 6.

5. Philip Selznick. "Foundations of the Theory of Organi-
    zations," American Sociological Review, (1948), Vol-
    ume 13, p. 29-30.

6. Ibid., p. 29.

7. Stanley J. Sarnoff, Physiologist, National Institute of
    Health, as quoted in Time Magazine, November 29,
    1963.

8. George Simmel. Conflict and The Web of Group Affilia-
    tions (Free Press, Glencoe, Illinois, 1955), p. 13-14.

9. Weber's criticism of the Marxian analysis in the devel-
    opment of capitalism is a case in point. Weber's
    thesis of the direct causal relationship between the
    advent of Calvinism and the rise of capitalism has,
    however, amassed its share of criticism too.

10. No doubt accelerated by political and social pressures
    in the City.

11. In most cases, he could not attend day classes even if
    he had those requirements.

12. Discussed in Chapter II, "Organizational Goals."

13. See Chapter II, "Organizational Goals."

14. Board of Higher Education of the City of New York,
    Minutes, April 17, 1950, Cal. No. 25, p. 207.

15. Ibid., p. 207.

16. The examples of the Special Baccalaureate Degree Pro-
    gram (the four-year baccalaureate degree) and the
    Nursing Science Program (the two-year Associate in
    Applied Science degree) illustrate some of the mech-
    anisms of interrelationship between SGS and the varie-
    ties of administrative and faculty roles within the Col-
    lege as a whole. See Chapter III, "Innovation through
    Cooptation."

17. These funds were used throughout the College for cleri-
    cal assistance, student aides and other professional
    and non-professional services not stipulated in the

Mayor's Executive Budget.

18. These non-matriculated students are, however, enrolled in the regular, approved courses and curricula of the College; the curricula and the standards for matriculation are responsibilities of the faculty.

19. "Working Paper" by Dean of Studies of the City University, October, 1963.

20. For September, 1970, the open enrollment policy was adopted in response to community pressures. All high school graduates will be admitted to one of the Colleges of the City University regardless of high school average or test scores. The threat of SGS dissolution has evoked mass protest meetings and demonstrations by SGS students and teaching staff.

21. Ibid., (emphasis added).

22. While somewhat removed from the proximate forces operating on the Schools of General Studies, it must be mentioned here that no small part of the stress on physical plant and facilities as well as on faculty and other personnel was emanating from the City University's policy to encourage growth in graduate programs. University status for the City's colleges carried with it emphasis on graduate programs, including Ph. D. programs which were being developed. While, in the long run, funds were to be secured for these programs in the City budget, in the transition period the major burden of staffing and providing classroom, laboratory and research space fell on the senior colleges campuses. "Working Paper," October, 1963.

23. Among the suggestions were: 1). Use of classroom space by scheduling of Friday evening and Saturday classes; 2). expansion of the Summer Session from six to eight weeks; 3). intensive use of large lectures, closed circuit T. V. and other teaching aids where feasible. "Working Paper."

24. Brooklyn College Newspaper KEN, October 14, 1963, p. 1. It was also reported that President Buell G. Gallagher of City College endorsed the "dawn-to-dark" proposal in the working paper.

25. The working paper had made no specific reference to the Schools of General Studies as such.

26. No essential change was suggested in this group.

27. The category was broken down to include: a) transfer students from other colleges; b) foreign students; c) other persons who give evidence of potential ability; d) mature persons (20 or 21 years of age or over) who give evidence of ability to redeem inadequate backgrounds; and e) persons interested in individual courses or a sequence of courses.

28. "The Schools of General Studies Look to the Future," November, 1963.

29. Ibid.

30. Ibid.

31. Reported in Legislative Conference Minutes, College Newspapers and Faculty meetings.

32. The Community College Presidents had objected to this category because "the proposed SGS pre-matriculant is by definition, the equivalent of the present Community College matriculant. . . . The students they propose to serve are precisely those now being served by the Community Colleges . . . there is ambiguity and lack of significant differentiation in their employment of the terms 'pre-matriculant' and 'non-matriculant'. . . . The proposal continues a dual system for dealing with students with confusion and overlapping." Memorandum of January 21, 1964, from C. C. presidents to administrative Council, re: SGS Directors' paper "The Schools of General Studies in a Master Plan for the City University," p. 1.

33. Master Plan, 1964, p. 80. See also Chapter II, "Organizational Goals."

34. In 1966, the University's senior and community colleges had 56,000 full-time students. President Francis D. Kilcoyne of Brooklyn College pointed out that "We are, in effect, operating with almost 10,000 students squeezed into a plant built for 6,000."

35. Laws of 1966, Chapter 782, Secs. 6278 et seq.

36. Convocation of the School of General Studies, 1964.

37. Applicants whose "averages" are slightly below the requirement for admission as matriculated students in CLAS frequently enter as non-matriculants in SGS with the objective of earning matriculation in college courses.

38. Myrtle S. Jacobson and Deborah Offenbacher. Accent on Adults (Syracuse University, 1970).

39. Amitai Etzioni. Modern Organizations (Prentice Hall, 1964), p. 7. "Goals are always intended; the difference is between stated intentions and real ones."

40. Letter dated March 16, 1966 from SGS Dean to Dean of the Faculties.

41. Letter dated March 16, 1966 from Dean of the Faculties to the SGS Dean.

42. See Chapter III, "Innovation Through Cooptation" for a detailed descriptive analysis of the processes by which new curricula are introduced.

43. This "hunch" was probably correct. A year later, a proposal to introduce a new four-year nursing program, which had strong Presidential endorsement, was postponed for a variety of substantive and procedural reasons.

44. The term "expansion" here is a misnomer. It is more correctly a case of "non-contraction."

45. Minutes of the Policy Committee, School of General Studies, September 30, 1965, p. 620. These minutes are circulated to all administrative officers of the College.

46. Minutes of the Committee on Space and Facilities, November 15, 1965, paragraph 283.

47. Minutes of the Policy Committee, December 9, 1965, p. 638, (Mimeo., emphasis added).

48. "Biennial Report of the President," 1963-65, p. 37, (mimeo.).

49. For example, only three out of twenty-five deputy chair-
    men are SGS faculty.   All of the deputy chairmen,
    including the SGS faculty members are assigned on
    a full or partial overtime pay basis.

50. Additional sums of money have been recently added to
    the salaries of deans, associate deans and assistant
    deans in CLAS.

51. The New School for Social Research in New York City
    is an example of the latter type of organization.

52. The maximum number of hours permitted was 15 per
    annum in 1949, 12 per annum by 1951; 10 per annum
    by 1963; 8 per annum by 1965.

53. Long Range Plan for the City University of New York
    1961-1975, p. 245-246.

54. Ibid. , (emphasis added).

55. Long Range Plan for the City University of New York
    1961-1967, p. 253 (emphasis added).

56. Board of Higher Education, Minutes, May 19, 1964.

57. Approved by Administrative Council, November 23, 1965,
    Calendar #6; recommended to the Committee on the
    City University and the Board, p. 1.

58. Ibid. , (emphasis added).

59. Ibid. , p. 2 (emphasis added).

60. Ten payroll hours; in effect twenty working hours are
    required by administrative rule.

61. For example, 12 hours per week on a 30 week basis
    (two semesters) are equal to 360 hours per year. If
    equated on a 40 week basis, the same 360 hours would
    be considered to be 9 hours per week.

Chapter VI

Image and Identity

Organizations, like individuals, construct self-images
of their nature and character. Often it is a composite, mental picture of what is and what is hoped for, a blending of
the here and now with the vision of the ideal. It is this
idealized image which organizations seek to project to their
internal and external publics.

The phrase "projecting an image" as applied to organizations has become associated with a slick Madison Avenue
approach. Thus Bankers Trust is painted as a "friendly" establishment where all of the employees smile: "You'll find a
welcome at Bankers Trust!" General Electric comes across
as an organization more concerned with scientific and industrial research than with sales or corporate earnings: "Progress is . . . (the) most important product." These images
of commercial good-will or technological development are projected to the general public. But unlike the proverbial man
"who is no hero to his valet," organizations are also keenly
aware that favorable images must be projected for internal
consumption to stockholders, managers, supervisors and workers.

Colleges and universities, too, are deeply concerned
with the institutional image held by many of their publics.
Through a variety of ceremonial, traditional and affective
means, the flavor and character of the institution are projected to the public at large, the academic community, alumni,

253

students, faculty, administrative staffs, private foundations
and governmental agencies.   Thus the "character" of Harvard, Antioch, Reed and Swarthmore can be distinguished
one from the other on the basis of projected images.[1] Each
institution actively seeks to mold the desired images reflect-
ing distinctive identity.

Evening College Images

To gain institutional support for their goals, operating procedures and aspirations, evening colleges, in general,
have a double task of image-making.   Not only must they
sedulously strive to project a favorable image and a positive
identity, but they must also counteract a traditionally-held
negative image of "second-class citizenship." This characterization of inferior treatment is an integral part of the basic vocabulary of evening college deans and directors.   For
example, at annual conventions of the Association of University Evening Colleges and in its publications the depreciating
words "second-class citizenship" are used over and over a-
gain in connection with "shoe-string" financing, inadequate allocation of resources, limitations on policy determination, and
other indexes of less than full recognition as "one among
equals." These views of unequal treatment naturally filter
down to students and staff.

In his 1960 annual report, the evening dean at Brooklyn College pointed out the invidious inferences of low status
that are drawn from "shoe-string" financing.   In a special
section entitled "Handicaps," he expressed objections to "step-
child" treatment and stated that it has "created the impression that the evening college lacks 'status' on the campus;
that its personnel are 'second-class citizens;' and the standards of excellence of the institution as a whole are being com-

promised." The obvious implication is that these impressions of low status, second-class citizenship and inferior
standards are not warranted despite inadequate financing.
Most important is the implication that these negative impressions would be dissipated if the financing were more liberal. [2]

Teaching staff documents similarly reflect concern
with the negative image of the evening college. Typical is
the statement of a group of Hunter College SGS line faculty
members that "the Evening Session, or School of General
Studies is a little understood branch of higher learning.
Those of us on full-time appointments in the evening (session) wish for a greater awareness of what it is that we are
doing and of our reactions to our assignment."[3] Grappling
with the negative image, the Hunter College document continues:

> That the Evening (session) has a large population
> of non-matriculated students has led to the false
> assumption that SGS is a second-rate branch of
> Hunter, that students attending it are inferior, and
> that the full-time faculty teaching in SGS are un-
> fortunately situated. [4]

The copious use of the pejorative words "second-rate," "inferior," "unfortunately situated" reveal the negative image
perceived by these SGS line persons. Significant is the observation that this image is based on false assumptions.

Student publications, too, struggle with the negative
images and frequently engender resentments. For example,
dedication ceremonies for the opening of a new Student Union
Building were held at C. W. Post College in Long Island but
apparently no invitation to participate was extended to any
student representative of the evening division "even at the
last minute with Student Council president, Joe Link, present

in the audience."[5]   While the Dean's reported explanation
was that this was "strictly an oversight" due to the last minute haste of setting up the ceremonies, editorializing is in-
jected in the news item by the statement that many evening
division students "are becoming rather touchy about being
'overlooked' by the college administration, not only in this,
but in other areas, too.   And we agree that EDS should not
be the 'step-children' of the college. . . ."[6]   The theme of
the students runs quite parallel with that of administration
and teaching staff regarding step-child imagery and treatment.

Sometimes evening colleges interpret an unfavorable
decision, though based on rational grounds, as unequal treatment based on a negative stereotype.   An example is the refusal of the Association of College Honor Societies to admit
Alpha Sigma Lambda, the evening college honor society, to
membership in the national Association.   Among the criteria
for admission to the Association was the requirement that student membership in the honor society be based on an outstanding scholastic record of at least sixty credits of work; Alpha
Sigma Lambda admits students on the basis of at least thirty
credits.   Not meeting the minimum credit requirements of
the Association, Alpha Sigma Lambda's application for membership was not granted.   However, the National Councillor
of Alpha Sigma Lambda reported other bases upon which the
application for membership was unfavorably evaluated:

> The majority of A. C. H. S. members think that part-
> time scholarship simply cannot be compared with
> full-time scholarship.   In addition, many A. C. H. S.
> members believe that there is really no need for a
> society such as Alpha Sigma Lambda because they
> think evening students who qualify should apply for
> admission to day school honor societies.   A third
> objection voiced by a few influential members of
> A. C. H. S. is that Alpha Sigma Lambda discriminates
> against day students because it was organized pri-

marily for evening students. [7]

Negative images pervade this evaluation, especially the
doubt expressed as to the justification for the very existence
of an evening college honor society.

Projecting a Positive Image

In common with other evening colleges, SGS at Brooklyn College also faces a dual task, that of counteracting a
negative image and that of projecting a meritorious image.
Support for and approval of its goals, academic standards,
curricula, students, teaching staff and administrative policies depend, to a large extent, upon a favorable image in
the eyes of the parent organization, its faculty and administration.   Budgetary allowances, resource allocations, scope
of authority to define and implement goals are considerably
influenced by the attitudes toward SGS.   The image symbol-
izes these attitudes.   Projection by SGS of a favorable image
is thus of major significance.

The image that SGS endeavors to project to its varied
internal and external publics is, in reality, its own "definition of the situation."   In the words of the SGS Dean, the
sub-organization is "basically a 'first-line' college and, at
the same time, a 'second-chance' school (that offers) expanding opportunities for baccalaureate education of adults, including not only those who are qualified for full matriculation, but those in need of readjustment to academic life."[8]
This terse description of SGS by its Dean as a "first-line"
college giving "second-chance" opportunities to adults is a
self-perception of its quintessence.   The dominant qualities
in this self-perception are excellence (first-line) in the performance of socially useful objectives (second-chances).   It
is this image of excellence and usefulness that SGS seeks to

project.

Many methods are utilized to establish and re-enforce the image of SGS as a separate organization with distinctive purposes, staff and student body.   Public relations
efforts, faculty-student social functions, honors ceremonies,
senior receptions, an evening honors society, an SGS convocation in full academic regalia, faculty conferences, faculty club, all sponsored and/or encouraged by administration, are a few examples.   While many similar events and
functions exist in CLAS and while SGS students and staff are
included, it is, nevertheless, the position of SGS that separate events are necessary.   The primary reason is that all
CLAS functions and social events are performed or held
during daytime hours.   Though SGS staff and students are
invited and included, they cannot realistically attend.

The explicit purpose for special SGS ceremonies and
socials is to give the SGS student and staff member an opportunity to participate during evening hours, usually the
only time they are free to come.   Another explicit purpose,
clearly intended, is to create distinctive functioning entities
for SGS students and staff.   The deliberate design is to re-
enforce identification with SGS, to promote group cohesiveness and esprit-de-corps so essential to effective group functioning.

Public Relations

In 1952, the Dean of SGS, with the approval of the
President, initiated a public relations program.   This was
the first, and only, such office in any of the schools of general studies in the municipal college system.   The purpose
of the office was officially stated:

> . . . to centralize responsibility for all public
> relations efforts in the School of General Studies
> . . . and . . . to secure for the School of Gen-
> eral Studies and its divisions the maximum de-
> gree of understanding and good-will from its pub-
> lics. [9]

The dean was concerned--and so stated unofficially--that
the unique programs in SGS could not be given sufficient
publicity in competition with the college-wide public relations program.   Both the volume of work and the lack of
detailed knowledge of SGS goals and programs precluded
such handling by the College public relations officer.   An
SGS "Coordinator of Public Relations" was, therefore, designated to center attention on SGS as distinct from the other units of the College.

Freshman Orientation, Honors and Senior Receptions

Once a year, entering CLAS students are greeted by
the President of the College during the day; SGS students
are greeted by the President and the Dean of SGS in the
evening.

Mid-semester each year, there is an honors tea held
under the auspices of the Dean of the Faculties for the students who have achieved scholastic distinction and are on
the Dean's Honor List.   All students who have earned hon-
ors--CLAS and SGS--are invited to attend.   Nevertheless,
SGS has its own reception in the evening for SGS students
only.   The Dean of SGS sponsors the event; the Dean of the
Faculties participates by recognizing SGS students on the
Dean's list.

At the close of the academic year, the President of
the College and his wife invite to a reception all students--
CLAS and SGS--who are being graduated with honors or who

have won special awards or scholarships. This event is
well attended by officers of administration, faculty and
staff, who participate in greeting and congratulating students. Although some SGS students attend, a separate Senior Reception, sponsored by the SGS Dean, is held during
evening hours. Both the SGS Dean and the Dean of the
Faculties, as well as other SGS officers of administration,
recognize students in formal and official ceremonials.

Annual Convocation

In March of each year, SGS holds an annual Convocation. It is a "full dress" academic ceremonial in which
officers of administration, deputy chairmen, coordinators
and full-time SGS faculty join in a processional in full academic regalia. All SGS students and staff are invited to
attend. Classes scheduled during convocation hours are dismissed and attendance is required for all students and staff
who have class schedules for that evening. The President
is usually the principal speaker of the evening.

Convocation is distinctly an SGS function. There is
no similar CLAS ceremonial. The SGS Dean customarily
addresses the audience on the theme of SGS, selecting news-
worthy topics from programs, student attainments, and institutional progress, problems or achievements.

Alpha Sigma Lambda

Alpha Sigma Lambda is a national evening college
honor society. Its scholastic standards are at least equal to
or perhaps higher than those of Phi Beta Kappa. The organization was originally fostered at Brooklyn College by SGS
officers of administration, a small group of whom formed
the charter membership. This honor society, which now has

student and alumni leadership, was nurtured and encouraged by SGS administration throughout its history.   The basic purposes are to provide leadership for the evening college student and the evening college movement.   Although SGS students are eligible (and many are elected) to Phi Beta Kappa, CLAS students are not eligible for membership in Alpha Sigma Lambda.

Staff Conferences

The SGS staff conference, consisting of faculty and staff, is held annually.   Its purpose is the exchange of ideas between administration and faculty as well as among faculty in the various disciplines.   Representatives of the part-time teaching staff are also invited.   Subjects have ranged from "Levels of Academic Achievement" and "Teaching Effectiveness" to "The School of General Studies in the Urban Community" and "Projecting the SGS Image."

The Dean views the Staff Conference as a contribution to SGS esprit de corps and states:

> The success of our (recent) Staff Conference argues that occasionally bringing the group together not only builds morale, but helps to crystallize-- if not solve--the problems that confront us. [10]

A cocktail party which usually follows the working and talking sessions helps, too.

Faculty Club

Although the SGS Faculty Club is essentially a faculty and staff voluntary organization, it has been encouraged and supported by administration.   Regular weekly teas are scheduled in the evenings in order to enable members of the staff to meet with their colleagues.   Special events--such as Convocation, Senior Reception, the Christmas Party, and Spring

Festival--receive the full support of the Club and help to
encourage a greater "sense of belonging" among the teaching personnel.   The Faculty Club has also sought to foster
social and professional fellowship among staff members.
Leadership constantly seeks to involve more members of
the staff in active committee and planning roles in the affairs of the club.

In addition, department meetings for SGS staff are
held by deputy chairmen during evening hours and special
SGS committees are appointed by the Dean to deal with a
multiplicity of matters in which SGS has a concern.   In
many instances these committees perform functions similar
to their CLAS counterparts, even though their titles are not
the same.   The theme, however, is always SGS.   The mel-
ody may be student activities, faculty-student relations,
scholarship, teaching effectiveness, aims and programs, or
it may be as broad as planning for revision of the Master
Plan of the City University as it pertains to SGS.

Over and over again, the attempt to construct, foster
and project an individual SGS identity for students and staff
is evident.

The self-perception is extensively revealed in the
SGS Staff Handbook which was written by an SGS staff member and distributed to all teaching and administrative personnel.   Content and form were approved by the SGS officers of administration.   As an instrument to project a favorable image, the Handbook was also widely circulated to
CLAS faculty and administration, to members of the Board
of Higher Education and to officers of administration of the
grandparent City University.   Under the bold heading "What
We Are," SGS is rendered in the following hues and colors:
We hope that the classical scholars among you

will forgive us if we describe the School of General Studies as Plato described democracy:
". . . a charming form of government, full of variety and disorder, and dispensing a sort of equality to equals and unequals alike. . . ."

Variety is probably our greatest wealth. . . .
Among our more than 10,000 students are young,
old, poor and rich of every race, religion, interest, and talent, with every sort of educational
background. . . .

We can offer something of value to each of these
students because we are committed to certain
ideas:

> that formal liberal arts curriculum is only one
> of the many kinds of programs properly called
> higher education;

> that age and job and home responsibilities
> should not necessarily bar a student from get-
> ting an education any more than lack of money;

> that those who need a second chance for educa-
> tion or a first chance late in life should be al-
> lowed to prove themselves;

> that academic standards must not and need not
> be sacrificed for our very special student body.

It should be clear by now that the School of General Studies is in no sense a replica of the College
of Liberal Arts and Sciences. It requires the
same academic standards, but in other ways it is
unique. Disorder? Or perhaps vitality. [11]

Image and Marginal Status

Like the marginal man exposed to two cultures simultaneously, SGS holds one status in the fellowship of evening
colleges and another status as a sub-unit of its own parent
institution. In the community of evening colleges, SGS enjoys a high reputation as an innovative, imaginative, efficient organization with high standards of academic excellence

and effectiveness.   Repeatedly over the years, the SGS
Dean and his associates have been invited to recount their
experiences and techniques to national and regional meetings
of the Association of University Evening Colleges, to the National University Extension Association, to the Center for the
Study of Liberal Education for Adults and to many other
professional groups.   Visiting teams from colleges and universities all over the United States and foreign countries
constantly visit SGS each year to learn about its curriculum,
students, teaching staff and administrative organization.
The Special Baccalaureate Program for Adults as well as
many of its two-year programs have served as models for
other evening and many community colleges.   In short, SGS
ranks high in the community of evening colleges.

However, the status of SGS is more precarious in
its home institutional setting dominated as it is by the larger, day college.   On its own campus, SGS is not one of a
group of like organizations sharing similar characteristics
and joined by a community of interests; rather it is a subsidiary unit that is judged by the criteria and norms of the
dominant unit regardless of differences in student body,
teaching and administrative staffs and curricular approaches.
While SGS regards itself as an integral part of Brooklyn
College offering the same baccalaureate degree, it nevertheless asserts claims to individual identity and rights to be
evaluated on individualized criteria appropriate for an evening college.   While the criteria may not be precisely the
same as those for CLAS, they may still be equivalent in
quality.   Thus in 1954, the SGS Committee on Aims and Objectives stated:

> Our problems are somewhat different from those
> that are agitating faculties elsewhere, for in our

> relations to the College of Liberal Arts and Sci-
> ences, we are like a chick following the footsteps
> of the mother hen.   Should we follow closely be-
> hind; turn when she turns, stop when she stops,
> or should we strike out in new self-determined
> directions?

Since 1954 SGS attempted to "strike out in new self-
determined directions" but these had to be molded into the
CLAS normative structure.   When SGS administration claims
that it is not identical with CLAS but is equivalent in academic standards, the day faculty and administration continue
to question the validity of this claim.   Regardless of the ap-
propriateness of day college criteria to SGS operating policies and innovative aspirations, CLAS continues to judge it
by these criteria.   Marginal status is thus accentuated as
SGS struggles for its distinct identity as an evening college
while retaining its identification as a valued unit of Brooklyn
College.

Image and Academic Standards

A major factor determining the image of SGS held by
day faculty and administration is the level of SGS academic
standards.   The level of such standards is obviously a critical issue because the reputation of the whole institution is
directly affected by them.   The crux of the issue is how to
evaluate the SGS standards.   Must they be identical with day
standards or may they be different, yet equally valid, in
view of the age range, maturity, motivation and needs of the
evening student?

The Deputy Commissioner of Education of the State
of New York critically questioned whether day and evening
programs should be identical in light of the marked dissimilarities in student bodies. [12]   Indeed, in speaking of institu-

tions which claimed to have the same courses and standards
for day and evening, he commented that he has "never evaluated an evening program where this statement has been
proved to any one's satisfaction in any convincing manner."
His position was that identity of standards was not the answer but rather that of _valid_ academic standards.   Essentially this is the view of SGS administration in common with
evening colleges administrators generally. [13]

The concept of _valid_ rather than _identical_ standards
involves a difficult problem of measurement.   Is a course in
mathematics specially adapted for technical students inferior
to one for liberal arts students solely because of differences
in scope and content?   Is a basic course in the natural sciences intended for students not majoring in that field of questionable quality because it is not identical with the more intensive science course designed for students majoring in the
discipline?   Seldom are such differences made the subject of
doubt on grounds of academic standards because the tailoring
of the particular course is in terms of student and instructional objectives.   Evening colleges assert that what is true
of individual courses is equally true of a total course of
study.

Since it is difficult to measure academic standards
comparatively, evaluators have focussed on the more measurable datum of the academic aptitude of evening college and
extension students.   According to a study of several universities made by Sorenson of the University of Minnesota:

> A comparison of the measured mental abilities of
> extension and non-extension students of a number
> of universities indicates that they are approximate-
> ly equal.   In some institutions the residence stu-
> dents are superior, and in others the extension stu-
> dents rank higher; but on the average the two groups
> may be considered about equal. [14]

In a comparative study of student aptitudes at the
University of Buffalo, similar findings that "there is not a
great difference in college aptitude" between day and evening students was reported. [15] The grading standards of
evening instructors were also studied. Though wide variations were found, "these variations are no wider than those
found in the campus divisions of the University. Therefore,
it is concluded that standards in both divisions are essentially the same." [16] Another study at the University of
Rhode Island compared the scholastic aptitudes of 68 extension students and 119 on-campus freshmen--both groups degree candidates in business administration. [17] No significant difference was found between the two groups in the
mean scores on the American Council on Education psychological examination. However, the extension students attained higher scores on the Cooperative Reading Comprehension examinations. The conclusion of the study was cast in
an a fortiori form that "since any differences which did exist between the two groups on these tests seemed to be in
favor of the extension students, it might be assumed that
(they) . . . were capable of doing college level work."

If the evening and extension students have the scholastic ability to meet the academic standards of the larger
institution, then the issue resolves itself to the question
whether the standards of the day and evening colleges must
be held congruent. Contrary to the view of evening college
administrators that academic standards may be validly equivalent though not identical with the day college, day faculty
and administration draw an inference of inferiority if academic standards differ. It is this inference that adds to the
negative image of SGS. Thus in 1966 the College Committee
on Course and Standing submitted to the SGS Dean a proposed

memorandum on "Comparability of SGS and CLAS Grading
Standards" prior to circulation to Department Chairmen and
Deputy Chairmen. In it the committee stated that four departments (out of a total of twenty-three) "presented objective evidence indicating wide discrepancies in grading standards."[18] Adding that "although members of the remaining
departments had no similar objective evidence to present,
the consensus of their impressions was in agreement."[19]
The source of these impressions appeared to be comparative
images of SGS and CLAS students: ". . . the major cause
for different grading standards undoubtedly lies in the lower
ability level of the average SGS student compared to that of
the average CLAS student."[20]

In his response to the memorandum of the Committee, the SGS Dean questioned the completeness of the data
on which the "underlying assumptions and conclusions" of
the committee were based.[21] "Thus, to speak of the 'lower
ability level' of SGS students," he declared, "it too sweeping in character unless supported by adequate evidence."
Recognizing that the Committee's conclusions were rooted in
a negative image of the SGS students, the SGS Dean emphasized that while he desires "to confront the problem squarely with the evidence on hand," at the same time he is eager
"to protect the School of General Studies against statements
that might prejudge the issues involved."[22]

The SGS Dean's request that the issues not be pre-
judged and that adequate evidence be adduced to support the
allegations that "lower SGS grading standards" prevail because of "the lower ability level of the SGS student" was
equally directed to the addendum of the committee which
stated:

> The committee is prepared to state <u>unequivocally</u>
> that grading standards in SGS and CLAS should
> be <u>identical</u>. Thus the number of correct an-
> swers on a multiple-choice examination, ability to
> supply one-word answers to fill blanks, and simi-
> lar objective criteria should be the same for a
> 17-year old freshman and a 40-year old freshman.
> . . . Since <u>insight and experience</u> are not subject
> to <u>such</u> methods of measurement, the Committee
> declares them to be <u>irrelevant</u>, or at least <u>too</u>
> <u>subjective to be considered seriously.</u> [23]

Having asserted unequivocally "that grading standards
in SGS and CLAS should be identical," the Committee then
declared that "Equivalence of SGS and CLAS standards probably cannot be attained until SGS <u>admission standards</u> become comparable with CLAS standards."[24] But the words
"equivalence of SGS and CLAS standards" as used by the
Committee really mean "identity of SGS and CLAS standards" and it is this requirement which SGS administration
challenges. Indeed, the suggestion that SGS admission standards "be comparable with CLAS standards" so that "grading
standards in SGS and CLAS . . . be identical" is directly
contrary to the purpose and spirit of SGS. Different admission policies and different grading standards of equivalent
quality are inherent in the statement of purpose and characterization of SGS in the Master Plan:

> The unique function performed by schools of gener-
> al studies is that they offer higher education to
> citizens worthy of the opportunity but unable to
> meet the conditions under which the normally quali-
> fied day-session enrollee studies. . . .
>
> Such citizens, given the opportunity to enroll in
> college-level courses, are as valuable and impor-
> tant to society as are the young high school gradu-
> ates beginning their college careers. [25]

CLAS insists on monolithic academic standards, in all

probability, because there is no simple method of measuring
whether academic standards that are different from those of
the day college are higher, lower, or on par.   As a result,
unfortunately the debate centers on the image of the student.

Comparability of Admission Standards

Variations in CLAS and SGS admission standards in
reality reflect fundamental differences in educational policy.
As a public, tuition-free institution, CLAS must legally base
its admission standards on identifiable objective facts.   Many
subjective standards that are normally accessible to private
institutions are just not legally feasible for public institutions.   Since the high school average together with the scores
on a nationally uniform examination, such as the Scholastic
Aptitude Tests, are generally recognized as reasonably valid
objective criteria, these form the bases for admission as a
matriculated student to the day college.   The same entrance
conditions are required for admission as matriculants in the
evening college.

However, there are broader conceptions of the proper role that a public institution in an urban community should
play.   Unless more flexible entrance standards are introduced, this broader social role cannot be performed.   Opportunities to the economically threatened, to those who were by-
passed in former years, to the culturally and economically
deprived and to the scholastically challenged were properly
conceived as appropriate roles of the Schools of General Studies.   For many of these lacking the usual entrance requirements, SGS was conceived as the locus where an individual
not fully qualified for admission could receive a fair chance
to realize new aspirations in a rapidly changing society.   Particularly in recent years, it was recognized that the wide-

spread advances in technology and automation were rendering old occupational skills obsolete. In addition, national
needs for trained personnel were sharply increasing. Adaptation to these dynamic changes required retraining and more
intensive explorations of human capabilities. In sweeping
terms, these are second-chances for new career adjustments
that the Schools of General Studies had to provide.

From a broader sociological point of view, the open-
ness of a society is seriously restricted if college education
is accessible solely to those who have performed adequately
in high school. Individuals gain in maturity at different rates.
High school years alone are not the exclusively magical years
constituting the final and decisive test of human potential.
The second-chance to the late-bloomer, to the wiser and more
sober adult, to the dreamer of a better and more fruitful life,
is the rationale for the SGS non-matriculated category in SGS.
Not to recognize the legitimacy of such provisional category
and to reject it in favor of an exclusive priority to an "intellectual elite" would be tantamount to turning the clock back to
a more closed society.

In academic terms, what does the second-chance
really mean? Simply it is the opportunity to earn matriculation through achieving a better than average scholastic record
in college courses during a limited probationary period. Current college regulations provide that a non-matriculated student may achieve full matriculation if, in two or three semesters, he attains a "B" average in at least fourteen credits in
an approved program of study. Alternatively, such full matriculation may be earned if in the first thirty or more credits
the scholastic index is 2. 75, the equivalent of a "B" minus
average.

No doubt the second-chance students of SGS are di-

verse and varied. Though the associate degree programs
are now being transferred to the community colleges, the
enrollment trends are clearly in the direction of a larger
proportion of more mature adults enrolled in liberal arts
programs.   This trend, rather than reducing the diversity,
tends to accentuate the diversity even more.

    SGS enrollment in the liberal arts areas, classified
by student status, reflects this marked diversity.   Indeed, it
is this multiplicity of student status that portrays the robust-
ly variegated character of SGS.   In effect, it is to this character that the CLAS Committee on Course and Standing looked
with a dim view when it stated that "Equivalence of SGS and
CLAS standards probably cannot be attained until SGS admission standards become comparable with CLAS standards."[26]

    The variety of student classifications in liberal arts
in the Fall, 1966, semester is typical:

SGS Enrollment - Fall 1966

Matriculated Students:

B. A. candidates in SGS	2, 005	
B. A. candidates from CLAS (on permit)	1, 203	
A. A. candidates in SGS[27]	2, 183	
Total Matriculated		5, 391

Non-Matriculated Students:

Holders of B. A. degrees	684	
Insufficient records filed	1, 149	
Admission standards inadequate	810	
SGS poor scholarship probations	408	
CLAS poor scholarship probations	162	
Total Non-Matriculated		3, 213
Total Liberal Arts Enrollment		8, 604

Of primary significance is the fact that about 3, 892
students or 45% of the student body were either fully matriculated for the B. A. degree or already held the baccalaureate degree.   Of these 3, 892 students, approximately
1, 203, though enrolled in CLAS, preferred also to take
courses in SGS for a variety of personal, job or other reasons.   Over 25% or 2, 183 of the students were matriculated students enrolled for the Associate in Arts degree
who, during the continuing phasing-out period, were still
striving to attain matriculation through superior scholastic
achievement in college courses.   Thus only about 30% of
the total of 8, 604 liberal arts students could be validly classified as non-matriculants.   It is on this small segment
that the negative student image of SGS is based.

Further analysis, however, indicated that this 30%
is not a homogeneously low level student.   The specific
categories have to be more clearly identified.   One-third of
them, or a total of 1, 149, happened to be classified as non-
matriculants simply because their high school or other college credentials were not received by the Registrar within
the required deadline dates to permit evaluation of status.
In the absence of such evaluation, they were automatically
classified as non-matriculants.   Less than one-third of the
total of 30%, or a total of 810 students, did have their records evaluated and were, therefore, properly classified in
the non-matriculated category.   Thus only 10% net of the
non-matriculants, a total of 810 students, did not fully meet
the scholastic requirements for full matriculation.   But it is
also noteworthy that within this overall non-matriculated category were 408 SGS students placed on probation for poor
scholarship and 162 CLAS students similarly placed on probation but consigned to SGS for that purpose.   In large

measure, this small number of CLAS "rejects" placed on
probation in SGS coupled with the opportunity for scholastic
redemption there on limited programs involves a particularly stinging stigma used against SGS.   It is characterized as
the "dumping ground" for CLAS failures.   Middle States Association insightfully alluded to this stigma when it ironically observed "that the 'penalty' connotation seems almost inescapable and it seems as a means of keeping the day program academically 'pure'." [28]

It is, of course, true that less than 50% of the non-
matriculants succeed in gaining full matriculation.   But significant it is that this attrition rate is not appreciably higher than the national average of college drop-outs.   Even as-
suming that this SGS attrition, though in conformity with national norms, is abnormally high, the evidence is by no
means conclusive that SGS academic standards are inferior.
Quite the contrary; the inference is equally valid that the
high attrition rate is convincing proof of high academic standards.   If academic standards were really lower, the attrition rate would be lower.   It is thus doubtful logic to infer
low academic standards solely on the basis of a high attrition rate among second-chance students.   The only necessary
implication is that many second-chance students do not succeed in the second chance.   Yet it is this unhappy implication that, in large part, is responsible for the poor image
of SGS.

The fact that the SGS attrition rate is higher than that
of CLAS is still an insufficient justification for the negative
image of SGS.   Students admitted as matriculants to CLAS
are the so-called "cream of the crop."   As a matter of statistics, a very low drop-out ratio should be expected.   Nevertheless, CLAS drop-outs do occur for many reasons: poor

orientation, poor adjustment, poor selection of courses, emotional conflicts, boy meets girl and other factors. Despite these impediments, the "cream of the crop" should statistically evidence a performance curve quite heavily skewed in the direction of high achievement.

SGS student body, on the other hand, represents more nearly the random sample of the college-going population. Its achievement distribution should more nearly fit a normal curve. Hence a higher ratio of failures. But it is upon this inadequate interpretation of statistical probabilities that the SGS image of inferiority is fashioned!

Image and Perception

The day faculty has been quite articulate in expressing doubts about the quality of SGS students, admission standards, grading practices, and, in general, comparability with monolithic CLAS academic standards. Indeed, the doubts question the feasibility or even possibility of a unit which is a "second-chance" school and at the same time a "first-line college." The CLAS view of SGS has been openly expressed in the action of committees as well as in the comments and actions of individual CLAS teachers and administrators.

While SGS administration has persistently attempted to project a favorable image, the SGS faculty and staff has, however, been far less articulate. For the purpose of ascertaining how the SGS teacher perceives his role, the students, the working conditions, the problems and challenges, a questionnaire was distributed to all members of the SGS instructional staff. [29] Responses were received from 258 staff members, representing 48% of the total staff. That these respondents constitute a representative sample is evi-

dent by the fact that the distribution of respondents, classified by position and title in SGS, corresponds almost exact-
ly to the percentages of these titles in the total SGS staff.

Table I

Percentage Comparison of Total Staff & Respondents

	% of Total Staff (N=600)	% Responding to Questionnaire (N=268)
SGS Line	13	13
CLAS Faculty	27	26
Lecturers	60	61

Characteristics of Students

Since much of the day session criticism had centered
around the characteristics of students in SGS, the first part
of the questionnaire was designed to determine how SGS staff
perceived its own students and, comparatively, how, in the
opinion of this staff, they differed from typical day students.
The questions regarding students were structured.   Prior to
the preparation of the questionnaire, a pilot survey of twenty-
five faculty members, chosen at random, was made to ascertain those characteristics which they believed best described
their students.   From these the most frequent were selected
and a list of sixteen characteristics was utilized in the questionnaire.   Included in the list of "characteristics" of students were "unprepared for college" (to test the allegation
that admission standards were too "loose"); "well-prepared
for classes"; and "hardworking" (to test the often voiced criticism that evening students simply do not do assignments "because they have no time").

"Off-campus lecturers presumably had little, if any,
contact with Brooklyn College CLAS students.[30]   Hence to

discover whether quality differences were perceived between
SGS students as compared to "typical full-time college students enrolled in day classes," specific reference in the
questionnaire to Brooklyn College CLAS students was avoided.

The two questions were in the following form:

1) Below is a series of terms which have been used
   by instructors to describe students. Please select
   those terms which you think best describe typical
   full-time college students enrolled in day classes.
   Please check.

2) Below is a series of terms which have been used
   by instructors to describe students. Think of the
   characteristics of the School of General Studies
   student body as you perceive it from your own experience here. Please select those terms which
   you think best describe SGS students. Please
   check.

As was anticipated, there were a greater number of
checks on the characteristics of SGS (1, 323) than on those of
full-time day students (835). Obviously, respondents reacted
with greater certainty to the characteristics of the students
they teach and, therefore, know better. The average number
of checks per questionnaire on SGS students was 4. 95 as compared to 3. 12 for full-time day students. [31]

Out of the total of 268 respondents, the percentage of
teachers that affirmatively noted each characteristic of SGS
students and full-time day students appears in Table II below.
The percentage points of difference in responses between the
two is shown in the third column.

Here are the terms which best describe the SGS student, listed in descending order of significance: mature
(54. 8%); having a respect for learning (50. 7%); over-anxious
about grades (49. 6%); challenging to instructor (42. 5%); responsibly adult (42. 1%); highly motivated (41. 7%); tired (38. 8%).
Lowest on the scale are these characteristics: well-prepared

Table II

Characteristics of Students
Responses (in percentages)

Characteristics	SGS Students	Full-time Day Students	% Points of Difference
Mature	54. 8	4. 1	50. 7
Respect for learning	50. 7	24. 6	26. 1
Over-anxious about grades	49. 6	50. 7	1. 1
Challenging to instructor	42. 5	30. 2	12. 3
Responsibly adult	42. 1	4. 1	18. 0
Highly motivated	41. 7	27. 6	14. 1
Tired	38. 8	1. 8	37. 0
Vocationally oriented	38. 0	28. 7	9. 3
Hardworking	35. 0	25. 3	9. 7
Unprepared for college	24. 6	11. 5	13. 1
Confused about goals	18. 6	37. 3	18. 7
Well-prepared for classes	17. 5	16. 7	. 8
Complacent	13. 0	16. 4	3. 4
Analytical	10. 4	10. 8	. 4
Fearful	9. 7	13. 8	4. 1
Rigid	5. 9	7. 4	1. 5

for classes (17. 5%); complacent (13. 0%); analytical (10. 4%); fearful (9. 7%); and rigid (5. 9%). In contrast are the terms which best described full-time day students: over-anxious about grades (50. 7%); confused about goals (37. 3%); challenging to instructor (30. 2%); vocationally oriented (28. 7%); highly motivated (27. 6%); hardworking (25. 3%). He is not considered to be either responsibly adult (4. 1%) or mature (4. 1%), but neither is he tired (1. 8%) or rigid (7. 4%).

Comparing SGS students with full-time day students, the following conclusions may be reasonably reached. In the opinion of SGS teachers:

  1. The SGS student is far more mature and more responsibly adult than the day student.

2. The SGS student is much more tired.

3. The SGS student has a greater respect for learning.

4. Both SGS and day students are equally over-anxious about grades.

5. The SGS student is more highly motivated but also less prepared for college than the day student.

6. While both SGS and day students are confused about goals, considerably more day students are confused about goals.

Working in SGS

The heterogeneous student body presents special problems for teachers; they are called upon to teach and to evaluate students at both ends of the academic ladder. This wide spectrum of students is challenging but, at the same time, difficult and often discouraging. In addition, day standards of evaluation are the "norm" at the college; evening standards as such are nowhere explicitly defined. [32] In order to elicit the views of the teaching staff as to "what they like best and what they like least about teaching in SGS," open-end questions were posed on those terms.

With respect to what he likes best about teaching in SGS, 46% of all responses centered on the type of student body, including maturity and motivation, diversity of background, and degree of appreciation. In this category, type of student body, there was minimal mention of student performance or achievement, except to characterize and contrast the "very good" with the "very poor." Half, or 23%, indicated that the enjoyment and challenge of teaching was what they "liked best." Only 19% of all comments were in the domain of working conditions. Some typical comments follow:

What I like best about working in SGS:

1. Type of student body (46%):

    A. Maturity and motivation of students.

       "Students are mature and well motivated."

       "Dedicated group of students well aware of opportunity who try to make the most of it."

       "Mature and serious minded students who realize the importance of learning."

    B. Diversity of student body.

       "Rich and varied background of students."

       "Wide spectrum of students. Good are more challenging. Poor are poorer and need more help."

       "Challenge of dealing with great variety of students."

       "By and large students are mature, serious, intelligent, whose varied interesting background makes class stimulating."

    C. Appreciative students.

       "Students' appreciation of a good course."

       "Appreciation of a job well done under more difficult conditions."

2. Enjoyment and challenge of teaching (23%):

       "I enjoy teaching."

       "Feeling of helping others most gratifying."

       "Challenging experience to work with students who are making many sacrifices to pursue a college education."

       "The chance to help students toward a college degree who otherwise would be unable to obtain one."

"Teaching students with deficiencies who are working hard to overcome them."

"It is somewhat depressing and not very stimulating to teach the type of student at the freshman
level, as the average is not as good as for day
people. Nevertheless, it is a challenge which
must be met."

3. Working conditions (19%):

A. Freedom

"Class is my own."

"Less pressure than day session."

"Free to vary course content and methods."

"Absolute free environment for pursuit of learning."

B. Hours and pay

"Convenient hours."

"The only time I can teach and still carry on my
regular program."

"The money."

"Supplement to my income."

C. The administration

"Cooperative administration and staff."

"Working with administration which is anxious to
make SGS as good a school as it can possibly be."

With respect to what the teacher liked least in SGS,
in contrast to what was liked best, the type of student body
is less significant than the working conditions. Considerations such as pay, hours, lack of job security, status of
SGS and other facilities and conditions under which the teach-

ing is performed loom large. Of all comments, 40% centered on working conditions; 33% of all responses were on type of student body. Some typical comments are:

What I like least about working in SGS:

1. Working conditions (40%):

   A. Hours and pay

   "Night work."

   "No free evenings."

   "Lateness of scheduling of last class."

   "Comparatively low salary."

   "Salaries not on a par with CLAS."

   "Inadequate compensation and recognition for equal work done under more difficult conditions."

   B. Status of SGS

   "Two sets of standards, one for CLAS the other for SGS, with the lower ones for SGS."

   "Second-class citizenship atmosphere."

   "The way the 'powers that be' treat the SGS."

   "Need to be on the alert to defend second-class evening students and staff."

   C. Tenure and security

   "Lack of tenure; in effect rehired each term."

   "After twenty-one years still as insecure as in first year."

   D. Other

   "Insufficient time for contact with students."

"Lack of opportunity to meet with and discuss problems with colleagues."

"No office space."

"Classes too large."

"True college environment lacking, causing lack of spirit and morale."

2. Type of student body (33%):

   A. Preparation and quality of student body.

   "Low level of preparation and basic deficiency in fundamentals."

   "Excessively large numer of students unprepared for college."

   "Generally lower caliber of students than in day school."

   "Non-matriculated students who are not qualified for college."

   "Some students, not prepared for college, slow down class."

   B. Heterogenity of student body.

   "Tremendous range of background and ability of students."

   "Too wide a diversity among students creates unfair burdens on both students and teachers in terms of growth of students."

   "Negative aspects of heterogeneous group. When good--very, very good; when bad--awful."

   "Lack of homogenity in intellectual capacity of matriculated vs. non-matriculated students, with the resultant lowering of standards."

   C. Tired student body.

   'Dealing with overtired individuals who require

extra motivation."

"Students tired and lack time and energy for extra-
curricular activities, library assignments, etc."

A comparison between the responses to what is liked
best and least indicates that while to some the diversity of
the student body provides a challenge and stimulation in the
teaching process, to others the heterogeneity creates unfair
burdens, is a negative element in the teaching and learning
process and results in the lowering of standards. Further,
those who included type of student in what was liked least,
emphasized "lack of preparation," "low calibre" and "deficiency in fundamentals." The statements that the students
are overtired merely confirmed the high percentage of response to the term "tired" (38.8%) in the first structured
question on student characteristics.

With respect to working conditions, many comments
simply added emphasis to those problems with which administration has been grappling, i.e., low salaries and lack of
job security (tenure) for evening part-time staff. It was also no surprise to learn that the image of "second-class citizenship" and lack of status as compared to CLAS are problems with which staff is deeply concerned. The factors of
"no office space," "classes too large," "insufficient time
for contact with students," etc., are "gripes" which abound
in day colleges as well; they are certainly not unique to the
School of General Studies, nor any more pronounced because
of the sub-unit relationship of SGS to the parent College.

The Most Important Problem

The responses to the open-end question "In my opinion, the most important problem the School of General Studies of Brooklyn College faces today is . . ." underscored

the views expressed in the two preceding questions about what was liked best and least about working in SGS. The caliber of the students, their lack of preparation for college and for specific courses were the most important considerations. Following closely a concern was expressed for selection of student body, standards of admission, the heterogeneous quality of such body, etc. Apparently, SGS teachers are impressed with the maturity, the respect for learning, the motivation, etc., of the SGS student. However, they are, at the same time, seriously concerned about his ability to perform, his lack of time for preparation of course materials and study.

The identity of SGS, the need to develop and preserve its unique quality and its "difference from CLAS" was also deemed to be a significant problem. This is undoubtedly linked to the concern for "status" of SGS. Caliber of staff was also an important problem as were working conditions such as pay, hours, lack of tenure, absence of retirement rights, and other status privileges.

The following table presents in descending order of dominant significance, the percentage of total responses to the inquiry of the most important problem. [33]

It is interesting to note the frequency with which comparisons with CLAS are manifested. They appear most distinctly with respect to caliber of students (17. 9%), selection of students (16. 4%), identity (12. 2%), quality of staff (11. 9%), working conditions of staff (10. 0%), particularly pay and tenure. Sensitivity to "inferior" status of SGS (9. 3%) also is important.

Table III

Problems in SGS
Responses (in percentage)
N=268

Problem	% of Respondents
Caliber of students	17. 9
Selection of student body	16. 4
Identity; need to define purpose, identity, function, preserve difference from CLAS, autonomy, separate administration.	12. 2
Quality of staff, SGS needs better staff, incompetent mediocre, etc.	11. 9
Working conditions; pay, tenure, hours, health insurance, etc.	10. 0
Status; lack of status relative to CLAS, lack of support by students, faculty, public.	9. 3
General conditions; more classroom and staffroom space, library facilities, etc.	8. 2
Class size; too large; reduce class size.	7. 0

A Differential Analysis

It was hypothesized that day faculty (CLAS) teaching during evening hours would be most critical of (1) caliber of students, (2) selection of students, (3) caliber of staff, and (4) working conditions in SGS. It was reasonably assumed that he would most probably be making comparisons with CLAS. On the other hand, it was anticipated that SGS line faculty whose full-time commitment is in SGS would be the least critical of these four elements. The off-campus lecturer group, itself so heterogeneous in background and other-than-SGS affiliation, would, it seemed, fall somewhere in-between.

This hypothesis was substantially verified in the relatively higher percentage of CLAS faculty who were concerned about the problems of caliber of students, caliber of staff and working conditions of staff. With respect to selection of student body, the SGS line person was more concerned with this as a problem. It may be inferred that the SGS line staff member whose primary commitment is in SGS identifies with and believes his own status on campus is linked with the nature of the SGS student body. Hence, it may be that, while he is less critical with respect to the caliber of students, he really would like to see a more selective process employed in admissions.

The responses by the three groups of staff, expressed in percentages, were the following:

Table IV

Problems in SGS
Responses (in percentages)

Problems	Weighted average of all respondents N=268	SGS "Line" N=34	Lecturers N=164	CLAS N=70
(1) Caliber of students	17.9	14.7	16.3	24.2
(2) Selection of student body	16.4	23.5	14.4	17.1
(3) Caliber of staff	11.9	11.7	8.1	21.4
(4) Working conditions of staff	10.0	5.8	10.6	11.4

With respect to positive and negative responses to student characteristics, the SGS line person is most positive about good student attitudes with lecturers expressing about

the same view and CLAS staff, less so.   All agree on the
fact that the students are <u>adult.</u>   On the negative side,
there is a great disparity between CLAS (31.4%) and SGS
line (17. 6%) on the characterization of the students as
<u>poorer.</u>   The lecturers' view here is close to that of the
CLAS faculty member.

Table V

SGS Students: Positive and Negative Responses
(in percentages)

Response	Weighted average of all respondents N=268	SGS "Line" N=34	Lecturers N=164	CLAS N=70
Positive:				
Good student attitudes	35. 0	38. 2	37. 1	27. 1
Adult students	24. 2	26. 4	22. 6	27. 1
Negative:				
Poorer students	27. 6	17. 6	28. 9	31. 4
Tired students	11. 1	5. 8	8. 8	18. 5

Choice Between Day College and SGS

The capstone question asked: "If somebody came to
you today stating that he has a choice between teaching in
the School of General Studies and a day college, what would
you advise him to do?"   It evoked a wide range of response.
These varied from "Are you kidding?" and "Stop asking fool-
ish questions" to "CLAS if married, SGS if single" and "Tell
him to make up his own mind. "   Of the 230 who responded
to this question, 149 (65%) chose the day college; 29 (13%)
would advise teaching in the School of General Studies, with

50 (22%) indicating "undecided" or "it depends."

The question also included <u>Reason for the choice</u>.
The reasons given by the 149 respondents who would advise
to choose day college are indicated in the following table:

Table VI

Advise to Choose Day College
(Reason for choice)
N=149

Reason	Number of checks	Percent of total
Type of student	80	53
Status	78	52
Time of work	73	49
Salary	49	33
Curriculum	33	22
Work load	30	20
Class size	20	13

Only 29 out of 230 respondents (currently teaching in
SGS) would advise teaching in SGS in preference to a day college!   While this very small number is in itself most significant, the distribution of the 29 answers by "Reason for
the choice" is too small to demonstrate any statistical significance of any particular reason.   Nevertheless, here again,
as with those who would choose a day college, <u>the type of
student</u> leads as a reason for the choice.[34]

The reasons given by the 29 respondents who would
advise to choose SGS are indicated in the table on the following page.

SGS Line Staff and Image

Of the 29, who indicated choice of SGS, 23 are lec-

Table VII

Advise to Choose SGS
by Reason for choice
N=29

Reason	Number of responses	Percent of total
Type of students	19	65
Time of work	11	38
Class size	6	21
Salary	4	14
Educational challenge	4	14
Curriculum	3	10
Work load	3	10
Status	1	.03

turers, 3 are from CLAS and 3 are annual line SGS teachers. It will be recalled that 34 "line" persons responded
to the questionnaire. Of these 34 SGS full-time staff members, only 3 (10%) would advise to choose SGS. In analyz-
ing the structure of SGS and, in particular, the elements of
internal stress in SGS based on its relationship to the day
college, it was pointed out[35] that SGS' hopes for a strong,
core faculty were pinned on its full-time "line" personnel
who would have commitment to SGS and be particularly oriented to the education of its heterogeneous adult population.
To be sure, the problems of the SGS staff were also recognized, i.e., the small number in relation to CLAS faculty,
status on campus, feelings of inferiority based on lack of
representation on department and college committees, concern about equality of treatment in matters of appointment,
promotion and tenure, etc. Nevertheless, it was from this
group that SGS administration hoped to elicit leadership and

therefore it was to this group that SGS directed its primary efforts to effect cohesiveness and esprit de corps. Of the thirty-four SGS faculty respondents, only three would advise to choose SGS over a day college!

It is interesting to note that each of the three cited educational challenge as the only reason for the choice. One stated:

> No "get in the groove" teaching here; requires considerable use of different teaching methods to reach the SGS students with their diversified business and educational backgrounds.

Perhaps "challenge" is not enough. Perhaps diversity presents too many problems. Perhaps concern with inferior status and discriminatory treatment are too overwhelming. Perhaps it was an over-optimistic SGS staff member who wrote:

> The Lord made the day and the night and He is not on record as saying which is better for work, for love or for college attendance.

Is There and SGS Image?

Is there an SGS image? Or are there, as in Roshomon, several different SGS images, each one a unique reflection of views held that are "corroborated" by projection of what the witness wants to see?

SGS Administration

Administration views SGS as a unique, identifiable unit, innovative in character, providing first quality higher education to part-time adult students and second chance opportunity to those who "didn't make it" the first time around. It sees the teaching staff as competent, though diversified, and appreciates the diversity as flavorful. SGS is also perceived as underprivileged with respect to budget, space, personnel and status on campus.   Although acutely aware of under-privilege and some staff dissatisfaction arising out of such handicaps as lower rates of pay, lack of tenure, lower stat-us privileges (retirement, health insurance, etc.), adminis-tration's view is that there is no real "quality" problem with respect to staff.   Administration is of the opinion that it is able to attract high quality instructional staff simply because of the prestige that stems from affiliation with Brooklyn College.   This is particuarly true for those teach-ers whose full-time day work is in business or the profes-sions.   However, there is implicit in administration's evalu-ation of SGS that there is much room for improvement if better fiscal and other resources were made available.   In short, administration's view of SGS is that, given its pres-ent budgetary and power and authority resources, it is doing a "first-rate" job.

CLAS Faculty

The CLAS view as expressed both informally by indi-viduals and in the criticisms of various committees is that SGS pays too heavy a quality price for its diversity in stu-dent body.   Both admissions and performance standards of students are seriously questioned.   To a large extent this CLAS "impression" is reinforced by the college regulation which gives the opportunity to students who are academical-ly dismissed from the day program to rehabilitate themselves in SGS on a part-time basis.   While the regulation is con-sistent with the "second chance" philosophy of SGS, it carries the high cost of being stigmatized as "inferior" by CLAS col-leagues.

SGS Teaching Staff

The view of the SGS teaching staff as expressed in the questionnaire is, itself, ambivalent.   The SGS student is the chief concern; he is mature, responsibly adult, has respect for learning, is challenging to instructors, etc. --far more so than his day session counterpart; however, he is less well-prepared for college than the day student and, while more hardworking, he is also more tired.   He is not well-prepared for classes, but neither is the day student. The maturity but also the great diversity in student body is recognized; to a larger percentage (46%) it provides exciting challenge; to others (33%) it becomes an unfair burden.

Working conditions in SGS (its inadequate compensation, lack of tenure and other status privileges) coupled with the second-class citizenship atmosphere and relatively low status are all part of the composite image of SGS.   As expressed by respondents to the questionnaire, the problems of "identity" or more correctly, "lack of identity" are also keenly felt.

Those who teach in SGS would overwhelmingly advise others, if a choice existed, to teach in a day college.   Type of student, status and time of work lead the reasons for the choice.   Though 53% of all respondents who would advise others to choose the day session indicated that type of student was the reason for the choice, status (52%) and time of work (49%) were reflected as strong factors to be considered. There is an apparent inconsistency here.   A higher rating is given to SGS students in an earlier question (see Table II above) yet the preference expressed for teaching in a day college has "type of student" leading the reasons for the choice.   It may be inferred that concern with "type of stu-

dent" is a more "acceptable" professional reason than "status" or "time of work." Given a set of multiple conditions
in choice making, there may well be rationalization of the
reasons for the choice.

Middle States Association Evaluation Team

The Middle States Evaluation Team provides yet another "image" of SGS. Its report was based on documents
submitted by the various units of the college as well as on
meetings with individual officers of administration and faculty, of CLAS, Graduate Division and SGS.

> The School of General Studies has performed re-
> markably well in meeting the higher education needs
> of the adult population of a large metropolitan com-
> munity. It has offered these important services
> to a vast student population, with minimal financial
> backing from the city and state.

> The School of General Studies, with 11,000 students,
> is an evening program and extends the use of the
> physical facilities to 10:40 P.M. This large enter-
> prise accentuates the crowded conditions at Brook-
> lyn College. . .

> The evening program has admitted some students
> into the Division of Liberal Arts on a non-matricu-
> lated basis. This approach serves students who
> have not met the baccalaureate admissions stand-
> ards and permits them to qualify for matriculation
> through developing satisfactory scholastic records
> in college. The approach is commendable, assum-
> ing the basic admission standards are realistic and
> defensible.

> Since the part-time faculty works for a lesser rate
> per course than do full-time members and since
> they also receive very limited "fringe" benefits, it
> is the faculty members who "subsidize" the program
> in a very real sense.

> Considering the general shortage of qualified faculty
> members, the absence of professional status and

tenure aggravates an already acute recruitment
problem.

The School of General Studies deserves much better support by way of additional regular faculty
positions.   Certainly the need for continuing education and for degree programs for adults will increase rather than lessen in the Brooklyn area.

The administrative officers of Brooklyn College
and of the School of General Studies are to be
commended for mounting this large and impressive
evening program.   They have worked diligently to
provide a manageable tie-in with the day program.
They have initiated programs and procedures which
have a ring of quality.   The enterprise simply deserves greater support by means of full-time faculty members, more counseling service, and sup-
portive services for the faculty including offices
and clerical assistance. [36]

Conclusion

This good report card from the Middle States Association evaluation team, however, probably has little effect on
the SGS image in its "task environment. "   Basically, the
"definition of the situation" by individuals and groups is influenced by their ideal and material interests.   Thus, CLAS
concern with maintaining the "purity" in quality of a Brooklyn College baccalaureate degree plus a safeguarding of its
space and other resources during periods of scarcity contributes to its view of SGS as "inferior. "   SGS administration, on the other hand, takes pride in its job and, hence,
views itself as a "first-line" college.   Faculty and staff image of SGS seems to depend on the context: when asked a-
bout SGS student image per se it presents a good one; when
questioned in the context of desirability of affiliation, the student image becomes less positive and factors such as "status" and "time of work" become more cogent considerations.

Images held by individuals and groups are strongly conditioned by their status positions in the social structure. Perspectives vary as the vantage point from which the observations of self and others are made changes the horizon.

Notes

1. Burton R. Clark. The Character of Colleges, Some Case Studies (Paper prepared for Conference on "Dynamics of Change in the Modern University") Syracuse University, June 13-17, 1965.

2. "Annual Report of the Dean," School of General Studies, 1960, p. 61.

3. A Commitment of Ours: Teaching in the School of General Studies, Hunter College, New York, p. 1. (off-

4. Ibid. , (emphasis added).

5. Evening Post, C. W. Post College, vol. 6, no. 5, April 1967, p. 4.

6. Ibid.

7. Report to Alpha Sigma Lambda Councillors from Dean Daniel R. Lang on Membership in A. C. H. S. , March 10, 1966, p. 2-3.

8. "Annual Report of the Dean," School of General Studies, 1966-1967, p. 1.

9. "Annual Report of the Dean," School of General Studies, 1953-1954, p. 28.

10. "Annual Report of the Dean," School of General Studies, 1962-1963, p. 7.

11. "Staff Handbook" School of General Studies, Brooklyn College, 1965-1966, p. 1-3 (emphasis added).

12. Ewald B. Nyquist, in Proceedings (Association of University Evening Colleges, 1952), p. 60.

13. G. Stuart Demarest, The Evening College at Rutgers, Notes and Essays on Education for Adults, No. 11,

(Center for the study of Liberal Education for Adults, 1955), p. 14; Ernest E. McMahon, The Emerging Evening College (Teachers College, Columbia University, 1960), p. 57-79.

14. Herbert Sorenson, Adult Abilities, A Study of University Extension Students (University of Minnesota Press, 1938), p. 70.

15. Earl J. McGrath and Lewis A. Froman, College Aptitude of Adult Students, University of Buffalo Studies, Vol. XIV, No. 1 (November 1936), p. 9.

16. Ibid., p. 34.

17. Hollis B. Farnum, A Comparison of the Academic Aptitude of University Extension Degree Students and Campus Students (The Journal of Applied Psychology, Vol. XLI, No. 1, 1957), p. 65.

18. Proposed Memorandum to Department Chairmen and (SGS) Deputy Chairmen, April 27, 1966.

19. Ibid., (emphasis added).

20. Ibid., (emphasis added).

21. Letter to Chairman, Committee on Course and Standing, May 9, 1966.

22. Ibid., (emphasis added).

23. Revised Memorandum to Department Chairmen and (SGS) Deputy Chairmen, May 2, 1966, (emphasis added).

24. Memorandum cited in footnote 18, (emphasis added).

25. Master Plan of the City University of New York, Second Iterim Revision, 1966, p. 15.

26. See footnote 18 (emphasis added).

27. Associate degree programs are gradually being transferred to the Community Colleges.

28. A Report of the Evaluation Team of the Commissioners on Institutions of Higher Education of the Middle States

Association of Colleges and Secondary Schools, October 31 - November 2, 1966, p. 23 (emphasis added).

29. The total number of the staff was 600.

30. It was expected, however, that CLAS teachers would use Brooklyn College CLAS students as a basis for comparison as would SGS line teachers, most of whom teach at least one course in CLAS each term.

31. In order to eliminate any distortion that might result from the sequence of the question, in half of the questionnaires respondents were asked about full-time day students first and in the other half, the question on SGS students preceded.

32. See "Image and Academic Standards," supra, p. 265.

33. Responses below the level of 5% were excluded as not significant.

34. In view of the fact that the impression of the SGS student was predominantly more favorable than that of the day student on the structured questions on student characteristics which appeared earlier in the questionnaire, how is it that type of student (53%) leads the reasons for choice of a day college? This appears to be a contradiction. The prior structured questions asked about student characteristics only. However, the capstone question above encompassed the total relationship of the individual teacher to the teaching unit by asking about reasons for choice of SGS or day college. It is significant that status (52%) is given almost equal weight to that of type of student. It therefore can reasonably be inferred that the SGS teacher really would prefer day session for status but legitimizes his choice by pointing to more socially acceptable reasons, i. e., type of student. Time of work is also indicated as an important reason for choice of day college (49%) but this is an apparent personal preference for a conventional working schedule.

35. See Chapter III, "Authority and Responsibility."

36. "A Report of the Evaluation Team of the Committee on
      Institutions of Higher Education," Middle States As-
      sociation of Colleges and Secondary Schools, October
      30 - November 2, 1966, p. 22-23.

Chapter VII

Retrospects and Prospects

> Though change is inevitable,
> change for the better is a full-
> time job.
>   Adlai Stevenson

The main analytical concerns of this study have been
the structural ties and interactive relationships of an educational sub-organization and its parent institution.   Specifically, it is an intensive case study of Brooklyn College as
the parent and the School of General Studies as one of its
component units.   While concentrated on a particular organization, the case study is intended to promote a better understanding of the organizational processes that engage similar
evening colleges operating under comparable conditions of
management and control.   Most evening colleges in the United
States are structured in a parent/sub-unit form similar to
that of Brooklyn College.

Existence of a sub-unit as an identifiable entity with
an administrative apparatus of its own, though intimately tied
to the power structure of the larger institution, implies a
special purpose to be served both by the parent and the component organization.   For more than half a century, the community need for evening colleges to accommodate a different
clientele from the day college has been recognized.   It was
in response to that need that the Evening Session and later
SGS came into being at Brooklyn College.   Once the sub-

unit is given life, it strives for growth and development on
the basis of its own aspirations and values.   However, the
formal arrangements are not sufficiently flexible in a domi-
nant-subservient relationship.   The subservient sub-unit constantly has to face the controlling restraints of the parent.

What the sub-organization is, what it hopes to become
and what, in fact, it does become are strongly conditioned,
if not determined, by the organizational milieu in which it
exists and operates.   The sub-organization, by virtue of its
quest for separate identity, seeks the freedom to formulate
its own goals and implementing measures under conditions
of coordinated control.   Polar forces of freedom and re-
straint are thus in an incessant state of tension; and it is
out of this dialectic that the interactive process must reach
a synthesis of viable balance.

The Problem of Goals

In broad scope, the goal aspirations of the component
must harmonize with those of the parent institution and must
gain its approval.   The processes by which goals are har-
monized and legitimated are the essence of the interaction
between colliding forces, those of superimposed managerial
control versus those of stirrings for managerial freedom.
In the final analysis, the extent to which the sub-unit is accorded the freedom to define particular goals and to organize particular means of attaining them is dependent on the
following factors:

1. The historical setting.
2. The scarcity of shared resources.
3. The essential nature of the goals.

These factors are, to a large extent, influenced by
pressures from the "external" environment, from sources

"outside" the nuclear relationship of parent and sub-unit.
In the case of Brooklyn College, for example, pressures
from the City University, the Board of Higher Education,
the City and State of New York, have played significant roles
in generating the conditions requiring new adjustments and
accommodations.   Thus, while the microcosm of this study
has been the School of General Studies and the institution in
loco parentis, the forces of the "external" environment have
been introduced at relevant points.

The Historical Setting

        The historical trend since 1950 in the municipal col-
lege system as a whole has been almost steady expansion
and growth.   The expansion was not only in the area of the
conventional liberal arts baccalaureate degree but extended
to wide diversification and experimentation with new programs.
        During the first decade, until 1960, the sub-unit, too,
enjoyed relative freedom in embarking on new goals and new
designs for their achievement.   While in part SGS growth
was mitigated by internal reorganization of its jurisdiction
by top administration, it was subjected to relatively minor
restraints by the parent body in seeking new goals.   Adoption of new programs and their implementation, to be sure,
required faculty, presidential and Board approval, but the
expansionist climate was conducive to a high degree of freedom for SGS growth.
        After 1960, the population bulge stimulated growth in
the City University system with even greater intensity.   In
fact, the pressure for expansion was so strong that new two-
year community colleges were created in order to take over
a portion of the functions previously within the jurisdiction of

the Schools of General Studies. Increased size and complexity made further "division of labor" and diversification
of function necessary. Administrative leadership in the
Schools of General Studies fought energetically for the retention of the programs they had instituted and nurtured but
it was to no avail. Historical forces in the City, as in the
state and nation, were in the direction of separating the
"junior" college curricula from the senior colleges; two-year
degree programs were thus relegated to the community colleges. As a consequence, SGS experienced a major goal
contraction.

SGS was powerless to resist this contraction. Nor
did the parent organization lend its support to combat the
contraction. In fact, the scarcity of space and resources,
combined with the increased pressure on the day college to
admit more students, were decisive factors contributing to
the parent's acquiescense in the jurisdictional contraction of
one of its sub-units.

The Scarcity of Shared Resources

When space and facilities are to be apportioned among
units of a complex organization, a ranking order of priority
must be established in order to achieve maximum efficiency
in resource utilization. In reality, the choices made in the
allocation of scarce resources constitute choices in priority
of goals. To allocate space for a new program or expansion
of existing programs is to evaluate them as more worthy
than competing claimants for the same space.

Decisions of this nature are so crucial at Brooklyn
College that they are reserved for top management. The
President retains the ultimate decision-making power in this
critical area. However, he relies heavily on the recommen-

dations of a faculty committee appointed by him. [1] Thus,
once again, control is exercised by managerial authority
"external" to SGS itself.   Once the severe competition for
shared space subsides through new building construction--a
three or four year prospect--SGS hopes that its drive for
greater self-determination and for realization of distinctive
goals will not be frustrated in competition with values
deemed superior by the parent.

The Nature of the Goals

        Approval of SGS goals varies in the degree to which
they are consistent with those of the parent organization.
The further the goal from the central purpose of the parent
organization, the less the burden of establishing propriety
and usefulness.   But when the goal comes within the central
purpose of the parent, (i. e. , liberal arts baccalaureate education) yet diverges with respect to essence, implementation
and clientele, a severe problem of legitimacy arises.   Although, as Burton Clark points out, "pluralistic societies
'tolerate' minority values," the tolerance is contingent upon
the legitimacy ascribed to the function. [2]   In the case of vocational and professional two-year degree programs, for example, the faculty accepted the innovations in large part because of the strong support of the President and the active
advocacy of the Board.   On the other hand, goals which are
clearly within the value system of the parent organization
but which involve differences in approach, variations in content, requirements and methods necessitate stronger proof
of legitimacy for they impinge more directly upon tradition.
The purity of the central purposes of the parent and the
sanctities surrounding these purposes are zealously guarded.
New proposals for special innovative programs leading to the

baccalaureate degree are, therefore, most rigorously scrutinized and often effectively resisted. Resistance of day faculty to change and experimentation that questions customary
and standardized goal definitions as well as the related procedures is a problem which SGS must always face if it wishes to continue to be innovative.

The Problems of Innovation and Cooptation

In a discussion of the academic community, Clark
Kerr succinctly states: "The external view is that the university is radical; the internal reality is that it is conserva-
tive."[3] Innovation comes hard at the university.

For SGS, innovation was a vital part of its self-image, an end in itself. SGS viewed itself and, to a degree,
was acknowledged as the innovative center of the undergraduate college. Structurally and administratively it is so constituted as to encompass programs and students which do not
precisely "fit" the traditional baccalaureate patterns. Of the
many proposals for innovation made by SGS, some of which
were accepted and some of which were rejected, two critical
examples were here selected for intensive analysis. These
examples not only demonstrate the institutionalized routes
which any proposal must follow but they also illustrate the
essential process of cooptation utilized to effect the adoption
of innovative ventures.

The first example, the Special Baccalaureate Degree
Program for Adults, had to pass rigorous faculty scrutiny;
there was faculty concern that the innovative aspects might
dilute the quality of the baccalaureate degree. Somewhat
helpful and reassuring were the program's support and sub-
sidy by a private, prestigious foundation. Significant also
was the spirited support of the President and the Dean of the

Faculties.   But to gain full CLAS support, faculty members
were cooptatively included in the major policy decisions
from the outset.   Not the least important, the original
group of faculty members who prepared the initial blueprint
of the program and who reported to the faculty at large were
highly regarded and respected professors of the college.

The second example, the Nursing Science Program,
was proposed by SGS in response to a strong, articulated
community need to reduce the shortage of nurses.   Two-
year degree programs were already institutionalized in the
college structure and the nursing science program could be
readily meshed into that structure.   Here, again, CLAS
faculty were invited to join with SGS administration to make
policy, to plan curriculum and to screen and select staff and
students.

While the process of cooptation was effectively utilized for both programs, the methods differed.   In the Special Baccalaureate Degree Program, the area of greatest
stress was in the curricular adaptation and in student evaluation.   In the Nursing Science project, on the other hand,
the greatest need for cooptation was to select personnel for
administration and faculty and to give them an acceptable
berth in the college.   For, in nursing, the qualifications of
available personnel necessitated substantial modification of
existing criteria normally utilized for full-time faculty of the
college.

Cooptation is a technique by which to obtain the support of the "task environment" for the realization of organizational goals.   Active participation by CLAS faculty in the
decision-making process not only contributes to goal realization but also maintains prescribed jurisdictional spheres.
Contravention and possible conflict is thus avoided.

Although the cooptative process is functional in goal
achievement there are some dysfunctional consequences.
First the process of cooptation takes time.   Members of
the "outside" group must be carefully selected with a view
to their potential constructive contribution.   Involvement of
many individuals and committees in the decision-making
process slows down the action.   Cooptation may result in
a laborious rate in having the innovation adopted and implemented.   Second, and more important, the original idea or
proposal usually has to undergo substantial alteration.   For
cooptation necessarily involves a meeting of minds and compromise solutions.   How different the resultant product is
from the original conception or design depends on the nature
of the project as well as on the dynamics of interaction.

The Special Baccalaureate Degree Program was indeed altered considerably from the original idea.   It was not
possible to take the broad giant steps hoped for in the initial
visionary plan.   Whether the program is "better" for the
moderation cooptatively introduced is a matter of value judgment.   The Nursing Science Program, too, experienced
many changes of format and implementing measures as a result of the cooptative process.   Most of these were highly
constructive.   The coopted CLAS faculty members became
staunch supporters of this two-year professional program and
strongly advanced its acceptance in a four-year liberal arts
college.   Yet, the Nursing Science curriculum and staff were
never fully integrated in the college structure.   As a result,
it was transferred to the community colleges in response to
forces external to Brooklyn College without significant opposition.

The Problems of Authority and Responsibility

Limitations on authority involve intervening control by agencies not totally dedicated to the aspirations and strivings of the sub-unit. They create conditions of dependency in manifold directions. This is essentially the core problem of authority and responsibility confronting SGS.

Central to the functioning of a college are its administration and faculty. In both areas, SGS has authority which is limited in scope. As to administration, the authority delegated by the President is primarily a concurrent one with the CLAS deans on student admissions, curricular planning, student counseling, extra-curricular activities, allocation of budgetary "lines" and staffing. As to faculty, SGS simply has no faculty separate and apart from CLAS. A minor segment of the SGS instructional staff occupies SGS "lines" but it does not constitute SGS "faculty." On the contrary, "line" personnel are, for all intents and purposes, members of the regular college faculty though budgetary lines stem from SGS.

The by-laws of the Board of Higher Education vest broad powers in the faculty. Most important is the authority to determine the composition of its own membership. Selection, retention, tenure and promotion are its prerogatives. Having no separate faculty, SGS is dependent on the regular college faculty for the performance of these crucial functions.

The administrative link between SGS and the college faculty, organized along departmental lines, is represented by the deputy chairmen. Choice of the deputy chairman is made by the CLAS department chairman with the concurrence of the SGS Dean. At most, the power of the Dean is to

withhold acceptance of a person nominated by the department chairman.   Amicable relations between the SGS Dean
and department chairmen are the informal means which
overcome the deficiencies of divided authority in appointing
deputy chairmen.   As a general practice, department chairmen usually confer with the Dean as to the acceptability of
a nominee or of several alternative nominees and they generally reach agreement.   Rarely do disagreements ripen into stubborn conflict.

Similar shared authority pertains to the allocation of
annual lines to individual departments.   Both the SGS Dean
and the Dean of the Faculties must jointly agree on the specific line allocation.   Allocation of a line must also be acceptable to the department which holds the authority and
bears the responsibility for recruitment and selection.   Informal personal contacts between the SGS Dean and departmental committees are also significant in avoiding intransi-
gent disagreements.   Consensuality is the dominant motif of
the operating relationships.

Certain dysfunctional consequences nevertheless flow
from the divided authority.   When identical professorial
ranks are available for staffing both in SGS and CLAS, the
priority of choice is usually retained by CLAS although, in
theory, the department should give equality of treatment to
SGS and CLAS.   In practice, CLAS usually makes the first
choice for itself.   Lacking authority, SGS is powerless to
prevent this "natural" but discriminatory practice.

Transfers of SGS line personnel to CLAS also exempli-
fy a tendency with which SGS cannot effectively cope.   While
the SGS Dean theoretically has the authority, with the support of the Dean of the Faculties, to block a transfer from
SGS to CLAS, as a matter of brute fact he is unable, in

terms of the practicalities, to exercise this authority. Requests of department chairmen, inspired by the one who desires the transfer, cannot easily be rejected. In addition, petitions and importunities by the applicant, who in almost all cases presents conditions of undue hardship, similarly cannot be lightly dismissed.

Efforts of the SGS Dean to stem the tide have taken the indirect form of erecting obstacles to easy transfer. Recruitment by the department of a person with qualifications comparable to those of the transferee has been made a condition of transfer. But this has been relatively feeble in ebbing the flow. Another developing technique is that of withdrawing the SGS line from the department. Whether this technique will prove more effective only the future can tell. In the meantime, transfer opportunities take their toll in undermining the stability of staff.

Normally, control of the purse strings brings a high level of power. While the total budget allocated to SGS may be considered shoestring financing, nevertheless the Dean's power to fix rates of compensation of part-time staff and to apportion funds to departments enables him to influence certain staffing decisions. Control of the budget affords him substantial power in scheduling sections and courses. These indirect means create the opportunity to mold the composition of staff to a high degree. This opportunity is most evident in the category of off-campus lecturers. While the department has the authority to appoint and to retain or dismiss, the Dean's power to allocate funds and to establish rates of compensation creates the boundaries for selection of staff.

The Dean's control of staff varies with the category of personnel involved. His authority is on a continuum, least with respect to line personnel (13% of staff), more with respect to CLAS faculty teaching on an overtime basis (27% of staff), most with respect to off-campus lecturers (60% of staff). The closer the category parallels the day college's formal prescriptions, the less the Dean's power.

On the surface, it would appear that the maximum control pertaining to 60% of the staff is a blessing in terms of authority, for it is this segment of the staff that provides highest flexibility in staff composition. But this blessing is not unmixed since the flexibility is acquired at an exceedingly high price. The off-campus lecturer category is the least stable, experiences the highest turnover, is the lowest paid and enjoys none of the fringe benefits of tenure, retirement, health insurance and other important working conditions.

These factors make it difficult to insist on the same graduate degree qualifications that reflect the conventional pattern of CLAS faculty. In a college milieu where social status and ranking is so directly related to such academic qualifications, the differences in credentials of many of the off-campus lecturers inevitably result in marginal status both to the group and to SGS as a whole.

The circle then becomes somewhat vicious in contour. Since lecturers are essentially part-time and temporary, it is difficult to expect them to assume comprehensive responsibilities in the operations of SGS other than the teaching of classes and counseling of students. Nor can they reasonably be expected to participate actively in policy-making decisions whether at the departmental or SGS levels. Even if such responsibility were imposed as a condition of employment, the absence in the by-laws of legal authority so to act is an insurmountable obstacle. Policy-making decisions in many

critical areas are reserved for the faculty and SGS has no
independent faculty.

The Problems of Stress and Strain

Stress and strain are revealed in the problems of
establishing goals, of introducing innovative programs and
of dealing with ambiguities and cross-currents in the patterns of authority and responsibility.   These are mainly internal stresses and strains.   But there are also forces external to both parent organization and sub-unit which exert
pressures on either or on both and which result in internal
stress.   Three significant examples of external pressures,
each of which evoked conditions of stress and strain on SGS,
have been analyzed.   Identified by source, these pressures
came from:

    1. The City University

    2. The College as Transmitter

    3. The Board of Higher Education

Pressure from the City University

Hampered by limited funds for new building construction and pressed by increasing demands for higher levels of
student admissions of an ever growing college-age population, the City University faced a serious dilemma.   Procure-
ment of construction funds and actual construction are necessary but they are arduous and long-term solutions.   In the
meantime, the colleges resisted increased admissions because they were already operating in excess of normal capacity.   How to solve the dilemma?

The Dean of Studies of the City University, aware
that priority choices would have to be made to enlarge "operation shoehorn," suggested that priority be given to the

"prime concern" of the colleges, namely full-matriculated
day college students.   He, therefore, proposed an admissions program in which first priority would be accorded to
the "prime concern" and lowest priority to SGS non-matriculated students.   In order to enlarge capacity for the admission of full-time matriculated students, he proposed that
the dividing line between night and day be erased.   Extinc-
tion of the evening colleges as separate entities would be
the necessary consequence.   This was a threat of major
proportions.

   The day colleges were strong enough to resist some
of the pressure for increased enrollments.   Day faculty
vigorously opposed those aspects of the proposal which would
have extended their working "day" far into the night.   In addition, the fees paid by non-matriculated students were not
expendable since the necessary budgetary appropriations anticipated were not granted.

   The proposals were thus not adopted but they left
their mark on SGS.   For the City University had expressly
stated its priority choices.   In the wake of this drastic evaluation by "top management," SGS administrators, faculty and
students suffered the pangs of insecurity and anxiety.

Transmitted Pressure from the College

   Another struggle was precipitated within Brooklyn College because of the failure of the Board to procure and the
City to provide ample funds for sorely needed new construction.   This failure of action by other authorities constituted
an external source of pressure.   Without new space and facilities, competition within the college for these resources
became more severe.   As a result, expansion of a segment
of the SGS student population as well as new program devel-

opment by SGS was threatened with curtailment.

In only the non-economy of heaven, where there is no scarcity of resources, is competition absent.[4] Competition among units of a college or university for scarce resources is reasonably to be expected. However, when competition becomes so keen that the larger organization blocks program development of the component unit, it is no longer competition but contravention. While competition may be stimulating, contravention can only be repressing.

An effort was also made to block SGS expansion of the non-matriculated student category. Only the intervention of the President frustrated this contravention attempt. Yet even this apparent affirmation of SGS interests by the President contained seeds of stress and strain. For it was believed--and rumor abounded--that the President's action was motivated less by a commitment to SGS objectives than by the college need for the fees paid by non-matriculated students.

Pressure from the Board

Pressures exerted from the "outside" on the day college as the primary target also reverberate into SGS. Multiple position regulations of the Board limiting the number of overtime work hours of day faculty had a severe impact on the available supply of personnel for SGS. Higher salary levels and reduced day teaching schedules which developed over a course of years made it feasible to limit overtime hours. In light of these developments, accrediting agencies were quite critical of the high level of "overtime" teaching permitted at the City University.

To comply with national norms as well as to respond to the criticism of accrediting agencies, the Board adopted a resolution providing for a gradual reduction, over a five

year period, of permissible overtime hours.   While the
Board's action was basically directed at the day college operation, it profoundly affected the availability of CLAS faculty for SGS administration and teaching.

Cooperation came into play to ease the stress and
strain.   Since additional SGS annual lines to replace CLAS
faculty (a necessary condition for the reduction of permissible overtime hours) did not eventuate at the rate anticipated, the SGS Deans of the various college units joined in
a petition to the Board to extend the timetable of reduction.
The Board granted the petition and retarded the planned rate
of reduction in permissible overtime work.   At Brooklyn
College, too, both the President and the Dean of Administration acted cooperatively by liberally interpreting the regulation for SGS administrative officers and by granting exceptions for teaching personnel when special circumstances
indicated undue hardship.

Consequences of Stress and Strain

Pressures from the outside which evoke stress and
strain place parent and sub-unit on a different level of being and becoming.   The impact of each varies in terms of
the nature of the pressure, its primary target and the consequences at stake.   Moreover, each entity has different
resources and abilities with which to cope with pressures.
Indeed, in some cases the power elite may decide to allow
certain pressures to bear more heavily on the sub-unit as
a way of alleviating the pressures upon itself.   In other
cases, the parent may join forces with the sub-unit in tac-
tics of resistance or delay.   The parent holds the controlling position and has the decisive choice as to the course to
follow.   Choice is not readily available to the subordinate unit.

As is true in any society, outside pressures affect different segments of the society differently and thus modify internal arrangements and relationships. Each segment endeavors to influence the direction and magnitude of change so as to maintain or to improve its position--of power, of resource control, of existence itself. External pressures are part and parcel of the dynamism of a changing scene and they generate the need for readjustments in relationships. An academic organization has to face these realities as do other institutions in the society.

The Problems of Image and Identity

One method of counteracting the varieties of internal and external pressures experienced by an organization is to project a favorable image to its publics. To SGS, a very significant public is the community of evening colleges throughout the nation. It is with this community that it identifies both in terms of basic objectives and implemental resources by which to achieve them. Another interest in common with other evening colleges is that of combatting the negative stereotype of relatively lower standards and status compared to the day colleges.

The publics to which SGS addresses itself more directly and intimately are included in its "task environment." To a large extent, the allocation of budget, space, designation of authority and responsibility as well as support and approval of goals rest on the confidence which SGS as a subunit is able to evoke, or, to put it another way, on the image it projects.

The image SGS seeks to implant is that of individuality, of distinct identity. The aims are to differentiate its being, characteristics, and goals from the total organization

and from other component units within that totality.   This
differentiation is frequently more than a striving for identity; it is a struggle for survival.   Its very being as a separate sub-organization depends to a substantial degree on its
distinctiveness in goals coupled with power and authority incorporating a reasonable degree of freedom in implementing
its goals.

In order to affirm its identity and, implicitly, to assure its survival, SGS utilizes a number of image-project-
ing and self-identifying techniques.   A public relations program, separate staff handbook, social functions, faculty conferences, separate faculty club, evening honor society, etc.
are all developed and supported to enhance the SGS image
and to re-enforce its separateness from the day college.
But this striving for distinct identity carries a high price
tag.   As a sub-unit with powerful kinship ties to the day college, SGS is constrained to conform in a large measure to
the normative structure of its parent.   Its students, staff,
admission and grading standards are evaluated by parent
norms in parent terms.

The claim by SGS administration that it achieves quality higher education for its adult population by "equivalent"
though not "identical" standards is seriously questioned by
day faculty and administration.   While SGS enjoys high status in the evening college community and is ranked in the
upper echelon by evening college national standards, on its
own campus it must constantly defend the quality and performance of its part-time students, particularly those in the
non-matriculated category.

An important segment of its internal public is its own
faculty and staff.   What does SGS faculty and staff think of
the students they teach as compared to full-time day stu-

dents? A questionnaire survey revealed that while the SGS
student is viewed as considerably more "tired" than his day
session counterpart, he is more "mature," more "responsibly adult" and has a greater "respect for learning." The
SGS student is also considered to be "highly motivated" yet,
at the same time, less "prepared for college" than the day
student.

The heterogeneous character of the student body was
viewed in both positive and negative terms. Affirmatively,
the diversity in student body is "challenging" and makes
teaching "more interesting"; negatively, the diversity presents a hardship and "unfair burden" on both teacher and
student. The affirmative statements regarding the heterogeneity of the study body (46%) outweighed the negative statements (33%).

Responses to questions on working conditions in SGS
revealed that what the teaching staff "liked best" about working in SGS was the type of student and the enjoyment and
challenge of teaching. What he "liked least" centered more
on low salaries, lack of job tenure and the disadvantaged
second-class status.

The questionnaire also posed a hypothetical choice between teaching in SGS and in a day college. To this question, 65% of all respondents chose a day college, while only
13% chose evening teaching in SGS. Type of student led the
reasons for the choice of a day college (53%) but status
(52%) was given practically equal weight in the decision.
Following closely was time of work (49%). Thus, when asked
to react to student characteristics, SGS staff rank SGS students comparatively higher than day students but they nevertheless cite type of student as the leading reason for choice
of a day college. The apparent paradox can probably be ex-

plained by the context of the question.   When the question
is not exclusively devoted to an evaluation of students but
rather to the all-encompassing decision as to the individual's choice of a place where he would prefer to work, he
evidently rationalizes his choice by citing type of student of
the day college as a recognition of the superior status of
the day college but at the same time as a socially acceptable reason for his choice.

Finally, it becomes clear that there is no one image of
SGS.   Just as there is no single account of an historical event
but rather a "variety of histories," so also is there a variety of
images.   The image is conditioned by the ideal and material interests of the individuals and groups who react to the situation.
Each has its own "definition" or "frame of reference." Thus
SGS is, to its own administration, a "first-line college;" its
character is diverse, richly variegated and innovative.   At the
same time, it struggles with underprivileged status and resources.   To CLAS faculty, SGS diversity is a liability for it
does not conform to the normative pattern and the quality standards set for full-time day students and faculty.   To an official
accrediting agency, [5] SGS is doing a creditable job within the
stringent limitations imposed by lack of adequate financing and
resources.

Thus SGS is confronted by a polar challenge.   While it
continues to stress the consistency of an image combining "quality" with "second-chance opportunity" and "diversity" with "role
integrity" these projections are directed to a community which
evaluates "quality" by the degrees of conformity with its own
standards.   It is clear that the very factors which give SGS its
raison d'être, --its second-chance philosophy and its multi-di-
mensional goals--coupled with a long history of underprivilege
with respect to fiscal and human resources, constitute the

major stumbling blocks in its struggle for a positive image and
an individual identity in its parent's home.

A Typology of Evening Colleges

Despite variations among evening colleges in structural relationships, authority and responsibility, teaching
staff composition, curriculum control, student admission
policies and budgetary financing, evening colleges throughout
the country can nevertheless be classified into three ideal
types.[6] These are:

1. Integrated fully with the parent institution
2. Autonomous as a separate college
3. Sub-unit under coordinated control

The Fully Integrated Type

The essential characteristic of this type, which comprises a small minority, is that of no organizational separation of day and evening operations. Authority and responsibility rest in the overall administration of the institution
though an evening dean or director may be designated minis-
terially to carry out policies and programs promulgated by
the central authorities of the institution. Regular faculty
teach either in the day or evening though temporary lecturers
usually supplement the regular faculty in the evening. Assignments to teach in the evenings rotate among permanent
faculty as part of the regular teaching load; overload compensation for evening teaching is not customary. Students
are free to choose day or evening attendance either for their
entire or part of their programs. Admission and academic
standards are the same for both day or evening. Curriculum and degrees are the same for both.

Implicit in the fully integrated type is the assumption

that dissimilarities between day and evening in student age
ranges, life experiences, primary or secondary commitments to education, full-time or part-time attendance and
other differential factors are irrelevant.   Hence all stand-
ards--admission, retention, curriculum, level of instruction,
requirements for the degree and other academic criteria--
are uniform for all.   To assure such uniformity, controls
are centralized in one administration and faculty for the total institution.

Autonomous as a Separate College

The most salient characteristic of this type of organization, also in a small minority, is parity of position of the
evening college with the other colleges of the university.
Sometimes the evening college has a distinctive name like
Millard Fillmore College of The State University of New
York at Buffalo; more frequently it is called University College such as the one at Rutgers University and that at Syracuse University.

In this autonomous type, day and evening colleges
have slight overlapping of administration and faculty though
a symbiotic relationship exists between the colleges.   Each
has its own independent administration and faculty.   The evening Dean reports directly to the President or to his deputy,
such as a vice-president.   Admission policies, academic
standards, curricula, degree requirements and all aspects of
student life are autonomously determined.   The degrees may
be the same as those of the day college though not in all
cases.   At Columbia University, for example, the B. A. degree is specifically identified as having been conferred by the
School of General Studies as distinguished from that of Columbia College.   The budget for the evening college is allo-

cated by the fiscal authorities in the same manner as for
any other college of the university.

   The autonomous type is pluralistic in organizational
philosophy. The view is that the dissimilarities of a heterogeneous student population require distinctive goals and implementing measures. Because day deans and faculty may
either not fully comprehend or may not actively support the
distinctive goals, approaches, or implementing measures of
the evening college, a separate administration and faculty
are essential. By placing authority and responsibility in an
autonomous unit single-mindedly dedicated to the interests
of its unique student body, the evening operation can be relatively immunized from the traditions and orientations appropriate for the day but not the evening unit.

Parent/Sub-unit Relationship

   This organizational type, which has been intensively
analyzed here as a case study, is distinctly the modal class
of evening colleges. To summarize the essential characteristics, administrative authority stems from the President to
whom the evening Dean is directly responsible. However,
the Dean's authority is subject to a variety of controls by
day deans and instructional departments. The evening college has no "faculty" of its own; teaching staff consists of a
small number of regular lines and, in part, of permanent
faculty recruited from the day on an overload basis. Temporary, part-time lecturers represent a large majority of
the teaching staff. Primary control for the appointment, retention and promotion of teaching staff resides in the college
instructional departments though the evening Dean shares in
the process through concurrence or disapproval opportunities.
Curriculum and degrees of the evening college are under the

control of the parent institution.

Between the antipodes of full integration on the one side and full autonomy on the other side lies the broad modal class of parent/sub-unit. This type is not peculiar to the academic sphere; many military, governmental, industrial, commercial and religious complex organizations are similarly structured. The object is to decentralize management while maintaining coordinated control. Management is decentralized in order to rationalize functions within manageable scales; control is coordinated from the top in order to harmonize the operations of each unit in accordance with the central purposes of the larger organization. Essentially the purpose is to keep each sub-unit in orbit.

Coordinated control, however, necessarily contemplates restraints on the sub-unit in goal-setting, in experimenting, in diversifying and in growing in conformity with its own visions. Greater self-determination is an organizational aspiration. But this wish for greater freedom meets the restraints of coordinated control and then tensions emerge. Parenthetically, a substantial body of opinion among evening deans and directors, as represented by views expressed at annual conventions of the Association of University Evening Colleges and in various publications, is strongly in favor of higher levels of autonomy in the evening college.[7] Though most evening deans and directors claim that they have strong allies in university and college presidents, they are critical of the shared authority with day deans and department chairmen.[8]

Adjustment of tensions is a basic law of organizational interaction. Mutual concessions and compromises have to be worked out in order to reach a state of equilibrium no matter how temporary it may be. Not the least important

means by which a sub-organization endeavors to attain its
objectives is that of amicable inter-personal relationships
with the power elite of the parent organization. These informal relations within the framework of the formal structure tend to moderate abrasive qualities inherent in shared
authority under conditions of coordinated control.

      Shared authority, however, is not a one way street.
The sub-unit also shares more or less in the parent's power, prestige, traditions, know-how and, most important, in
its human and material resources. SGS, for example, gains
many benefits from the superior bargaining power of the
College as a whole vis-à-vis the Board, the City and the
State in relation to legislative, budgetary and a vast array
of policy matters. SGS also gains stature for itself and for
its students on the basis of the prestigious Brooklyn College
degree with which it is identified. Talents, experience and
skills in many areas--administration, faculty, library, counseling, audio visual, etc. --are garnered by the evening college from the parent college as are a considerable amount of
physical and material resources. In short, the totality of
human and material resources in the possession of the parent are shared with the evening college on some viable basis.

      In the case of the City University in general and
Brooklyn College in particular, the Board in its by-laws and
the President in his delegations of authority to the day and
evening deans, respectively, have decreed the parent/sub-
unit type of organization. Taking this type then as the one
officially sanctioned, the basic question is how the structural
and operating relationships can be modified in order better to
serve the interests of both decentralized management and coordinated control. Necessarily it will be assumed that budgetary allocations for SGS will be consistent with its fiscal

requirements. While distribution of a common fund always
involves questions of fairness and equity, reliance has to be
placed on sound budgetary policies and procedures re-en-
forced by sound and customary accounting practices.

A Blueprint for Better Balance

Better balance might be achieved if administrative and
faculty relationships were reorganized in the following manner:

1. Authority and responsibility of the SGS Dean should
   continue to stem directly from the President.   But
   the administrative authority of the SGS Dean over
   all aspects of the evening programs, including policies on student admissions, curricular structures,
   academic standards, instructional staff, counseling
   and other auxiliary services, should be independent of the day college deans.

2. The SGS instructional staff should consist primarily
   of full-time annual line personnel in professional
   ranks attached to the day academic departments.
   This "core" staff may be supplemented to some extent, as conditions warrant, by CLAS permanent
   faculty (either on an overload or exchange basis)
   and by part-time, temporary lecturers.   These lecturers should be classified in adjunct professorial
   ranks based on qualifications.   Selection, appointment, promotion and tenure should continue to be
   functions of the day academic departments in consultation with the SGS Dean.   The "core" staff
   should have the authority and responsibility of a
   "faculty" on all SGS policies and procedures of an
   academic nature.   An internal committee structure

of the core staff should be coupled with proportional representation on departmental and college-
wide committees.

These two proposals are designed to achieve two
basic purposes: first, in accordance with sound administrative practice, to vest in SGS administration the independent and full authority necessary to carry out its responsibilities; second, to establish an SGS "core" instructional
staff sufficiently large in numbers so that representation of
the SGS interests is significant in the decision-making processes of the college faculty.   Thus, while these proposals
maintain the essential character of the parent/sub-unit type
of organization, they would rationalize authority, controls
and responsibility in terms of evening college goals, program development, individual and institutional status, and
operating procedures.

Administrative Authority of SGS Dean

The scope of authority delegated to the SGS Dean is
determined by the President.   While he made the evening
dean directly responsible to him, he limited the evening
dean's authority to one of concurrence with that of the day
deans.   It is this power of concurrence by day deans that
gives rise to duality of authority harboring a multiplicity of
overlaps, intersections, criss-crossing and ambiguities.
Duality of authority in the same broad areas of concern, particularly when means and ends are not always congruent, necessarily invites stresses and strains.   Informal friendly relations, cooptation, bargaining to settle differences, and other informal measures to reach a modus vivendi frequently
moderate stresses and strains.   But when policy positions between deans become intractable and fixed, an impasse devel-

ops and then only the President can make the final decision.
The situation in that case is an adversarial one, each dean
competing for the crucial support of the President.   In the
role of arbiter between contestants, the President may find
a solution satisfactory to both sides and save the respective
faces of the vying deans.   However, he may arrive at a
solution satisfactory to neither dean, in which event both
feel the disappointment of inadequate support by the President.   Such feelings have the tendency of impairing friendly
relations among the deans.   These feelings are intensified
when the President fully supports the position of one dean
and rejects the position of the other.   Then there is a vic-
tor and a vanquished.   It is this eventuality that sound administrative practice seeks to avoid.   Authority must be as
broad as the responsibility.

A recent resolution of the Board of Higher Education
to establish the Bronx Center of Hunter College (Lehman
College) as an autonomous college in the Bronx is grounded
in the same principle of sound administrative practice.
Since 1931 Hunter College had operated on two widely separated compuses, the parent at midtown Manhattan and the
branch in the upper Bronx.   Enrollment at the Bronx branch
had in the meantime grown roughly to the level of the original Manhattan campus with a substantially similar scope of
curricular offerings.   Reports of several study committees
"identified the weaknesses inherent in the present split-campus arrangement and the educational desirability of college
status for the Bronx campus.   Separation would meet student
and community needs for a four-year municipal college in the
Bronx with sufficient flexibility to meet expanding enrollment
needs. "[9]   In adopting the proposal for separation, the Executive Committee of the Board of Higher Education noted that

"The full complement of a college administration would permit better planning for facilities, library, office space and a graduate program presently recognized as deficient because of the administrative control exercised at the geographically separated parent campus. "[10] The Executive Committee also expressed the view that "Better quality faculty could be recruited because of greater promotional opportunities that would result from college status. . . . Faculty at the Bronx Campus was generally concentrated at the lower ranks with the result that the most competent faculty sought transfer to the parent campus where a fuller range of opportunities was found. "[11] This reference is vividly reminiscent of the plight of SGS instructional staff.

The administrative and faculty weaknesses of a split-campus arrangement are quite analogous to the split-authority arrangement in the parent/sub-unit relationship in the same organization. Briefly and simply to paraphrase the language of the Executive Committee of the Board of Higher Education in the Hunter College situation: The full complement of administrative authority in the evening dean, independent of the day deans, would permit better planning to meet student and community needs by the evening college.

Redefinition of the evening dean's authority to make it coextensive with his responsibility requires the acceptance by the President of the wisdom of the basic administrative principle. Furthermore, his support of the experimental and innovative drives of the evening college as well as its search for self-identity and integrity must receive his positive affirmation. This means, in essence, the approval by the President of the organizational philosophy that monolithic standards and procedures are not apodictic for both day and evening but that varying standards and procedures, though not

identical, nevertheless may be equivalent in quality.   To
attain these, the evening dean's authority must be as broad
as his responsibility and this is within the executive powers
of the President to grant.

SGS Instructional Staff

Of grave concern is the small number of annual lines
in SGS in relation to student enrollment.   If the faculty-student ratio in SGS on a full-time equivalent were the same as
the 1:15 ratio of CLAS, a full-time staff of about 330 teachers for the approximate 10,000 students would produce parity.   The actual number of full-time annual lines is about
58.   Thus if all SGS students, whether matriculated or non-
matriculated were counted, a deficit of 272 full-time annual
lines results.

Though projected on the student-faculty ratio of 1:15,
SGS annual lines are limited by budgetary authorities to the
full-time equivalent of matriculated students only.   Thus non-
matriculated students are excluded from the 1:15 ratio.   In
part, this exclusion rests on the consideration that the State
does not provide financial aid to the City for non-matriculated students; the State aid formula is cast in terms of matriculated students only. [12]   It is substantially for that reason that non-matriculated students are charged tuition fees.
But at present these tuition fees are pledged to the Construction Authority to guarantee the payment of principal and interest on bond issues for new construction.   It would, therefore, appear fair and equitable that the allocation for the
SGS Tax Budget should reflect this pledge of fee funds used
for a purpose beneficial to the institution as a whole and not
solely for SGS.

It is, however, hardly likely that sufficient budget

would be provided by the City to create SGS annual lines in
accordance with the 1:15 faculty-student ratio also embracing non-matriculated students.   Moreover, there would be a
loss of the cross-fertilization advantages of having a cadre
of CLAS faculty teaching in SGS as well as a reduction of
desirable staffing flexibility represented by part-time temporary lecturers.   Nevertheless, the goal should be a domi-
nance of numbers in SGS annual lines supplemented by a
reasonably small minority of CLAS faculty and temporary
lecturers.   Such dominant number in its instructional staff
would then constitute for SGS a core nucleus of full-time
faculty members devoted to evening college goals, developments and standards.   Moreover, this core nucleus could
internally organize a committee structure in order to deal
with SGS goals, developments, and standards.

Equally important is proportional or other reasonable
representation by members of this SGS core nucleus on departmental and college wide committees in order to have a
significant voice for SGS instructional staff in selection, appointment, promotion and tenure which remain the functions
of the college academic departments.   This proportional or
other reasonable representation should also apply to the
whole gamut of committee concerns, from curriculum to
space, which are within the jurisdiction of departmental,
presidential and faculty committees.

It must be repeated that this proposal does not involve
alteration of present faculty authority and responsibility for
the college as a whole.   Only one faculty would exist; in it
a larger number of SGS line personnel would be incorporated.
But this SGS sector would be concerned for SGS with the usual functions of a faculty; and through adequate representation
on departmental, presidential and faculty committees would

constitute a bridge in curricular and other matters of common interest.

The contribution to the teaching staff of the part-time lecturer is of considerable importance to SGS.   Adjunct professorial titles for part-time staff who meet the college's requirements have recently been established. [13] These titles are intended for persons who are engaged full-time in professional, technical, and business activities in the work-a-day world and who devote part-time to college teaching. They bring to SGS their learning and practical experience in areas intimately related to their major fields of activity.

However, adjustment of rates of compensation for adjunct professorial and lecturer titles is still essential. Equity requires that they be proportionate, in relation to departmental teaching load, to the annual salary and incremental steps of the corresponding regular ranks.   Thus, if the departmental teaching load is 12 contact hours, a teaching schedule as an adjunct professor of six contact hours would be equated to a course rate resulting in 50% of the regular line earnings.

If adjunct professorial titles and ranks were joined with commensurate levels of compensation, SGS would be in a position to expect responsible participation in SGS committees, study and task groups, and other functions that are usually within the ambit of a "faculty's" concerns.   Such expectation would then not rest on a pious hope of individual dedication but rather on the firm sociological bases of status and role prescriptions.

To Mold the Future

The modification in organizational relationships recommended in the blueprint would not only correct existing de-

ficiencies of the present parent/sub-unit structure; it would
also enable SGS better to achieve its educational objectives
of providing opportunities for quality higher learning to a
large segment of society unable to attend college during the
day.   Night is the SGS domain and it is at that time that
SGS seeks, subject to the obvious provisions of adequate financing, to provide adults with the legacy endowed through
centuries past by creative and reflective minds.

Notes

1. The Committee consists of the Deans of the Faculties,
   Students, and Studies, Registrar and Supervisor of
   Buildings and Grounds.   The SGS Dean is not a mem-
   ber of the Committee.

2. Burton R. Clark, "Organizational Adaptation and Precarious Values," in Amitai Etzioni,   Complex Organizations (Holt, Rinehart and Winston, 1965), p. 161.

3. Clark Kerr,   The Uses of University   (Harper and Row,
   1963), p. 94.

4. Walton Hamilton,   "Competition,"   Encyclopedia of Social
   Sciences, Vol. IV (Macmillan, 1930), p. 141-147.

5. Middle States Association of Colleges and Secondary
   Schools.

6. These three ideal types and their relative distribution
   were confirmed by a mail survey of forty representative institutions, members of the Association of University Evening Colleges.   Total membership of the
   Association is about 150 evening colleges.

7. Ernest E. MacMahon,   Emerging Evening College,   Ch.
   VII (Columbia University, 1960); and Brigham Young
   University,   A Self-Study of the Department of Evening
   Classes (April 1966), p. 19-65.

8. Association of University Evening Colleges, Salary Survey
   of Administrative Personnel (June 1965), footnote 1,
   p. 3.

9. Board of Higher Education, amendment to the Third Interim Revision (1967) of the 1964 Master Plan for the City University of New York, Sec. 10, p. 20.

10. Ibid.

11. Ibid.

12. New York State Education Law, Sec. 6215.

13. Under contract with the United Federation of College Teachers, effective October 1, 1969.

Appendix

Questionnaire

For School of General Studies Teaching Staff

I. General Information

    A. Division: Liberal Arts ___ Vocational Studies ___
    B. Instructional Department _____
    C. Number of years in SGS ___
    D. This semester in SGS, I teach
        1. elective course(s) ___
        2. introductory course(s) ___
        3. both ___

II. Brooklyn College Affiliation

    Please check all that applies to you.

    A. Annual line:

Rank	College of Liberal Arts and Sciences (CLAS) annual line	School of General Studies (SGS) annual line
Professor		
Assoc. Prof.		
Asst. Prof.		
Instructor		
Lecturer (sub.)		

    B. Lecturer in SGS (not annual line): _____

        What is your highest academic degree? _____

III. Outside Affiliation

    If you are a Lecturer in SGS (category "B" above),
    please check and fill in what applies to you in your out-
    side work.

    A. I work
        1. at another four-year college or university ___

335

2. at a community college ___
3. at an elementary or high school ___
Position held (i. e. , teacher, principal, etc.) _____

B. I am engaged in business or a profession _____
   1. Type of business or profession _____
   2. Position _____

C. I am a graduate student ____

D. Other? Please state _____

IV. Below is a series of terms which have been used by instructors to describe students.   Please select those
terms which you think best describe typical full-time
college students enrolled in day classes.   Please check:

     1. highly motivated   ____
     2. vocationally oriented   ____
     3. respect for learning   ____
     4. tired   ____
     5. complacent   ____
     6. mature   ____
     7. rigid   ____
     8. fearful   ____
     9. responsibly adult   ____
    10. hardworking   ____
    11. over-anxious about grades ____
    12. confused about goals   ____
    13. unprepared for college   ____
    14. well-prepared for classes ____
    15. analytical   ____
    16. challenging to instructor   ____

Add others if you wish _____

_____

_____

V. Below is a series of terms which have been used by instructors to describe students.   Think of the characteristics of the School of General Studies student body as
you perceive it from your own experience here.   Please
select those terms which you think best describe SGS
students.   Please check:

1. highly motivated   ____
2. vocationally oriented   ____
3. respect for learning   ____
4. tired   ____
5. complacent   ____
6. mature   ____
7. rigid   ____
8. fearful   ____
9. responsibly adult   ____
10. hardworking   ____
11. over-anxious about grades ____
12. confused about goals   ____
13. unprepared for college   ____
14. well-prepared for classes ____
15. analytical   ____
16. challenging to instructor ____

Add others if you wish _____

_____

_____

VI. What I like best about working in SGS is _____

_____

_____

_____

_____

_____

VII. What I like least about working in SGS is _____

_____

_____

_____

_____

VIII. In my opinion, the most important problem the School
       of General Studies of Brooklyn College faces today is

       _____

       _____

       _____

       _____

       _____

       _____

       _____

IX.   If somebody came to you today stating that he has a
       choice between teaching in the School of General Stud-
       ies and a day college, what would you advise him to
       do?

       _____

               What is the basis for your advice? Please check:

                   Type of student   _____
                   Salary   _____
                   Time of work   _____
                   Curriculum   _____
                   Status   _____
                   Work load   _____
                   Class size   _____

               Other?   Please state _____

       _____

Bibliography

Books and Articles

Homer D. Babbidge. "The Outsiders; Some Thoughts on
    External Forces Affecting American Higher Education,"
    paper delivered at a Syracuse University Conference
    on Dynamics of Change in the Modern University,
    June 15, 1965.

Chester I. Barnard. The Functions of the Executive. Har-
    vard University Press, 1938.

Howard S. Becker. "The Teacher in the Authority System
    of the Public School," in Amitai Etzioni, Complex
    Organizations, Holt, Rinehart, Winston, 1965.

Peter M. Blau and W. Richard Scott. Formal Organiza-
    tions. Chandler Publishing Co., 1962.

David Boroff. "A Kind of Proletariat Harvard," New York
    Times, March 28, 1965.

Brigham Young University. A Self-Study of the Department
    of Evening Classes. April, 1966.

Theodore Caplow. Principles of Organization. Harcourt
    Brace, 1964.

Burton R. Clark. "The Character of Colleges: Some Case
    Studies," paper delivered at a Syracuse University
    Conference on Dynamics of Change in the Modern Uni-
    versity, June 13, 1965.

---- The Open Door College; A Case Study. McGraw Hill,
    1960.

---- "Organizational Adaptation and Precarious Values,"
    in Amitai Etzioni, Complex Organizations, Holt, Rine-
    hart, and Winston, 1965.

339

Phillip H. Coombs. "The University and Its External En-
    vironment." Mimeo, 1960.

G. Stuart Demarest. The Evening College at Rutgers.
    Notes and Essays on Education for Adults, No. 11.
    Center for the Study of Liberal Education for Adults,
    1955.

Nicholas J. Demrath. Changing Character of the University.
    Center for the Study of Liberal Education for Adults,
    1959.

Peter Drucker. The New Society. Harper and Row, 1962.

Amitai Etzioni. Complex Organizations. Holt, Rinehart,
    Winston, 1965.

---- Modern Organizations. Prentice Hall, 1964.

William M. Evan. "Toward a Theory of Inter-Organization-
    al Relations," Management Science, Vol. II, No. 10,
    August 1965.

Evening Post. C. W. Post Evening College Newspaper, Long
    Island, New York, April 1967.

Hollis B. Farnum. "A Comparison of the Academic Apti-
    tude of University Extension Degree Students and
    Campus Students," The Journal of Applied Psychol-
    ogy, Vol. XLI, No. 1, 1957.

John M. Gaus. "A Theory of Organization in Public Admin-
    istration," The Frontiers of Public Administration,
    University of Chicago Press, 1936.

Samuel B. Gould. "Quality in Adult Education," an address
    to the Association of University Evening Colleges,
    Louisville, Kentucky, November 17, 1958.

Walton Hamilton. "Competition," Encyclopedia of Social Sci-
    ences, Vol. IV, Macmillan, 1930.

Myrtle S. Jacobson and Deborah Offenbacher. Accent on
    Adults: the Small College Program at Brooklyn.
    Syracuse University, 1970.

Talcott Parsons, (ed.). The Theory of Social and Economic

Salary Survey of Administrative Personnel.   Association of
    University Evening Colleges, June 1965.

Philip Selznick.   "Foundations of the Theory of Organiza-
    tions," American Sociological Review, Vol. 13, 1948.

---- Leadership in Administration.   Row, Peterson and
    Co. , 1957.

---- The Organizational Weapon.   Free Press, 1952.

---- TVA and the Grass Roots.   University of California,
    1949.

George Simmel.   Conflict and the Web of Group Affiliations.
    Free Press, 1955.

Herbert Sorenson.   Adult Abilities, A Study of University
    Extension Students.   University of Minnesota Press,
    1938.

Edwin H. Spengler.   "College Life Begins at 40."   Unpub-
    lished, 1954.

Bernard H. Stern.   "Degree Seeking Adults: A Preliminary
    Report on an Experimental Project at Brooklyn Col-
    lege."   Unpublished, April, 1954.

---- How Much Does Adult Experience Count?   Center for
    the Study of Liberal Education for Adults, 1955.

---- Never Too Late for College.   Center for the Study of
    Liberal Education for Adults, 1963.

Bernard H. Stern and J. Ellswerth Missall.   Adult Experi-
    ence and College Degrees.   Center for the Study of
    Liberal Education for Adults, 1960.

Herbert Stroup.   "Intellect Incorporated," The Journal of the
    Association of Deans and Administrators of Student Af-
    fairs, July, 1965.

Richard J. Thain.   "Teaching on the Swing Shift," On Teach-
    ing Adults, Center for the Study of Liberal Education
    for Adults, 1958.

Official Documents, Reports and Laws

By-Laws of the Board of Higher Education of the City of
    New York.

Board of Higher Education of the City of New York,
    Minutes: April 1950, May 1954, December 1958,
    May 1964.

Diploma in General Education Announcement, Brooklyn Col-
    lege, 1953.

Long Range Plan for the City University of New York,
    1961-1967.

1964 Master Plan for the City University of New York.
    Board of Higher Education of the City of New York;
    Second Interim Revision, 1966, Third Interim Revi-
    sion, 1967.

Men's Division Announcement, Brooklyn College, 1930-1931.

New York State Education Law, Sec. 6215.

---- Sec. 6304 et seq.

New York State Laws of 1966, Chapter 782, Article 125B.

School of General Studies Announcement, 1950-1951.

Unpublished Documents

Administrative Council of College Presidents, City Univer-
    sity of New York, "Minutes," November 23, 1965.

Admission and Evaluation Committee, School of General Stud-
    ies, Brooklyn College, "Adults as College Students,"
    October 1954.

Advisory Council of the School of General Studies, Brooklyn
    College, "Minutes," July 11, 1950.

"Annual Report of the Director," Evening Session of Brook-
    lyn College, 1948-1949.

"Annual Report of the Dean," School of General Studies,
  Brooklyn College, 1950-1951; 1953-1954; 1954-1955;
  1960; 1962-1963; 1965-1966; 1966-1967; (title changed
  from Director to Dean in 1966).

Board of Higher Education of the City of New York, "A
  Broader Mandate for Higher Education," Report of
  the Chairman, 1946-1948.

---- "Higher Education on the Offensive," Report of the
  Chairman, 1943-1944.

Brooklyn College Nursing Science Program, "Report, 1954-
  1958."

Brooklyn College of the City University of New York, "A
  Report to the Middle States Association of Colleges
  and Secondary Schools," June 1, 1966.

Brooklyn College, School of General Studies, "Experimental
  Degree Project for Adults, Accreditation of Informal
  Study for Adults," January, 1957.

Budget Request of the Dean of the School of General Studies
  to the President of Brooklyn College, 1953-1954.

Committee on Space and Facilities, Brooklyn College,
  "Minutes," November 15, 1965.

Dean of the School of General Studies to President of Brooklyn College, "Memorandum on Nursing Science Program," May 1, 1959.

Dean of Studies of the City University of New York, "Working Paper," October, 1963.

Deans and Directors of the Schools of General Studies of the
  City University of New York, "The Schools of Gener-
  al Studies in a Master Plan for the City University,"
  January 1964.

---- The Schools of General Studies Look to the Future,"
  November 1963.

Harry D. Gideonse, President, Memorandum to Deans, Directors, Department Chairmen, Deputy Chairmen,
  "Responsibilities of the Director (Dean)," School of

General Studies, October 1, 1959.

- - - - Memorandum to Deans, Directors, Chairmen of De-
    partments, "Appointments to Annual Lines in the
    School of General Studies," June 9, 1960.

- - - - Memorandum to Deans, Directors and Department
    Chairmen, "Administrative Responsibility," April 22,
    1963.

- - - - Memorandum to Department Chairmen, "Appointments
    on Instructional Lines," May 27, 1967.

Hunter College of the City University of New York, "A
    Commitment of Ours: Teaching in the School of Gen-
    eral Studies," 1967.

Daniel R. Lang.   "Report to Alpha Sigma Lambda Council-
    lors on Membership in the American Council of Hon-
    or Societies," March 10, 1966.

Middle States Association of Colleges and Secondary Schools,
    "A Report of the Evaluation Team of the Committee
    on Institutions of Higher Education," October 30 -
    November 2, 1966.

Policy Committee of the School of General Studies of Brook-
    lyn College, "Minutes," September 30, 1965.

Special Baccalaureate Degree Program for Adults Research
    Committee, Brooklyn College, "Memorandum on Cur-
    riculum," November 1960.

Edwin H. Spengler and Glenn Howard.   Joint Memorandum
    to the Administrative Council, "Nursing Science Pro-
    gram," 1958.

"Staff Handbook," School of General Studies, Brooklyn Col-
    lege, 1965-1966.

State Education Department, Division of Professional Educa-
    tion, University of the State of New York, "Report
    of Visit to Associate Degree Program in Nursing at
    Brooklyn College, School of General Studies," Oc-
    tober 1 - 2, 1963.

Index

Compiled by Ilse B. Webb
Drew University Library, Madison, N. J.

academic probation 272, 274
academic rank (professional) 131
  Nursing Science 132-135, 137-139, 147
  SGS 158
academic standards 39, 86-87, 94, 96, 107, 265-270, 273-
    274, 317
Accent on Adults 233
accounting education 35, 58, 82
accreditation 26
Administrative Council of College Presidents 67-68
  and Nursing Science 131, 132
  and SGS 220, 242
administrative organization 149-150
  academic 150-151, 320-325
  Brooklyn College 27-28, 43-45, 63, 68, 152-154, 302
  CUNY 47, 71, 206
  SGS 31-34, 62-64, 90, 151-154, 177-185, 203-204, 205,
    308-309
    recommendations 325-332
admission criteria
  associate degree programs 118
  Brooklyn College 26, 32, 74, 270
  CUNY 217
  Nursing Science 129
  SGS 269-271
  Special Baccalaureate Program for Adults 100
admission (school)
  SGS 32, 33
adult education 52, 54, 74, 92, 223, 228-229, 231-233, 250
Adult Education Division 54, 55-56, 62, 63
Advisory Council, SGS 33, 124
Alpha Sigma Lambda 229, 256, 260-261
  Committee on New Students 230
American Association of University Professors
  Brooklyn College Chapter 26

345

American Association of University Women 26
American Council on Education 26
American Council on Education Psychological Examination
     102, 267
American Medical Association, Council of Medical Education
     and Hospitals 26
Anthropology Department 89
Assistant Commissioner for Higher Education 107
Assistant Supervisor of Vocational Studies 130
Associate Dean, SGS 32, 99, 115
Associate in Arts diploma see degrees
Association of American Colleges 26
Association of American Universities 26
Association of College Honor Societies 256
Association of University Evening Colleges 254, 264, 332
athletics 30
attrition
   CLAS 274-275
   SGS 274
audiovisual aids, SGS 54, 60, 64

Baruch College 40
Baruch School of Business Administration 58, 82
Basic Program for Adults, SGS 230, 232
Biology Department
   and Nursing Science 128-129, 136-137
Board of Education 40
Board of Higher Education 24, 28, 33, 37, 40, 57, 58, 63,
     67, 70, 71, 75, 79, 88, 108, 120, 121, 327
   and Nursing Science faculty 131
   and SGS 214, 312, 314
   [annual] report, 1944 51
   [annual] report, 1946-48 52
   appointive power 207
   approval of Nursing Science curriculum 127, 132
   by-laws 308, 324
   Committee to Look to the Future 72, 74, 220
   dissolution of Division of Nursing Science 140
   Master Plan see Master Plan for the City University of
     New York
   regulation of faculty teaching loads 236, 240, 242, 314-
     315
book store 30
Boroff, David 201
Bronx Community College 71
Brooklyn College

and Brooklyn Community College   68-70
and SGS   15, 17, 51-52, 55, 72, 80, 94, 264-265, 274,
   285-296, 300, 312-314
by-laws   28, 30, 41
history   25
objectives   48-50, 304, 313
see also   specific topics
Brooklyn College Committee [of Board of Higher Education]
   27
Budget Director, New York City   37
   and Nursing Science   133, 136
   and SGS   157
budgets
   Brooklyn College   30, 212
   CUNY   24, 37, 212, 223
   Division of Audio-Visual Services   64
   SGS   37-38, 39, 40, 212, 216, 227, 248, 329
Buffalo, State University of New York 267
   Millard Fillmore College   321
business education   35, 54
business enterprises, Brooklyn College committees   30
Business Manager, Brooklyn College 27, 29, 30, 68

C. P. A. license examination, N. Y. State   58
C. W. Post College   255
Center for the Study of Liberal Education for Adults 60, 92,
   97-98, 101, 108, 264
   Research Associate   93
ceremonials
   Brooklyn College
      committees   30
      SGS participation 259
   SGS   259-262
      faculty participation 176, 262
children's theater   53, 61
choruses   61
Christmas Party, SGS   261
City College   25, 40, 63
City University Construction Fund   25, 223
City University of New York (CUNY) 23-25, 27, 37, 72,
   302, 312
   Chancellor   30
   Legislative Conference 186
   Long Range Plan   74-75, 81, 239-240
   Master Plan 75-76, 79, 81, 84, 140, 214, 223, 233-234,
      269, 333

City University of New York (cont.)
  SGS directors 67, 72, 315
  see also specific topics
CLEAR (Community Leadership Through Education and Re-
    sponsibility) 231
clubs 30
College Committee on Course and Standing
  see Committee on Course and Standing
College Committee on Long Term Curriculum Development
    96, 97, 109, 230
college credits 104, 112-113, 116-117
College of Liberal Arts and Sciences (CLAS) 31, 34, 53, 65
  Economics Department 58
  Education Department 190
  faculty 155, 185-192, 236-237, 306
  involvement in SGS 39, 58, 62-66
Columbia University 321
Commencement 176
Commissioner of Hospitals 122, 136
Committee on Admission and Evaluation
  see Special Baccalaureate Program for Adults. Com-
    mittee on Admission and Evaluation
Committee on Committees of Faculty Council 29
Committee on Course and Standing, Brooklyn College 32,
    105, 113, 267, 272
Committee on Faculty Personnel and Budget, Brooklyn Col-
    lege 30, 31
Committee on Long Term Curriculum Development
  see College Committee on Long Term Curriculum Devel-
    opment
Committee on Review, Brooklyn College 31
Committee to Look to the Future
  see Board of Higher Education
Communications 109
community colleges, CUNY 24, 37, 42, 67-77, 302
  faculty 68, 70
  objectives 69, 73-76, 250
community relations 59
community services, SGS 53, 54, 61
concerts, SGS 54
Convocation, SGS 176, 260, 262
Coombs, Phillip 209
cooperative programs, Division of Vocational Studies 57
Cooperative Reading Comprehension examination 267
cooptation
  and Nursing Science 119, 306-307
  and SGS 141-143

and Special Baccalaureate Program   96, 101, 117, 306-307
   defined 90-91
Coordinators
   Division of Vocational Studies   124
   Nursing Science   125-126, 130
   of Public Relations   259
   SGS   33
core courses   59, 108, 230
   objectives   109
costs
   academic facilities and operations   65, 67
Council of Coordinators, SGS   33
Council of Deans and Directors   32, 70, 78-79, 84, 220, 240
Council of Deputy Chairmen, SGS   33
Council of Executive Officers, community colleges   68
counseling services, SGS   54
courses
   Adult Education Division   56
   Division of Audio-Visual Services   60
   Division of Vocational Studies   57
credit courses   59, 64
culturally disadvantaged   213, 217, 232, 270
curriculum
   Brooklyn College   40, 51, 82, 113
      planning   88-89
   College Committee on Long Term Curriculum Development   96, 97, 109, 230
   Nursing Science   127-128
   SGS
      planning   32, 33, 92, 108-109
      research   114
Custodial Engineer, Brooklyn College   68

dance, SGS   54
Day Session, SGS   75
Dean of Administration, Brooklyn College 27, 243, 315
Dean of Students, Brooklyn College   27, 30, 32, 64, 130, 332
Dean of Studies
   Brooklyn College   27, 332
   CUNY   216
Dean of the Division of Graduate Studies, Brooklyn College   27
Dean of the Faculties, Brooklyn College 27, 30, 39, 64, 88,

349

Dean of the Faculties, Brooklyn College (cont.)
89, 95, 105, 113, 115, 175, 206, 230, 259, 260, 305,
309, 332
Staff Bulletin   110
Dean of the School of General Studies   27, 31, 37, 41, 53,
58, 64, 68, 69, 70, 72, 77, 96, 98, 107, 108, 259,
260, 264, 268, 332
and Dean of the Faculties   159
authority to appoint faculty   196-198, 310
designation of admissions committee, Nursing Science 130
designation of Appointments Committee, Nursing Science
126
functions   152, 166, 172, 206, 308-311
recommendations   325-329
deans
Brooklyn College   27, 29, 30, 152
and Nursing Science faculty   131
Queens College
and Nursing Science faculty   131
deans, assistant, SGS   32
degrees   53, 72
Associate in Applied Science   54, 56, 57, 60, 66, 73, 82,
118
Associate in Arts   34, 35, 37, 50, 53, 66, 71, 118
associate programs   51, 73, 74, 75, 77, 141, 236, 272
Bachelor of Science in Nursing   120
bachelors   68, 71, 73, 86, 117
honors   115, 117
candidates, SGS   33, 34-37
experimental baccalaureate   60, 87
jurisdiction over programs   64, 72, 94
masters   117
Ph. D.   87, 117, 143
Department chairmen
Brooklyn College   29, 30, 164, 308
Biology Department   126, 130, 133
SGS   see   Deputy chairmen
Department of Personnel Service   64
Deputy chairmen, SGS   32-33, 41, 177-185, 205, 207, 244-
245, 308
diagnostic tests   109
Diploma in General Education   59
Director of Admissions, Brooklyn College   129
Director of Teacher Education, Brooklyn College   27
Director of the School of General Studies
see   Dean of the School of General Studies
discipline, SGS   32

Division of Audio-Visual Services, SGS 54, 60, 62, 64
Division of Community Services, SGS 54, 55, 61, 62, 63
  Director 64
Division of Counseling and Guidance, SGS 54, 64, 100
Division of Liberal Arts, SGS 32, 53, 57-60
Division of Program Development, SGS 78, 230
Division of Vocational Studies, SGS 32, 33, 54, 123-124
  and Nursing Science 133
  enrollment 35, 56
  facilities 69
  programs 56-57
doctoral programs 40
Dodds, Harold 23
Drucker, Peter 18

Early Childhood Center 28, 190
economically disadvantaged 81, 270
Economics Department 58, 89
Education Department 190
Educational Clinic 28, 190
Educational Testing Service 102
equivalency tests 94
evening colleges 254-257, 263-265, 316, 317, 320-325
  administrative structure 320
  objectives 323
Evening Lecturer's Song 195
Evening Session 50, 300
  community colleges 76
  Directors 52
Executive Officers, community colleges 68
expenditure per student 38
Experimental Degree Project for Adults
  see Special Baccalaureate Program for Adults

facilities
  Brooklyn College 65, 70, 128, 223, 226, 249, 303
    committees 30
    laboratories 128
  community colleges 70
  CUNY 223, 312
  SGS 39, 70, 74, 227, 303, 324
faculty
  Brooklyn College 26, 28-31, 154, 160, 163-165, 170-
    173, 238-240, 306, 308, 319
    appeals 31

faculty (cont.)
  Brooklyn College
    committees 30, 88, 95, 206
    promotions 172-173
  CUNY
    teaching load 236-240, 314-315
  SGS 39, 41, 154-177, 192-203, 225-226, 237, 239, 298, 308-311
    appointments 195-198
    attitude questionnaire 275-296, 298, 318, 335-338
    committees 33, 206, 262, 330
    faculty-student conferences 185, 207
    morale 226
    Nursing Science 125-126, 131, 132, 138
    promotions 172-176
    recommendations for the future 325, 329-331
    recruitment 162-165, 196
    retention 165-169, 198-200, 310
    tenure 170-172
    working conditions 279-286, 311, 314, 318
Faculty Club 176, 261-262
Faculty Committee on Curriculum and Admission Requirements 89
Faculty Council, Brooklyn College 28-31, 33, 55, 88, 89, 95, 97, 109, 110, 113, 115, 127
Faculty Day 176
Faculty Personnel and Budget Committee 170, 172
Faculty Wives Club 176
Fashion Institute of Technology 67
financial support
  CUNY 24
  for students 26
Food Service Administration 57, 82
food services, Brooklyn College 30
Ford Foundation 59, 60, 97
Fund for Adult Education 60

G. I. Bill of Rights 51
Gideonse, Harry D. 28, 89, 219, 226
graduate study 87, 249
guidance services, SGS 54
Guidelines for Second Quadrennium, 1968-72 75

high school graduates, New York City 217
Higher Education Act of 1965 231

Holy, Thomas C.   240
home study   60
honor societies
    Brooklyn College   26-27
    SGS   256, 260-261
honors curriculum   87, 116
Humanities   109
Hunter College   25, 40, 63
    accounting curricula   82
    Bronx Center   327-328
    Lehman College   40, 327
    nursing science program   120-121
    SGS   255

image   see   public relations
individualized programs   97
industrial relations education   35
innovation   305
Institute of International Education   26
insurance education   35
International Association of Student Evening Councils   20

Jewish Chronic Deseases Hospital, Executive Director   136
John Jay College of Police Science   40

Kellogg Foundation   136
Kerr, Clark   22, 23
Kings County Hospital   122
Kings County Medical Society, Nursing Committee   136
Kingsborough Community College   71, 77
    President   77

laboratories   72
Lecturers
    graduate students as   196
    Nursing Science   131
    SGS   192, 203, 208
Lehman College   see   Hunter College
liberal arts
    Brooklyn College   48
    community colleges   68, 73
    SGS   52, 53, 58, 73, 272
    Special Baccalaureate Program for Adults   101
libraries   28, 68

library facilities 72, 82
"life experience," academic evaluation of 93, 103
Link, Joe 255
loans, SGS 32
Long Range Plan 74, 75, 81, 239-240
Long Term Committee
    see College Committee on Long Term Curriculum Development

Manhattan Community College 71
Master Plan for the City University of New York 75-76, 79,
    81, 84, 140, 214, 223, 233-234, 269, 333
mathematics 109
Mathematics Department 89
Mayor, New York City 40
Men's Division Announcement 81
Middle States Association of Colleges and Secondary Schools
    26, 159, 185, 238, 274, 294, 319
Millard Fillmore College
    see Buffalo, State University of New York
multiple employment 238-245
multiversity 22, 23

National League of Nursing 127, 133
National University Extension Association 264
National Youth Administration 26
natural sciences 109
New School for Social Research 252
New York City Community College of Liberal Arts and Ap-
    plied Sciences 67, 69, 71
New York City
    Department of Hospitals 120, 121
    pressures on the City University 212-213
New York State Board of Nursing 127
New York State Education Department 58, 71, 121, 231
    A. A. S. degree requirements 127
    Division of Professional Education 138
New York State Education Law 67, 71
New York State License Examinations for Registered Nurses
    131
New York University
    Sunrise Semester 60
noncredit courses 59
Norwegian Lutheran Deaconess Hospital 57, 120
Nursing Science 32, 57, 77, 87, 91, 133, 306-307

Nursing Science (cont.)
   administrative organization 123-124, 132
   Associate degree program 118-141
   curriculum 127-128
   funding 122, 135-136, 147
   historical background 120-121
   laboratory facilities 128
   objectives 121-122
   staff 125-126
   staff selection committee 125-126
   student admissions 129-130
Nyquist, Ewald B.   107, 265

Office of Exemption Examinations 99
open enrollment 249
orchestras 53, 61

petitions, Brooklyn College faculty 31
Phi Beta Kappa 26
plant operation and maintenance, Brooklyn College 30
police science 35, 40, 57, 82
Policy Committee, SGS 34, 124, 229, 230-231
Port of New York Authority 57
President of Brooklyn College 27, 29, 30, 31, 37, 39, 53,
      63, 68, 77, 88, 95, 126, 133, 206, 243, 259, 260,
      303, 305, 314, 315, 324, 326-327, 329
President of the Board of Education 40
Presidential advisory committees
   Brooklyn College 30
      Space and Facilities 226, 233
programs, SGS 73-80, 215
Prospect Heights Hospital 57, 120
Psychological Corporation test 130
Psychology Department 89
public relations 253-254
   evening colleges 254-257
   SGS 258-259, 262-265, 275, 316-317
purchasing, Brooklyn College 30

Queens College 40, 63
   accounting curricula 82
   nursing science 120, 121-122
Queensborough Community College 71
questionnaires 275-292

355

Race and Culture Contact [course title]   89
radio   60
real estate education   35
refunds, SGS   32
Registrar, Brooklyn College   28, 29, 332
research, CUNY   47
Research Committee
    Special Baccalaureate Program for Adults   114
retention policy, SGS   32, 37
Rhode Island, University of   267
Richmond College   40

safety, Brooklyn College committee   30
salaries
    Brooklyn College   135, 244, 252
        administration of   30
    Nursing Science faculty   135
    SGS   38, 39, 185-186, 201, 207
Scholastic Aptitude Test   270
School of General Studies   (SGS)
    administration attitudes   291-292, 319
    and community colleges   67, 70-77
    annual report, 1950-51   53
    description   16
    designation   52-53
    history   302-303
    objectives   50-55, 62, 69, 74, 78-80, 85, 141, 214, 220-
        222, 228, 257, 263, 269, 271, 302-304, 319
    see also   specific topics
school schedules, Brooklyn College   224
Schwertman, John   92, 98, 106
secretarial studies   35
Selznick, Philip   90, 228
seminars   109-110, 114-115
Senior Reception, SGS   260, 261
Simmel, George   211
social sciences   109
social security   189
Society of Sigma Xi   26
Sociology Department   89
Sorenson, Herbert   266
Speakers' Bureau   61
Special Baccalaureate Program for Adults   87, 91-118, 144,
        234, 264, 305, 307
    administrative structure   99
    admission criteria   100

Special Baccalaureate Program for Adults (cont.)
 Committee on Admission and Evaluation 99, 105, 106-
  107, 110-112, 114
 credits 104-108
 funding 92, 95, 97-98, 107-108, 114
 objectives 92-93, 97, 101
student evaluation 104-105
special courses, SGS 32
Speech and Hearing Center 28, 61
speech therapy 53, 54, 61
Spengler, Edwin 219
Spingarn, Edward 207
Spring Festival, SGS 261
Staff Bulletin 110
Staff Conferences, SGS 176, 261
Staff Handbook 262
state aid 67, 71
Staten Island Community College 71
statistics [curriculum] 89
student applications, CLAS 66
student enrollments
 policy
  Brooklyn College 227
  CUNY 216, 223
  SGS 49, 76, 227
 statistics 15, 65
  Brooklyn College 25, 28, 70, 223, 250
  CLAS 34-36
  community colleges 76
  CUNY 24, 223, 250
  SGS 16, 34-36, 39, 65, 205, 272-273
   Adult Education Division 56
   Division of Vocational Studies 56
   Nursing Science 130
   Special Baccalaureate Program for Adults 100, 102,
    108, 117
Student Services Department, Brooklyn College 30
students
 CLAS 34-37, 276-279, 318
  ability 266, 268
  credit load 41
 CUNY 217-219
 SGS
  characteristics 34-37, 50, 73, 76, 81, 221, 250, 266,
   268, 272-280, 283, 318
  credit load 41
  non-matriculated 49, 52, 53, 73, 221-223, 235, 271-
   273, 313
357

students (cont.)
   Special Baccalaureate Program for Adults
      characteristics 102
      evaluation 103-106
Sunrise Semester 60
Superintendent of Buildings and Grounds, Brooklyn College
   30, 332
Supervisor of the Division of Vocational Studies 126, 130

teacher rating, SGS 33
Teachers College, Cooperative Project for Junior College
   Nursing Education 121
teaching load 207, 236, 238-245, 252
   SGS 32, 331
Tead, Ordway 51, 156
technical education
   community colleges 68
   CUNY 47, 53
   SGS 86, 87, 271
televised instruction 60, 227
theater, SGS 54, 61
   see also children's theater
trustees, Brooklyn College 27
tuition and fees 25, 66
   Brooklyn College 30
   CUNY 224
   Nursing Science 122
   SGS 216, 313
   Special Baccalaureate Program for Adults 114, 145

United Federation of College Teachers 186, 332
University College
   Rutgers University 321
   Syracuse University 321
University of Buffalo
   see Buffalo, State University of New York

veterans education 51, 113
vocational education see technical education

women's education 234

York College 40